ROUTLEDGE LIBRARY EDITIONS:
ETHICS

Volume 29

MORALS AND REVELATION

MORALS AND REVELATION

H. D. LEWIS

LONDON AND NEW YORK

First published in 1951 by George Allen & Unwin Ltd

This edition first published in 2021
by Routledge
2 Park Square, Milton Park, Abingdon, Oxon OX14 4RN

and by Routledge
52 Vanderbilt Avenue, New York, NY 10017

Routledge is an imprint of the Taylor & Francis Group, an informa business

© 1951 H. D. Lewis

All rights reserved. No part of this book may be reprinted or reproduced or utilised in any form or by any electronic, mechanical, or other means, now known or hereafter invented, including photocopying and recording, or in any information storage or retrieval system, without permission in writing from the publishers.

Trademark notice: Product or corporate names may be trademarks or registered trademarks, and are used only for identification and explanation without intent to infringe.

British Library Cataloguing in Publication Data
A catalogue record for this book is available from the British Library

ISBN: 978-0-367-85624-3 (Set)
ISBN: 978-1-00-305260-9 (Set) (ebk)
ISBN: 978-0-367-49910-5 (Volume 29) (hbk)
ISBN: 978-1-00-304809-1 (Volume 29) (ebk)

Publisher's Note
The publisher has gone to great lengths to ensure the quality of this reprint but points out that some imperfections in the original copies may be apparent.

Disclaimer
The publisher has made every effort to trace copyright holders and would welcome correspondence from those they have been unable to trace.

MORALS AND REVELATION

By
H. D. LEWIS

London
GEORGE ALLEN & UNWIN LTD
Ruskin House Museum Street

FIRST PUBLISHED IN 1951

This book is copyright under the Berne Convention. No portion may be reproduced by any process without written permission.

Inquiries should be addressed to the publishers.

PRINTED IN GREAT BRITAIN
in 11 *point Georgian type*
BY THE BLACKFRIARS PRESS LTD.
LEICESTER

TO
MY WIFE

Preface

THE ESSAYS included in this volume have been brought together in their present form in amplification of some of the views advanced in my *Morals and the New Theology*. They have appeared mostly in philosophical journals, but I venture to hope that they may be of some interest also to students of theology. Each paper is self-contained and was written in the first instance for a particular audience, but the series as a whole represents the development of a fairly continuous theme, and the papers have thus been arranged, not in the order of their first publication, but in the order which best brings out this underlying unity of theme. The closing essays outline a view of truth and imagination in religion of which I hope to provide an ampler presentation elsewhere.

There are again many persons to whom I am much indebted, and two in particular, namely, Sir David Ross and Professor C. A. Campbell. It will be evident how much I owe to the work of these writers, not least where I have ventured to criticise their views; and I have received much personal kindness from them. Professor John Macmurray, Dr. A. C. Ewing, and Professor Dorothy Emmet have also put me much in their debt by reading some of these papers before publication, and I am glad of this opportunity to thank them. I wish likewise to express my gratitude to my colleague Mr. D. A. Rees for putting his considerable experience at my disposal in correcting the proofs. He also prepared the index.

Acknowledgment must finally be made to the Editors of the various journals in which these papers made their first appearance for permission to reproduce them here. The original place of publication is indicated in each instance, together with a note, in some cases, of the audience for which the paper was first intended. Some passages have been added to the closing section of Chapter VI, and in Chapter VII I have availed myself of the valuable comments made by Professor Broad on the occasion of delivering the paper. Apart from this there are few alterations.

July, 1950.   H. D. LEWIS

Contents

	PREFACE	*page vii*
1.	Morality and Religion	1
2.	Revelation and Reason—a study of Emil Brunner	28
3.	Obedience to Conscience	47
4.	The Present State of Ethics	78
5.	Collective Responsibility	102
6.	Moral Freedom in Recent Ethics	121
7.	Guilt and Freedom	148
8.	Some Ambiguities of Mystical Thought	179
9.	Revelation and Art	204
10.	On Poetic Truth	232
	INDEX	257

Chapter I

MORALITY AND RELIGION[1]

BELIEF in the ultimacy and distinctiveness of ethical principles has been challenged in many ways today. The advance of science, especially in the fields of psychology and anthropology, has provided the relativist and the sceptic with many new weapons to put in their armoury; and the positivist has launched a very subtle attack. The present state of society, both in the internal affairs of the peoples of the world and in their interrelations, has brought many moral principles into contempt. But there have also been notable advances, especially where more self-effacing virtue is concerned. Philosophers have also rebutted the attacks of the sceptic with peculiar incisiveness and vigour; indeed we know better today than at any other time just what we must hold if the objectivity of ethics is to be maintained. How the battle is going is by no means easy to determine. But there is one corner of the field, and that the one from which the most powerful attack of all may be delivered, which the upholder of the ultimacy of moral truths has left almost wholly undefended, so lightly does he estimate the danger from that quarter. That is the religious one. Account has been taken of the arguments of the sociologist and the Freudian psychologist, but it has been assumed, with astonishing naïveté, that religion is an ally to be wholly relied upon. But morality and religion have often been in conflict, and they seem to be so as much as ever today. For some of the most powerful forces in our religious life, and those which are in some ways most attuned to our needs, seem to be wholly inimical to the moral life. It is with this aspect of the vast problem of morality and religion that we can best concern ourselves in a course with the general title of 'Moral and Political Conflicts of Our Time'.

The distinctive feature of religious thought at the present time is the emphasis on the transcendent character of God. Theories

[1] *Philosophy*, January 1949. Series: *Moral and Political Conflicts of our Time*.

which seek to describe the nature of God exhaustively in terms of the nature and activities of man himself are entirely out of favour, even among the most liberal type of theologian. The change has indeed been rather sharp. For it is not so long ago since leading religious thinkers turned with great eagerness to William James's idea of a 'finite God', a God himself courageously taking his place in the van of the battle which man has also to wage; thinkers even accorded a welcome to crude and obscure ideas of God as a Life Force or as an emergent God, a God gradually coming to be in the process of history. It was even believed that the idea of God as a 'useful illusion' or a mere projection of man himself was not incompatible with the highest interests of religion. But it is generally understood now that humanistic conceptions of this sort, though by no means everything that has gone under the ambiguous name of humanism, do not accord at all with what we mean when we think of God or with the testimony of religious experience. We learn rather that God is 'above' or 'beyond' the nature of man, or, as in the terms already employed, 'alien' and 'wholly other'. There can be no identification of the human and the divine.

This emphasis on the transcendent character of God is opposed, not merely to the more overt forms of humanism which we have noted, but also to idealism, as this term is technically used. For idealism holds that the clue to the ultimate nature of the universe is found in our reason. Reality, on this view, is an entirely rational system, and the nature of each part is determined by the 'whole' or absolute to which it belongs. A sufficiently discerning mind could see the rational necessity for all that is; it could read the riddle of the universe in the tiniest part. But this raises two main difficulties for a religious view, neither of which has been successfully met by idealist writers. *Firstly,* it seems to cast doubt on the reality of finite life and the 'distinctness of persons'; and if all is some phase of the absolute, how can there be room for suffering, error, and sin? Idealists have sought to cope with this problem by regarding all evil as good out of its place. But even if this could be done, the fact that there is maladjustment would remain to stain a universe supposed to be perfect throughout. The positive character of moral evil, evil which involves a deliberate choice of what we know to be wrong, seems particularly hard to accommodate within the idealist view, and although some prominent idealists have put considerable strain on their main assumptions in their anxiety to preserve the reality of moral struggle, the real drive of their arguments has been in the direction of presenting the adventures and hazards of the moral life as a mere appearance, even that being, of course, an uncertain solution of their problem; for the appearances do appear. A feature of this is the elevation of the community to the position of an entity more real than its individual members. But along with these doubts of the ultimacy of finite existence, and especially the threat to the finality of men's responsibility for their own actions, idealism also fails, in the *second place,* to account for the sense of God as a mystery, present to us indeed, but also altogether eluding our grasp and remaining essentially 'alien' and 'other'. For idealism there is nothing in the nature of God which is not in principle present in the nature of man. The 'Absolute' is the extension and perfection of the finite. When it is more than this, idealism has passed its bounds, as it tended to do very markedly in the case of Bradley.

The belief that the real is the rational goes back, of course, a long way. It began with the Greeks, and Parmenides was led by it to some very strange views of the universe. Plato, coming to the rescue of Parmenides and pointing the way out of some of his main difficulties, concluded that the nature of what is fully real is best discerned in mathematics; every truth depends on every other, and we are thus drawn away from the world of sensation and change to the contemplation of immutable principles. But if every truth is true because it belongs to a whole or system, we seem driven to the view that system presupposes system *ad infinitum,* and thus there is some incompleteness in the notion of a thoroughly rational universe. Plato was therefore led to the view that the supreme reality, the 'Form of the Good', is 'beyond being and beyond knowledge'. This brought an important mystical element into his philosophy, and this accorded well with his character and that of Socrates. But it was a mysticism which took us altogether out of the world of experience. It allowed of no mediation, although it required an intellectual and moral discipline. And the theory and practice of mysticism (affected by Plato much more than is commonly realised) has followed that course in the main ever since. But what we really need is some way to lay hold on reality in its alien irreducible nature, but yet not taking us away from the world and the life that we know from day to day, a mystery which remains a mystery but does not entirely elude us, a 'wholly other' which is at the same time 'within'.

Herein lies the special force of the recent emphasis on the transcendent character of God. But it is fraught with a very grave difficulty. For if we are not to reduce the idea of transcendence to some meaning which idealism might give it, it is hard to see how the transcendent can have any significance for us or enter into our experience. This seems to me much the hardest, as well as the most important, problem in the philosophy of religion. No answer to it seems possible until we have a clearer view of the nature of religious symbolism, and perhaps the most hopeful and revealing feature of philosophy today is the concentration on symbolic thinking. But we have to remember that there is a very sharp difference between symbolism in logic or mathematics or science and symbolism in art or religion. The former can be fully rationalised, for it is a short-hand for what could be presented, but, of course, not so revealingly, in much more complicated ways in ordinary terms. Some scientists and mathematicians will, no doubt, deny this, the former in particular hankering after some esoteric interpretation of atoms and electrons, etc., although these seem plainly convertible into phenomenalistic terms or statements of what can be observed in experience. But symbolism in art makes us aware of reality in some way quite different from normal observation and science. It is some kind of revelation and links up in this way with the distinctive problem of religion. When we have reflected further on the meaning of this sort of symbolism, we may be able to appreciate better how there can be a witness or revelation actually within our own experience of what is altogether beyond it.

But where this approach is not carefully followed, there remain the most serious pitfalls, created by the temptation to appeal wholly to special revelation. This is the course pursued by Barth and others of the so-called 'Continental' school of theology. They deprecate any suggestion of a natural theology, and affirm that God is known only by the Scriptures, and by the Scriptures as they become the revealed word of God to each individual. The Divine message must be known immediately and has no echo in ordinary thought and experience. But this makes it extremely difficult, indeed quite impossible it seems to me, to give any content to the word of God. That appears to be the strait to which the Barthians in particular are reduced, but of course they cannot rest happily in it; for they wish also to give to God's revelation and to our thought about Him the content which religion has traditionally given to them. And so, to every question we may ask about God they have to answer 'it is and it is not'. God is omniscient, just, gracious, the Father, etc., but not in any ordinary meaning of these words, nor by analogy with their normal use. A special language seems to be coined in this way for religion, but it seems hard to see why we should retain for the purpose words which are already current in ordinary intercourse. To do so leads to the most astounding paradoxes and makes it extremely hard to comment on anything in Barthian theology or to criticise it. For that theology becomes so elusive, and so dangerously near to sheer prevarication that there does not seem to be any point at which we can firmly lay hold of it. And this seems, moreover, inevitable so long as we think of God as a truly transcendent being and yet find no way in which he can be present in the common encounter of men in this world.

Just what is the function of reason and natural experience has never been properly clarified by Barthian theologians, although of late, taking alarm at the bankruptcy of their position and its negation of their own office, they have been more inclined to stress the task of reason as systematiser of what is given to us in the 'Word of God'. But even this concession— and slight though it is, it is rather apt to undermine the whole position—leaves our natural faculties so discredited that man can hardly look for substantial guidance about what he should be and do anywhere outside of special revelation. There seems to be no room, therefore, for ordinary ethical thinking, and the 'Continental' theologians, however much they may have shunned the excesses of Barth in other regards (and lacked the consistency which underlies his paradoxes), have been very unfaltering in their denunciation of any autonomous ethics, that is of any ethics which is not immediately derived from religion or is not a part of revelation. How far this involves an open indifference to ethical questions is of course very hard to determine. In some cases it seems to carry with it the deepest concern about the way men should conduct themselves in this life. Barthianism, we should remember, is a 'theology of crisis' and not of other-worldliness, its spirit is dynamic and not passive, and it came to birth in the upheaval of a world war and as a protest against the impotence of the churches. Nor will recrimination take us very far in mutual understanding. But the upshot of this peculiar type of transcendentalism is to bring ordinary ethical thinking into complete contempt and to dismiss it openly as 'mere moralism', a term of abuse apparently coined for the purpose.

One curious argument has recently been used in support of complete reliance on special revelation for purposes of conduct, namely that it makes for unanimity and harmony. This seems to be just the reverse of the truth. For those who make an appeal to special revelation are notoriously at variance with one another and with their fellows generally. This is not surprising, for, while we normally seek to correct our ethical judgments by taking account of the views of others, the person who believes that he is directly guided by God is hardly likely to pay serious heed to what his neighbours think. Neither will he be ready to compromise and make the adjustments we normally consider necessary when we fail to reach agreement on ethical questions. How could he compromise, how could he feel other than bound to obey when he believes that his course is directly mapped out for him by God? Intolerance and persecution, often to the point of hideous cruelty, have therefore been the normal accompaniments of a complete reliance upon divine guidance. And, therefore, instead of making for harmony and patient understanding of one another's problems, the abjuration of ordinary ethical thinking in favour of reliance on immediate revelation has just the reverse effect. It breeds dissent and encourages a fanatical dogmatism.

One hardly needs to pause here to indicate how serious this

is bound to be at the present time. A successful issue to the crisis of Western Civilisation, in its strictly ethical and political aspects, turns very largely on our ability to agree to differ in a spirit of mutual respect and to find ways of co-operating with those who are seriously at variance with ourselves on fundamental questions of principle. If we fail at this point our hopes of retaining the essentials of democracy become very slender, and it might not be too grave a view to say that the survival of human society, in any form in which we have a serious interest to preserve it, is in the balance. This has been repeatedly stressed of late and is one of the main reasons why we regard our age as an age of crisis. Little would be gained here by adding to the grim warnings which have already been uttered with ominous unanimity by leaders of thought, and which may be echoed by any who give the slightest thought to the present plight of human society. Scientific progress has made the world so much more completely a single unit than ever before that tolerance and agreed methods of settling differences have become essential as never before for the peace and prosperity of mankind. This is why problems of peace and democracy are also problems of survival. It is, therefore, extremely distressing that the theological thinking which is, in one regard and that religiously the most fundamental, most alive and creative, and which is most effectively addressed to the deepest needs of men, should also encourage, in the social and political field, those very attitudes of opinionatedness and fanaticism which constitute at present the greatest immediate threat to civilisation and which have already taken their heavy toll of human life and world resources in the course of two devastating wars.

It makes little difference here that the content of religious dogmatism is not likely to have much in common with the sort of political fanaticism which makes the individual today a prey to despotic movements. It avails little to denounce particular forms of tyranny if we make no effort to condemn and oust the spirit which makes it possible. Subservience and bigotry, the willingness to adhere blindly to doctrines which are never subjected to critical discussion, lose little of their inherently evil nature, and their power to harm us, when we vary the ends to which they are directed. It is the dogmatic spirit itself that is most injurious and hardest to counteract. And this is what makes it so exceedingly serious, in an age which has in so many ways an unrivalled opportunity for the spread of enlightenment and culture, that the main weight of religious thought should be thrown on the side of reaction and the barbarous dogmatisms which have found such fertile ground in the confusions and anxieties of an age of rapid progress and transition.

The assumption, moreover, that one has some infallible hold on the truth, even when that is most sharply opposed to the opinions of others, is itself a form of that spiritual arrogance which the theologians I have primarily in mind, in conformity with the main religious tradition of the past, have singled out for special condemnation. To suppose that we can set aside the age-long endeavour of men in the past to arrive at the truth, in pagan as in Christian communities, and proceed without regard to the experience accumulated by our fellows at the present time, is to ascribe to ourselves a position of quite unwarranted importance. And this seems especially evident when we remember the complicated social contexts in which we have to decide what is our duty. Those who uphold the privileges and responsibility of seeking to form an enlightened ethical opinion of our own are often denounced as individualists by their opponents. But it seems to me that there can be no more vicious form of individualism than that which supposes that God has entrusted his message to each individual in a way which does not require the co-operation of other members of society for its full elucidation.

One must of course admit that a great many of the dissensions by which society is rent today could speedily be ended if there were more universal willingness to approach our differences in the spirit of true religion. And this is why religious leaders are apt to assure us that the first condition of social regeneration is spiritual conversion. But how far is conversion possible to those who do not address themselves seriously to practical problems? May not the preoccupation with personal conversion produce the spirit which makes religious rebirth peculiarly remote? One is reminded also of a penetrating observation of Mr. Basil Matthews when he refers to "the not uncommon fallacy of saying that what we desire is a change of heart, while meaning that what we do not desire is a change of anything else". But setting these objections aside, and admitting, as, surely, those who have any appreciation of religious truth must admit, that to proceed in a spirit of Christian charity, especially if that were done on both sides of a controversy, would lead to a just and speedy solution of a host of practical problems, that is by no means the whole of the battle. For it seems evident that those who are already imbued with a spirit of Christian charity are likely to find themselves for a considerable time in a great minority in a world of bitter opposition and mistrust. And even if this were not the case there could still be a possibility of serious disagreement among the most truly Christian peoples. For a truly religious spirit is no guarantee of infallible knowledge of the facts on which our practical decisions must be based. Nor does it carry with it always the soundest appraisal of the facts. Honest and devout persons have also been frequently biased and affected by irrational considerations. To ensure the right religious attitude is thus no guarantee of unanimity in regard to practical issues. Nor is the spread of true religion ever likely to bring about conditions in which men will not be subject to moral perplexity and find themselves compelled to adjust their conduct to that of persons who are far from sharing their own convictions. Nor is this desirable, if life is to retain its savour, however great the need to overcome bitter dissension and malicious antagonism. But finally, and, for the present purpose most important of all, a spirit of Christian trust and forbearance is hardly likely to be engendered when men turn away from rational consideration of one another's problems, and wrap themselves up in a cloak of spiritual self-assurance. Irritation and frustration are much more likely to ensue if we cultivate this attitude.

The Barthian may, of course, retort, at this point, that it is quite unfair to accuse him of encouraging overweening self-assurance. His intention, he will maintain, is quite the reverse, namely to encourage greater humility and to emphasize the complete dependence of man upon God. But does he not overreach himself? For the upshot of his doctrine is to induce individuals to make what cannot fail to be a highly arrogant claim to an exclusive monopoly of truth, at least in some matters, even in defiance of quite contradictory opinions of other persons. And even if this attitude were not bound to carry with it smugness and contempt for the views of others, is it not a subtle form of inverted pride to disdain the exercise of ordinary human powers and to demand, in their stead, infallibility and a more immediate, but less exacting, access to the mind of God than appears to be vouchsafed normally to finite creatures?

A word may be interpolated here about the alleged sinfulness of pride to which such prominence is given in attempts to discredit the natural faculties of men. If any reliance on our own capacities is to be discouraged, then it would seem that joy in personal attainment must always be condemned; more bluntly, pride must be always and inherently sinful. But to maintain this, I submit, is nonsense. Pride in some forms is even a quality we ought to be at pains to cultivate. And we all of us do feel proud on some occasions without the slightest sense of impropriety or sinfulness. If one wins a race or comes out first in an examination, one is naturally and very properly proud, and we show that we do not consider this in any way reprehensible by proceeding to congratulate those who have had a marked success. Theologians have not been lacking in this grace; on the contrary they have been quite forward with praise and encouragement where deserved. Neither, be it said to their credit rather than maliciously, have they been indifferent to them themselves. It seems, therefore, very hard to maintain that natural pride is inherently evil. To have an exaggerated estimate of the importance of our own achievement is, of course, another matter, and to seek personal aggrandisement at the expense of others is clearly reprehensible. But there is nothing here to suggest that joy in the exercise of human powers and reliance upon them is inherently vicious.

I know that I shall be told here that my objection is very naïve, and that it altogether misses the point of the theological doctrine. It is pleasing to know this, although it certainly will not hold true of the harsher and more uncompromising affirmations of the sinfulness of pride among prominent religious thinkers, not excluding some of the most notable of our contemporaries; for if the religious doctrine is put forward in a way which directly incurs the criticism made in the preceding passage, its advocates are really committed to quite impossible and ridiculous reactions. But if the doctrine is not to be taken in a literal sense, then how are we to understand it? As a sense of creatureliness in relation to the perfection of the Creator, we shall be told. But any sense of unworthiness of this sort which may be present in religious experience, carries with it no aspersion on the worthwhileness of marketing the talents which have been put in our keeping. We cannot at one and the same time consider it a duty to cultivate our powers and condemn the exercise of them. That is just downright contradiction which no peculiarity of religious truth can justify. And if the radical sinfulness of pride is not to be interpreted in the more obvious ways which I have noted, it is the duty of those who affirm it to take much greater pains to show just what it does mean. And they seem peculiarly reluctant to do so.

But, to return to the main course of our discussion, it will be urged, in defence of the Barthian doctrine, that the reliance on special revelation is not to be understood as involving an aloof withdrawal of ourselves from the turmoil and perplexities of the present life into some exclusive inner sanctuary. Has not Barth himself quite explicitly condemned this sort of other-worldliness? Admittedly he warns us not to seek the divine message in the course of history as such. "Whoso says history, says non-revelation." But the 'Word of God' comes to the individual in the agitation and stress of historical circumstances, in *crisis*. But if this means anything at all, it surely presupposes some appraisement of historical events which leads to the judgment that they are critical, when they are so. And if the divine message is addressed to man in a peculiar historical context, will it not also depend on a fair appreciation of the facts in a particular situation? But is that ever guaranteed? Will the most scrupulous honesty and the profoundest piety give us an infallible knowledge of matters of fact? Quite obviously not, and any doctrine which maintains that it does, condemns itself at the start. But if it be admitted, as it must, that religious persons, as much as any others, may be mistaken about matters of fact, then we seem bound to admit also that we may be mistaken about the course we should follow, unless it is maintained that we receive guidance in a way not related at all to the specific nature of the situations in which we find ourselves.

This comment of course implies that we never do know with absolute certainty what we should do. And it is uneasiness on this particular score that drives many persons to seek in religion an infallible guide. The advocates of the theory of special revelation refer often to our unhappy plight if we are not lifted out of 'the relativities of history'. They denounce the 'relativism'[1] which seems to beset us the moment we rely on an autonomous ethic. They warn us of the danger of "atomising God's commandment, destroying its unity, making it correspond to, and identifying it with, a multitude of different life situations. The inference might be drawn", from the fact that God's command is "given to each man in the special, concrete, crises and decisions of his own life" that "there was a special law for special people, special times and special stages of culture. This inference would, however, be wholly incorrect. The divine commandment is the commandment of the one God, springing from the one election of grace, which includes all men and is directed to every situation. It therefore possesses at all times the same character and the same quality". So writes Dr. F. W. Camfield,[2] one of Barth's closest followers in this country. He continues: "When the moral law is made to consist in general rules and prescriptions whose particular and individual application is left over to man's disposal and choice, it inevitably divides men. The real decisions become the affairs of different men, classes, and stages of life. One man's right is set over that of another, and there is no way out of the situation save by conflict". Several matters in these passages invite comment. But to keep to what concerns us most, there seems to be no appreciation of the sense in which relativism is vicious and the sense in which it is not. If it be held that moral principles vary directly with the attitudes and beliefs that we ourselves adopt from time to time, then we are committed to the sort of subjectivism which places morality in very serious jeopardy. But to affirm that our obligations vary with circumstances, and that there is, in this sense, 'a special law for special peoples' etc., is in no way

[1] cf. F. W. Camfield, *Reformation Old and New*, p. 28.
[2] op. cit. p. 97.

inconsistent with there being genuine ethical principles which call for one course of action, and no other, in a given situation. Variation of the second kind is inevitable and in no way to be deplored. And any theory which seeks to repudiate it shows that it has lifted itself out of the sphere in which ethical problems arise and decisions are made. Similarly with regard to the complaint that 'one man's right is set over that of another'. If this means that there are no absolute or unlimited rights, or that we should not allow claims of right to develop into bitter antagonism, it is, of course, very true and very timely. But if it means that there is no proper sense in which one man's right may conflict with that of another, it clearly flies in the face of the obvious facts. We are often uncertain what we should do, and this uncertainty arises from the fact that we are confronted with incompatible claims; shall I contribute to a charity or give my friend a much-needed holiday, shall I obey the law and discharge my obligation to the State when I consider the law to be seriously harmful, shall I vote for this or that, shall I take part in war or become a conscientious objector? Such questions, sometimes more, sometimes less, important, confront us every day; they are of the very stuff of the moral life, and they are quite unavoidable. Just how we are to describe a claim which is overridden by another claim, is indeed a very difficult ethical problem which has been much discussed of late.[1] Is it proper to call such a claim a right—perhaps a *prima facie* right? But this is largely a matter of nomenclature. For it is something of an ethical nature that is being over-ridden in cases of this sort. And there seems to be no way, even if that were desired, in which human life would be possible without conflicts of this kind, leading in some cases to most painful decisions. And, again, a theory which disregards conflicts of this kind is turning away from the obvious facts of the human situation, the facts which give morality its meaning.

It has to be added that, when confronted with the sort of practical problem we have noted we find ourselves subject to perplexity and error, we are not immobilised ethically. For, in the first place, we can continue our efforts to make our ethical judgments as sound as is possible. Our own fallibility

[1] cf. E. F. Carritt, *Ethical and Political Thinking*, p. 3.

does not affect the truth itself. There is a right and wrong to every situation, as every opinion must be true or false. And just as we can be 'morally' or practically certain that some matters of fact are as we take them to be, so we can have all the certainty we need about a great many ethical questions. Where this is lacking there is often a reasonable presumption that we are right; and when in serious doubt, there are open to us various ways of seeking to make our opinions sounder. Furthermore, even if we are in doubt or mistaken, we can always set ourselves to pursue the course which our consciences set before us as the most likely to be right. And when we have done this there is nothing more that we can do. Good men are always at one in the loyalty of each to his own ideal, but it is a great mistake to suppose that they must also be at one in their opinions about what is right. To require that is to rebel—may we not add, in a spirit of arrogance?—against the conditions of finite existence, and to demand in ethics a royal road to truth which we would hardly expect to find elsewhere.

Much that is peculiarly instructive has been written about these matters by notable ethical thinkers of the present day, and the progress that has been made recently in ethics is one of the most distinctive and promising features of modern thought. But religious thinkers, in the main, have been curiously indifferent to these important advances in a field closely akin to their own. This is especially true of the Continental Theologians and the Neo-Protestant writers in general. For however we may finally view their central position, it seems evident that many of the arguments to which they attach most weight themselves depend on assumptions which a little acquaintance with the recent clarification of ethical concepts would show to be very confused. But this failure to take account of matters which bear so closely on their own work, when these have been fully accessible and much publicised, affords further evidence of a lack of interest in the problems of practice which a somewhat too clamant disavowal of other-worldly preoccupation does little to dispel.

This bears on a further, and most important, feature of recent theological controversy, namely the assumption that there is no alternative to the theory of special revelation other than that of making ethical ideas dependent on the nature of man himself. This is perhaps the main weapon in the armoury of the Neo-Protestants. Dr. Camfield writes:[1] "How can a law which is rooted in man's nature be a real command? If the 'ought' is to be a genuine ought, it must come from without, it must command; it must be the word of a Lord; it must be given to man, and it must not be compromised by being changed, however circumspectly, into an 'is'." It is the Catholic doctrine of natural law that Camfield has before his mind in this passage, a doctrine which Barth himself treats with much respect as the main alternative to his own; and of this we shall have something to say later. But it is none the less evident how easy is the transition for Camfield from the rejection of any view which equates value with being, ought with is, to the assumption that 'ought' has no significance except as the Word of the Lord—and the Word of the Lord, moreover, in the special sense that he gives to the term. The spectre of subjectivism is in this way constantly held before us. But the alternatives suggested are not, in fact, exclusive. There is a *third* possibility which will enable the moral life to escape complete absorption in religion without perishing in the swirls of subjectivism. And it is here that the course of recent ethics proves exceptionally helpful.

For although there is deep disagreement among moralists to-day about the meaning of conceptions like 'ought' and 'goodness', some very formidable arguments have been advanced against the attempt to define these conceptions in terms of some interest or reaction of our own. These arguments seem to me very sound, and I do not think they can be avoided by making goodness, for example, depend on some general nature of man, or 'man as such', as idealist writers suppose.[2] But what is of most importance now is that it is possible to carry on this controversy without recourse to any distinctively religious notions. For we can think of 'ought' or 'goodness' as unique non-analysable notions whose meaning we perceive directly by moral intuition and which do not require to be translated into terms of our own likes and reactions. This gives us a command which comes from

---

[1] *Reformation Old and New*, p. 90.
[2] cf. H. J. Paton, *The Good Will*, and C. A. Campbell, "Moral and Non-Moral Values", *Mind*, vol. XLIV.

without, but which is not peculiarly religious, and which does not require any religious belief or practice for its apprehension. The ablest recent protagonists of moral objectivity, rarely, if ever, mention religion. And if it is argued, as is done by some religious writers, that these refutations of subjectivism rest ultimately on some distinctively religious foundation, it is incumbent on those writers to show why this is the case when it is possible to make the refutations so effective without the introduction of any religious ideas.

The same point may be pressed by noting that we continue to consider those who have no allegiance to any religion as responsible as any other persons for their conduct. And this would be preposterous unless we credited those persons with an understanding of right and wrong, good and bad, which is not affected by failure to embrace a religious doctrine—much less the peculiar doctrines of Neo-Protestants. This does not by any means imply a complete divorce of ethics from religion. The refinement of ethical ideas usually comes from religious sources, and we have derived our noblest ethical ideals directly from religion. But this can well be allowed without any merging of ethics in religion. It is very natural that profound religious experience should carry with it a quickening of other faculties, and, in particular, of the moral consciousness. And morality in its turn, as we shall stress especially before the close, is essential for the continuance and deepening of religious awareness. But the fact remains that it is possible to be moral without being religious. To deny this is just perverse, for it is an assumption we make every day in our dealings with irreligious people among whom there are many for whom we must have the highest esteem. We may also bear in mind that there have been persons of a deeply religious nature, and some religious geniuses, in whom the flame of the moral life flickered very faintly, and others whose ideas of moral values were very distorted. Thus the normally close relation between ethics and religion appears to be by no means an invariable one. But what we have to emphasize here is that there can be no fusion of ethics and religion, and that it is quite possible, indeed most usual to-day, to appreciate moral distinctions and live a very moral life, without subscribing to religious beliefs or being touched by religion.

This seems quite beyond dispute, and furthermore, those of us who do hold religious views could think them away without thinking away our normal[1] obligations; in a godless universe it would still be wrong, for example, to be cruel. It seems evident therefore that ethical ideals cannot be regarded as immediate commands of God, and that they need not lose anything of their distinctiveness and objectivity when we turn away from religion. The alternative to the Barthian view, which is shared in this matter by many others, the view, namely, that ethics has no significance apart from religion, is not, therefore, of necessity humanism or subjectivism. And it is hard to see how this can fail to be evident to any who deign to pay careful attention to the writings of those who have made the most successful recent attacks on ethical subjectivism.

The view that there can be no standards for the guidance of our conduct other than those which are immediately given us by God encounters yet graver obstacles in another regard. For it is not merely that doubt is cast on our ability to determine, without the immediate aid of God, what courses of action to pursue, but also that the very significance of the notions of right and value, as we normally think of them, is blunted. For the ultimate reason why the guidance of 'natural' moral sense is distrusted is that ethical thinking as such is discredited. It thus seems impossible to retain any distinctively ethical conceptions, and the irreligious person, nay even a professedly Christian person who puts his trust in any human power in his usage of the notions of right and ought and value, becomes simply the prey of delusions. In this matter the scepticism of the Neo-Protestant is very complete; it brings him into the closest alliance with the nihilists. For the meaning is emptied out of most that we consider significant in our ordinary contacts, an accusation that could not be brought against the far less radical scepticism of the subjectivists.

This is reinforced in a further, and even more fundamental, distrust of human power. For, in stressing the dependence of man on God and seeking to avoid any humanistic account of the ministration of His grace, it comes to be assumed that the

---

[1] There may, of course, be distinctive religious obligations, but that is quite another matter.

life of man is of no account except in the immediate impact of 'the transcendent' upon it, the 'wholly other' does not establish itself within the human context but annihilates it. The natural activities of man, as well as his understanding, are annulled as completely as in any nihilistic philosophy,[1] it is all struck out under the 'hammer of God'. God is all, man is nothing, and this is maintained, not as the reflection of certain religious moods, but as unqualified truth. In no regard, therefore, does the effort of man himself avail him anything; if he is free it is only to discover his own impotence, to feel himself obliged and yet know that all attempts to discharge the obligation are essentially self-defeating. As Brunner puts it,[2] in a typical paradox: "My duty to do good is precisely the sign that I cannot do it. It is true, as Kant showed, following the Stoic line of argument, that the imperative of obligation is the principle by which I come to know my formal freedom, i.e. my responsibility. But it is at the same time—and no philosopher has recognised this —the ground on which I become aware of my lack of real freedom. For the good that I do, because I ought, is for that very reason not freely done, and therefore it is not really good". This contradicts all that we seem bound to think about duty, and the very conception of duty is altogether absorbed in a different religious conception. All that is left to man is to witness to, or, rather vaguely, to 'mirror' 'the right act of God', to be justified by his faith and yet know that the very acceptance of this justification, while it leads to good works (but by what standards?), is itself the gift of God, to know that, even here, "God himself is the agent".[3] "Every freedom", we are told, "other than that which is found in dependence upon God is illusion and slavery".[4] "Therefore faith also, thus understood, *is the end of all ethics.*[5] For the obedience of faith comes not from the law, not from general principles, but from the address and gift of God alone. Therefore it is also the real good, because

[1] One should note here also the close similarity between Barth's teaching and that of the Vedantic writings. cf. W. S. Urquhart, *Humanism and Christianity*, Chap. VI.
[2] Brunner, *God and Man*, p. 78.
[3] op. cit. p. 81.
[4] op. cit. p. 83.
[5] Italics mine.

it is that which God does to us and through us, by his Word and his Spirit. For they who believe are led by the spirit of God. It is not that they *ought,* they must".[1] There is much that is obscure in doctrines of this kind, even when we view them in a religious rather than an ethical context; there is also confusion to which a corrective could be found in elementary ethical distinctions. In particular it is hard to see what significance 'justification' can have if it does not presuppose any specifically ethical notions, and the relevance of the process of 'justification', even when it is held, somewhat inconsequently it seems to me, that it leads to 'good works', to the business of living from day to day, is in no way evident. Nor does it seem possible to make these matters plainer without surrendering the initial assumptions about 'special revelation' and man's dependence on God— is not that the essence of the rift between Barth and Brunner? But however we are to understand these doctrines, and whatever their importance in a properly religious reference, it seems that little, if anything, can be left of ethics to those who subscribe to them.

This cannot fail to have a peculiarly unfortunate effect at present. For it is hard to think of any age when there was greater need for men to lay hold very firmly on their ethical principles. It is a commonplace to note how easily the confidence of men, not merely in this or that particular ethical view, but in all morality, is undermined in periods of transition; these are the periods when selfishness is most swift to exploit the prevailing uncertainties, when honest doubt gives way to cynical opportunism. But how much more is this the case in times of tremendous upheaval like the present. The damage to the moral fabric of Western civilisation is already recorded very grimly in the woeful pages of recent and contemporary history. Nor is it easy to determine whether private or public morality has received the greatest hurt. But these are matters too obvious to need to be laboured in this essay. What concerns us here is the support, no less powerful because unwitting, which the most influential and stirring religious thought of to-day inevitably gives to the moral nihilism by which society is so seriously threatened. Instead of looking to religion for

[1] op. cit. p. 85.

moral stability, and for the refinement of the moral consciousness which we require to cope with new and bewildering problems in almost every sphere of interest, we have, for the most part, to consider how best to counteract the influence of religion itself.

It should be stressed here that the teaching to which I take exception is that which leaves its stamp most plainly at present on religious thought and practice in general, as well as on theological thinking. Evidence of this may be found in abundance in authoritative religious pronouncements such as the report of the Oxford Oecumenical Conference. Nor is the hurt to morality mitigated much by half-hearted formulations and illogical concessions to common sense. The strict Barthian, having the courage and consistency of his convictions, may do less harm in the long run. For the effect of his teaching, being less insidiously established in the midst of more rational doctrines, is less likely to receive wide endorsement and be perpetuated.

But the worst of it is yet to mention. For, as it is essential to take some account of natural human capacities, the more especially when it is held that man was originally created in the image of God, we are given the view that the mind and the will of man alike have suffered corruption in consequence of man's sinful rebellion against God. How exactly this conception is related to the original difficulties of the view that man, being finite, is yet aware of the infinite and in fellowship with that which transcends his own nature, is not made very plain. For it seems clear that, whatever our prospects of solving this fundamental problem of religious thought, its difficulties are such as appertain to the problem of truth and knowledge in ways which are not directly affected by moral considerations; and of this far too little account is taken in theological writings. But when recourse is had to the view that our natural powers are not to be relied upon in any way where ethical or religious insight is concerned, if indeed they should be trusted in any regard (but should we forswear them altogether?), because of the way man has sinfully alienated himself from God, then we seem committed to an extremely radical denunciation of human powers; they are not merely unreliable but *evil*.

It is this inherently evil character of human action that theologians have primarily in mind when they affirm that the very effort of man himself to do what is right is an expression of sinful pride. This is the main way in which it comes to be affirmed that man stands under the 'condemnation' of standards with which it is impossible for him to conform, that, paradoxically, the 'ought' is a sign of unfreedom. But the position is fraught with quite exceptional difficulties. For, apart from the matters mentioned in the preceding paragraph and earlier, it is hard to see what is the relation of the sinful rebelliousness of 'man', and the evil which characterises 'the human situation' to the particular actions of each individual. On some views it is boldly declared that the Fall is 'prior to any human action'; and of that I find it very hard to make the slightest sense; but it is hardly less difficult to see how there can be any wickedness which is not the specific wickedness of this or that man, but of an abstract humanity—at least if ethical conceptions retain anything of their ordinary meaning.

One consideration which is often urged in support of the view that human action is inherently evil is closely related to the matters we have discussed earlier, namely the admitted fallibility of the moral consciousness. Although we can have practical certainty in some regards that we are acting rightly, we can never be fully certain, and we are sometimes seriously in error. But, it is argued, if we can never know what is right we can never do what is right. And if we never do right our actions are always evil.

This argument is, however, highly fallacious. In the first place, although we have no absolute assurance that our action is right, we are by no means subject to unmitigated ignorance. There is the presumption that the greater part of our ethical judgments are sound, and that, therefore, in obeying them, we have acted rightly. There is thus much to be put to the credit side.

But, secondly, it has to be stressed that no one is morally to blame for what he does in ignorance. On the contrary, if he is loyal to the duty that presents itself to him, his conduct, albeit misguided and harmful, may be very worthy of praise. This is the main point of the distinctions which have figured so prominently in recent ethics, the distinction between what is objectively right and what is subjectively or 'putatively'[1] right, and the closely connected distinction between 'the worth of the agent' and 'the rightness of the act'. Reflection on these distinctions will help to make it plain that moral ignorance is not itself morally evil nor any direct indication of moral evil. That it is evil in other ways need not be denied; so is lack of aesthetic taste. Of these two moral ignorance is more to be deplored, both in itself and for its effects. But the two have this in common, that, however they may grieve and distress us, the question of blame (and the special sort of praise which is correlative to blame) does not arise in respect of them at all. Ignorance may of course be due to neglect in the past or to failure to take sufficient pains to discover where our obligations lie. Conscience needs to be cultivated, and it is also apt to be blunted when its behests are set aside. But when this happens, it is for our neglect in the past or for some similar wilful lapse which has caused us to have a faulty judgment now, and not for anything which now proceeds from our own ignorance, or for the ignorance itself, that we are to blame. If we disregard this we shall find ourselves in very queer straits, as men have often done in the past. For we shall find it impossible to dispute about ethical matters without immediately calling one another to account. Controversy has often been embittered in that way to the ruin of tolerant and patient solution of complicated questions. Nor is it easy to avoid that in practice, for denunciation of persons and opposition to policy are very apt to go together. But we know, when we think about the matter, that they ought to be sharply distinguished, and that political and social problems would offer much better prospect of solution if we did so. It is widely acknowledged, at least where democratic principles survive, that an opponent must be respected as a person, however deluded and mischievous his view and however severe the measures we must take against him, provided we are sure that he holds to his way with honest intention. We can conclude, therefore, that defective ethical judgment is no direct indication of an evil will. And even if it were, we should be still far from proving that men's actions

[1] cf. E. F. Carritt, *Ethical and Political Thinking*, Chap. II.

are invariably and essentially evil. For, as I have stressed, there are sound as well as erroneous ethical judgments.

The seriousness of spreading the view that men's actions are essentially corrupt can hardly be exaggerated. For to encourage so gloomy and distorted a picture of human nature is plainly not conducive to the vigorous effort required to establish society again on a firm foundation after its recent upheaval. Yet this is in fact, not merely the incidental result of much contemporary Christian teaching, but its open aim. It is not merely that we are cautioned not to take too utopian and unrealistic a view of our immediate prospects, a wise if somewhat unnecessary counsel, but, rather, that the disparagement of all thought of progress and the inculcation of utterly despondent views of all human endeavour, the representation of history as a series of inevitable and cumulative disasters, is considered an essential preparation for the utter reliance of the individual on divine grace and guidance thought to be required by religion. And of the ill-effects of this sort of teaching at the present critical juncture in the history of man it is hardly possible to speak too severely.

Moreover, by obliteration of all ordinary ethical distinctions and the merging of all wicked actions in some communal guilt or 'universal sinfulness of man', we encourage reactionary tendencies in another way. For we give endorsement immediately to the crude and barbarous doctrines of collective responsibility which identify the individual very completely with a group or society. To weaken the sense of personal responsibility in this way is a peculiarly grave disservice to society at present. And no one who has viewed the course of recent social and political disorders with a glimmer of understanding can fail to appreciate this. Extensive, almost unqualified, collectivism seems to be the barbarous alternative to a successful issue to the crisis of civilisation. And they build strangely who bring religious forces to its support.

Encouragement is also given to reaction when the repudiation of ordinary ethical conceptions takes away the basis for criticism of accepted standards and the limitation of state and other public enactments. For the notion of 'justification' is too vague and too uncertainly related to specific problems to provide any alternative. The history of the Lutheran Church, especially in recent years, fully bears this out. And so do the statements of leading Neo-Protestant writers, for they take little pains to disguise their counsel of complete submission to 'powers that be' in all matters except those which directly concern the preaching of 'justification'. Dr. Urquhart points out that Barth himself has modified his attitude a little in this regard. Barth had formerly taught: "The Church's proclamation cannot permit . . . a question as to whether it is making the necessary contribution towards the preservation or even to the overthrow of this or that form of society or economy. A proclamation which takes up responsibilities in these or similar directions spells treachery to the Church and to Christ himself. It only gets its due if sooner or later its march is stopped by some kind of delicate or brutal godlessness".[1] He now declares "what is a choice of faith, if it never becomes a political choice? And what is the choice of faith today if in this thing it never becomes *this* political choice?"[2] But this is still highly ambiguous. A much more complete repudiation of Barth's earlier attitude is needed, including a clear admission that there is a Christian obligation to interfere in secular matters independently of their immediate effect on the teaching and practice of religion. Barth justifies his former attitude by noting that "the political experiment of National Socialism had to be given its chance to declare what was in it", but "it has now disclosed itself as an out-and-out rival to Christianity . . . It cannot be regarded as simply a 'higher power' to which we must be obedient so long as we are in the world. It has shown itself to be a rival 'religious institution of salvation' ". So writes Dr. Urquhart.[3] But this is a very inadequate defence. For Hitlerism was offensive, not merely as a rival institution of salvation, but because of inhuman practices and oppression whose character was obvious long before the Lutheran churches decided that National Socialism was also a rival in the strictly religious field.

There are, however, matters to be put to the credit side of these doctrines. And among them is the consistency and ruth-

[1] *The Doctrine of the Word of God*, p. 80.
[2] *The Church and the Political Problem*, p. 58.
[3] *Humanism and Christianity*, p. 125.

lessness with which they develop the implications of positions to which Christians commonly subscribe without fully appreciating whither they lead. This gives Neo-Protestant theology peculiar importance, for, in this way, it has helped to clarify fundamental issues and bring them to a head in a fashion which may well make the present period, in this as in other respects, a turning point in the history of theological thinking. This seems especially clear with regard to the Catholic doctrine which the Barthians usually take to be the main alternative to their own view. That doctrine is based on the ultimate identity of being and value, and thus involves the notion of "natural law" by which ethical standards are derived from the nature of man himself, the Aristotelian notion of good as end or purpose being here followed very closely. But this, as has already been stressed, does not give us a truly objective standard. Neither has it room for freedom of choice, in spite of the prominence most commendably given to that principle in Catholic theology. For it is implied that man is bound to act in conformity with certain ends. Furthermore, Catholic theology retains within a restricted sphere, or as the completion of the theory of natural law, ideas of special revelation and grace substantially the same as those of the Lutheran. This involves it in a fundamental dualism and leads to the representation of "natural law" as only "relative" and not absolute, relative, moreover, not merely in the sense that it is the best compromise possible in the circumstances, but also, and primarily, in the sense of being inherently imperfect. This latter supposition is bound up with ideas of the Fall and of man's "tainted" nature which make it very hard to stop short of the Barthian denunciation of all ethics which is not strictly theological. Here, as in the controversy with those liberal Protestant theologians who make concessions to traditionalist or "orthodox" doctrines, the Barthian has the best of it in point of consistency, however great the violation of ethical principles. It seems therefore that Neo-Protestant theology has done us the great service of bringing all these matters to a head and showing that there is no middle position between the complete absorption of ethics in religion, with all the consequences we have described, and the full admission of the autonomy of ethical ideas and of man's independence in making his moral choices.

The clear affirmation of these latter principles seems to me to be as essential for religion as for ethics, and to be peculiarly important at present. For the drift of the masses away from religion in those countries where Christianity was most firmly established, is due, in no little measure, to the adherence of the Churches to doctrines which it becomes increasingly hard for anyone with an open mind to accept or to treat with seriousness, so repugnant are they to our understanding and moral sense. In some cases, indifference and contempt gives way to sharp opposition, not without some justification in view of the support which religion tends to give at present to reactionary forces. There can be no effective "recall to religion", and indeed the very attempt may defeat itself, until we take bolder steps to discard those doctrines which are quite unacceptable to our moral consciousness.

But that is not the main point. The main point concerns the peculiar achievement of the new Protestant theology in making us more aware of the need for infusion into the ages of enlightenment of a sense of reality as "wholly other" and not to be dissolved into the categories of our own thought. The appeal to special revelation will not, I am sure, avail here. The divine must be laid hold upon within a properly human context and in the fullness of the life of man. But Protestant thought is none-the-less truly prophetic, both in its accent and in its message, in its urgent insistence upon our need to raise ourselves to a new level of spiritual life by deepening our sense of "the transcendent nature of God". But this very aim is itself defeated at the start when the moral life is weakened. For it is just in that discipline of the moral life which is quite unlike that of any other experience that the soul is most surely turned outward from itself to the awareness of a reality which impinges upon it without a surrender of its own character and complete externality. If, therefore, we are to meet the challenge of our time, and if the urgent cry of our religious writers is not to go unregarded, we need above all to raise the prestige of morality and to inculcate in men generally a more vigorous straining after high ideals than at any time in the past. For the same reason, the crucial question for the churches is that of the relevance of the ethical teaching of the Christian religion to the problems of today. This they are far from tackling as they should, and if they defer much longer, the opportunity, so far as they are concerned, may well be lost altogether. But this I will not amplify at the moment. Suffice it to insist that, although religious thought today shows us so surely what is the real malaise of Western Civilisation, its achievement will have been in vain if, in its own teaching or in the attitude of the churches, the vitality of the moral life is sapped.

Chapter II

REVELATION AND REASON—A STUDY OF EMIL BRUNNER[1]

THE evangelical view of religious faith could hardly find a more powerful advocate than Emil Brunner. For while Protestant theology numbers among its protagonists today some of the most discerning thinkers of our time, there are not many theologians of Brunner's stature who show the same breadth of outlook as he or rival his competence and vast range of scholarship in matters outside the strictly theological field. The present work[2] gives us a comprehensive statement of Brunner's views on the main problems of religion, designed to interest the layman as well as the scholar. It lacks nothing of the incisiveness of his earlier writings, and should the reader feel, as is certainly the case with the present reviewer, that the author has been committed by certain initial assumptions to a peculiarly desperate defence of impossible positions, there can still be little doubt that this book will remain for some considerable time a work of outstanding importance for students of religious thought.

Brunner's main concern is to stress the unique and absolute character of the Christian revelation. He urges that something is given to man in this way which is wholly inaccessible to his natural faculties for research and discovery—"a mystery is mysteriously manifested, a knowledge that comes from outside the normal sphere of knowledge, which cannot be achieved by man, but must be given to him, enters suddenly and unexpectedly into his life".[3] But there is nothing analogous to this outside the sphere of specifically Christian experience. This peculiar 'encounter' of man with God, however, itself presupposes a 'primal' or general 'revelation in the Creation' of which idolatry is an important indication. This is not something

[1] *Hibbert Journal*, Oct. 1948.
[2] *Revelation and Reason*.
[3] op. cit. p. 22.

given in the past; it is ever present and common to all men in virtue of their being made in the image of God. There is thus a sense in which every man must know God, for he could not deny God, so it is argued, "had he not an original knowledge of Him".[1] Atheism is itself a kind of theology and contains much that is important for a right understanding of religion (cf. Chapter XXIII). But this primal revelation must not be confused with rational argument. It also, as must be stressed in opposition to the Catholic doctrine, is a 'gift' or 'disclosure' and not the result of any process of thought. For it is the "invisible Being (of God), His Transcendence, which is manifested in His works of creation".[2] At the same time "there is no revelation for the creatures without reason",[3] and reason as "the subjective capacity of man to receive this knowledge" is "the unmistakable sign that man comes from God".[4] But the knowledge itself is not possible except as God wills to manifest himself. A special form of primal revelation is man's knowledge of good and evil: "all men know what is commanded and forbidden",[5] for God has written it in their hearts and consciences. But this knowledge, like all primal revelation, has been darkened and corrupted by the influence of sin. As a sinner man is 'in revolt' against God and thus alienated from him; he 'holds down the truth in unrighteousness', this being the essence of his sinfulness and guilt. But it is only for sinners that God's supreme revelation of his love in Christ's atoning act is possible. Christian revelation is also redemption, and thus has no meaning apart from man's responsibility and guilt. "Responsibility is the core of human existence, of personality",[6] and nothing must be allowed to obscure this. But responsibility is always 'towards God' and thus "the doctrine of general revelation is implicit in the doctrine of salvation in Jesus Christ".[7] Without the former there would be no guilt to be removed, and it is in the removal of guilt, in the 'vicarious' suffering of Jesus, that we have the

[1] op. cit. p. 56.
[2] op. cit. p. 67.
[3] op. cit. p. 68.
[4] op. cit. p. 56.
[5] op. cit. p. 71.
[6] op. cit. p. 55.
[7] op. cit. p. 70.

final revelation of God's mercy which "keeps faith even with the unfaithful".[1] But there is an even closer relation between the two forms of revelation. For "the Revealer is the same" in both cases, "the Father of the Lord Jesus Christ".[2] "The Creator God is none other than the Redeemer".[3] This is why there can be no natural theology, and for the same reason, Brunner maintains, it is only the man "whose eyes have been opened by the particular historical Word of God"—'the saving revelation in Christ'—"who is now once more able to see what God shows us in his revelation in the Creation. As we know, men might have seen it all along, the fact that they did not do so was due to their incomprehensible, sinful blindness".[4] But through faith in Christ "the eyes which had been blind begin to see again". Christ is therefore the centre and principle of all revelation.

This raises very many questions. How, for example, does reason become the 'subjective capacity' for the receiving of that which has to be 'given' because it is 'altogether above' and "hidden from the natural knowledge of man"? And in what sense may we be said to have a revelation and yet, in our sinful blindness, not see that we have it? There are indeed some senses in which it would be meaningful to say that we know something and yet do not know it—as Plato showed in the *Sophist*—but none of them seem to be relevant here. Again, if there is an essential unity of atonement and revelation, if Creator must also be Redeemer, how can it be maintained, in consistency, that "did sin not exist, man would always live in continual contemplation of God in the majesty of his Revelation"?[5] In this context we are also induced to raise a further and very old question in connection with doctrines of the atonement, namely whether it is not being implied that our sinfulness is itself willed by God as part of 'His Plan for the world'. But the point at which Brunner's teaching seems to present the most overwhelming difficulties is in connection with his conceptions of sin and guilt. For apart from the fact that Brunner appears to be thinking of sin in some vague, corporate sense as the 'sin of man', that

[1] op. cit. p. 193.
[2] op. cit. p. 197.
[3] op. cit. p. 75.
[4] op. cit. p. 76.
[5] op. cit. p. 73.

is, as some general condition of mankind, and not as the actions of this or that person (a collectivism which is but little ameliorated when we read also that 'the believer' "ceases to be an individual"[1]), we seem also to be told both that our sinfulness is due to blindness and that our blindness is due to our sinfulness. Is a vicious circle avoidable here? In any case it is quite mistaken to ascribe sin to blindness, for neither moral ignorance nor the wrongful acts which result from ignorance are themselves culpable. Ignorance bears upon questions of properly moral worth only to the extent that it is due to neglect or some other blameworthy conduct in the past. Brunner's view can only be made consistent if we adopt a frankly Socratic ethic. But that means that we must also give up the belief in responsibility, guilt, remorse, etc., as we normally think of them. This Brunner is altogether unwilling to do. He goes out of his way to emphasize man's responsibility and guilt, he regards this as a factor of exceptional importance for 'Reformation Theology', and his own system would obviously crumble if the notion of the guilt of man were abstracted from it. It is because of his 'revolt' that man stands under the 'wrath of God', is 'banished' from His presence and condemned to "death, disaster, ruin, destruction".[2] But is it possible for us to take guilt and responsibility as seriously as this if they are not also rooted in some quite unambiguous betrayal by the individual of an ideal which presents itself to him?

A subsidiary difficulty arises in regard to the presumption that all men have knowledge of the law of God. It is argued[3] that the moral sceptic invariably gives his case away by resenting injustices done to himself. This argument, stated more clearly and with better grasp of its limitations, has, very deservedly, been given much prominence in recent ethics. But what does it show? At most that we have a general awareness of right and wrong, not that we know in particular cases what is our duty. The plain fact seems to be that we are often seriously mistaken about the content of our duties and much troubled by moral perplexity. The obvious genuineness of such

[1] op. cit. p. 137.
[2] op. cit. p. 28.
[3] op. cit. pp. 71-72.

perplexity makes it very strange, if not, indeed, invidious, to say that we are simply 'holding down the truth in unrighteousness'. And the fact that Brunner pays such little attention to diversities of opinion about specific ethical issues, much though the problem calls for discussion by any who adhere to his notion of 'sinful blindness', together with his failure to distinguish between doubt about particular courses of action and fundamental ethical scepticism (and may not this also be very genuine—in the case of the Freudian, for example?) shows how little he is thinking in terms of ordinary ethical distinctions and individual conduct. Moral distinctions have been assimilated very fully to religious ideas which obscure their particular presuppositions.

This becomes very plain in two chapters which have crucial importance for our understanding of Brunner's treatment of ethical matters. The first is concerned with 'The Problem of Doubt'. Here it is roundly stated that "Doubt is a form of sin; rightly understood it is the root of all sin, sin in its original form."[1] But this doubt is essentially doubt about the truth of the Christian revelation. It comes about because man arrogates to his reason a function for which it was never intended. The sceptic demands that the truth of revelation be proved, regardless of the fact that revelation essentially precludes rational presentation of this kind. He rejects revelation on *a priori* grounds. And he does this because he wishes to set himself at the centre of things, he is too proud to restrict his reason to the matters with which it is competent to deal. But how far, we must ask, is this an adequate picture of genuine scepticism? It seems plain, in the first place, that not every religious sceptic denies the claims of revelation outright. Many, of course, do so. But there are others who retain an open mind about the possibility of revelation but deny that they have had it. There are again many who deny the claims of revelation but who would not usually be regarded as unbelievers, and there are yet others who would reject revelation in Brunner's sense, but would claim to be in receipt of revealed truth. Are all these attitudes equally sinful? Apparently, for Brunner; but what he seems to have most particularly in mind is the *a priori* rejection of revelation

[1] op. cit. p. 206.

as such. But even if this were the only form which scepticism could have, to regard it as peculiarly sinful is markedly out of accord with all that we feel normally bound to think. For whatever view we hold of the soundness of a completely rationalist view, it seems altogether clear that such views are held by persons of unmistakable integrity and great disregard of self. 'Sin' and 'wickedness' are hardly appropriate terms in such context. We should need at any rate to make it plain that we were departing altogether from the ordinary usage of these terms. That is certainly not Brunner's intention. If it were, his position would be more intelligible, but his procedure would hardly be one we could commend, for it could only lead to great confusion. But it is clear that Brunner claims to be describing what we normally mean by sin. In that case it seems particularly hard to make his position meaningful. We may readily admit that a certain kind of preoccupation with the attainments of our reason may unfit us for certain other forms of awareness; and Brunner, in common with other theologians of his school, appears to me to have something of distinctive importance to address to our age in this connection. But his message cannot be properly delivered so long as he continues to dress out his views on epistemological and metaphysical matters in ethical terms. The confusion between ethics and epistemology is particularly marked in the present work; and this incidentally makes the task of the reviewer more than usually difficult. For he may find himself in agreement with the author's views on a point of epistemology and, at the same time, be repelled by the quite inappropriate ethical form in which they are presented. It is the same ambiguity, to my mind, which makes it possible for Brunner himself, on the one hand to write as if he had in mind our normal ethical reactions to specific individual enactments, and, on the other, to insist in emphatic, but highly obscurantist terms, that the man whose sin he describes is "Adam, man as a whole".[1]

The absorption of ethics into the problem of religious revelation meets with difficulty also when we consider how little our ordinary ethical judgments turn on matters of religious belief. If the essence of sin is religious doubt, how can we condemn

[1] op. cit. p. 214.

instances of cruelty, deceitfulness, greed, etc., without ascertaining anything about the agent's religious life? But in point of fact we do so, just as we continue to distinguish, in the case of believer and unbeliever alike, between good and bad qualities of conduct. This brings us to the second chapter to which special reference must be made.

This is the chapter entitled 'Revelation and the Moral Law of Reason'. It is here that Brunner makes the most determined attempt to reconcile his theory with the apparent autonomy of ethics. He frankly admits that, "although religion helps to determine the moral consciousness . . . it may be stated as a proved fact that the moral sense of mankind is to a high degree independent of any religious tradition, whether Christian or pagan".[1] Not only the Decalogue, but even "the so-called Golden rule, the command to love one's neighbour, and indeed to love one's enemies, have been formulated on different levels of culture, quite apart from the Bible".[2] "Through moral reason", therefore, "man can know that the rule of loving one's neighbour, not merely the rule of justice, should be the standard for his conduct, and that in this all morality consists".[3] Nothing, one feels, could be plainer than that. But Brunner immediately proceeds to argue that there are fatal limitations to moral knowledge of this kind. It cannot, he contends, maintain itself in the absence of religion, the main reason adduced for this belief being that morality, in practice, is menaced and perverted in periods of religious decline. But this fact is capable of more than one explanation. It may be the case, for example, that conditions inimical to religion happen also to be inimical to morality and there are some who would urge that the decline begins at the moral level—at least in some instances. Brunner does not consider these possibilities, neither does he pause to consider any possibility of an interdependence of religion and morality subtler than his own and more favourable to morality. A more direct indictment complains of "the abstract character of the rational ethic" whereby we are induced to treat another person "as a case", and not as an object of love, "as an occasion

[1] op. cit. p. 324.
[2] op. cit. p. 323.
[3] op. cit. p. 325.

for acting according to one's duty".[1] But there seems to be little foundation for this. For it can plainly be one of our duties to cultivate love of one's neighbour and sympathetic understanding of his needs, and the more we are mindful of our duties to others, the more, it seems to me, are we likely also to love them. But it is just here that we come to the crux of the matter. For Brunner seems to believe that all duties are summed up in love of one's neighbour, and he does not think that love of this kind is possible at any human level. The reasons for this belief are not altogether clear. Brunner seems to think that there can be no love of our neighbour except that which is prompted by that love of God which comes with the knowledge that 'He has first loved us'. Of this love "man knows nothing" except as it "defines itself in Jesus Christ".[2] But surely, even if that latter love is the highest and most complete, genuine love wells up in all manner of ways outside the Christian community, and some understanding of love at this natural level seems indispensable for an appreciation of love in its completer religious form. But Brunner seems also to be impressed by the fact that love cannot be summoned up at will or commanded. Here it is not a case of inability to know our duty but of the power to fulfil it. Both these are matters which seem to be peculiarly connected in Brunner's thought, but he does not make it plain just what is the relation between them. And this makes it hard to comment on his view. But we can at any rate very readily and fully agree that, provided the statement be taken in its ordinary meaning, and not in relation to a particular view of revelation, love cannot be commanded, not only because we cannot, in point of fact, summon up any emotion at will, but also because the spontaneousness of love is essential to its worth. It excludes all compulsion, from within or without. But what follows? It is here that Brunner takes up his main stand by concluding that we are commanded by our conscience to do that which simply cannot be fulfilled in obedience to a command. "Love", it is stated, "cannot be commanded". And yet again it is the "only thing that is really good".[3] "The law cannot

[1] op. cit. p. 330.
[2] op. cit. p. 336.
[3] op. cit. p. 336.

awaken love; it can only demand it", and "the great illusion of morality consists precisely in the fact that it does not see this impotence of the moralist's demand".[1] "So long as man stands under the law he cannot do what he ought to do".[2] This curious position has at least one merit which Brunner may claim as against recent ethical writers who have been much concerned with the same question. It does not try to save the categorical imperative by urging that we are free to act in certain ways although, on the views in question, our actions spring from emotions and desires which it is admitted we cannot control directly.[3] But the position is none the less flatly contradictory. Brunner may find some consolation in this, belonging to a school which glories in paradox. But there will be others not sufficiently inured to these daring procedures to acquiesce in downright contradiction. They will contend, very rightly to my mind, that if the morality of duty is as contradictory as Brunner suggests, the proper course will be, not to retain it, as one element in a theory which transcends morality, but to discard it altogether. If the discharge of duty is impossible, then let us no longer speak of a guilty failure to fulfil the law. Let us regard our failure simply as failure, and not as wickedness, and let us take up some theology of grace which does not presuppose sinfulness and guilt in the ordinary sense, a procedure by no means unattractive to those who can accept the Socratic ethic already mentioned. But the contradiction is in point of fact easily removable. For we have only to point out that love is one thing, duty another. There is room for both, we can admire one action because it is the discharge of a distasteful duty, and accord a very different sort of praise to another which is the spontaneous expression of affection. Morality is not the whole of life; there are other values, such as those realised in art and knowledge as well as in personal relations. They all have their place, and their conditions are different. It is only when we fail to make these differences plain, and roll all our values into one, that we find ourselves in the sort of impasse which Brunner sets before us and which he seeks to exploit in the interest of a certain view

[1] op. cit. p. 331.
[2] op. cit. p. 332.
[3] Ross: *Foundations of Ethics*, Chapter VI.

of religion. So plainly is this the case that one can but marvel at the confidence which builds so elaborate a structure on so slender a basis. For the alleged contradiction is fundamental to Brunner's system.

The emphasis upon the absolute uniqueness of the Christian revelation, and the view that there can thus be no revelation apart from Christ, raises also the question of the claim to revelation in other forms, for example in the Old Testament. Is there not revelation here as well as in Jesus? Brunner, of course, believes that there is, but he maintains that it has no significance except in relation to the Messianic office of Christ which had to be the fulfilment of a promise conveyed in the dealings of God with Israel. There is thus an essential unity of Biblical revelation, but it is not the unity of doctrine. Brunner himself is very contemptuous of ingenious attempts to elicit a thoroughly coherent body of doctrine from the Scriptures as a whole, and he reminds us that there are sharp inconsistencies, not merely between the teaching of the Old Testament and the New Testament, but, also, within the latter, between the teaching of Christ and that of the Apostles, and between the views of one Apostle and another. But underlying this variety there is "a unity of divine revealing action",[1] the work of Christ being the culmination of God's self-communication in 'saving history' —not to be confused with a mere progressive initiation into correct ideas about God, for the prophetic 'word' is at the same time an 'act', and the teacher, above all in the case of Jesus, does not, as a good teacher should, make himself superfluous. But although God imparts himself with absolute finality in Jesus, giving us, not 'a word from God' but 'God himself', the 'Person who speaks' and the 'content of his teaching' being one, yet the process of revelation is not complete. For there are some things which Jesus, in the role of Messiah, cannot say about himself. There is thus needed 'the witness of the Apostles' without whom "the story of Jesus would not have become a revelation to humanity".[2] "Had a Jewish or a pagan chronicler transmitted to us the deeds and words of Jesus, we should not be able, through their 'historically faithful' account, as eye-

[1] op. cit. p. 195.
[2] op. cit. p. 122.

witnesses, to know Jesus as the Son of God and Redeemer", any more than the "record of events under the Old Covenant", "had they been handed down by an unbelieving chronicler", would have been more than "a fragment of quite ordinary Oriental national history".[1] The apostle is thus "absolutely essential", his testimony and its peculiar authority being known by 'the signs of an apostle', and not admitting of overt definition. He is thus marked off from other 'eyewitnesses of the resurrection', and in him the divine revelation has 'reached its goal'; "the circuit is now complete".[2] The apostles thus stand "on the border line where the history of revelation becomes the history of the Church".[3] But it is only as proclaimed by the Church, and made the living word of God by the 'illumination of the Holy Spirit' which breaks down our 'sinful arrogance', that the truth is disclosed to the individual and becomes the means of his regeneration. Belief being, however, still 'a venture of faith', since God has appeared, not in his compelling majesty, but in 'the form of a servant' that we may freely (*sic*) accept him, it looks forward to the 'complete unveiling', the 'Revelation in Glory' which is "not 'faith' but 'sight' ". We have thus all the essentials of traditionalist theology *but with a difference.* And what one finds hard to determine is just what is the difference. It is clear what Brunner rejects—the ideas of an 'infallible book', an 'infallible dogma', an 'infallible Church'. But it is by no means easy to understand what he wishes to put in their place, his procedure consisting so much of the repudiation of positions obviously open to objection that it is not only the hostile critic who will find it hard to lay hold upon his view, but also everyone else. Let two examples suffice.

The 'Word' of God, it is held, requires as 'a mediating witness' the 'word of the Church'. But "The Church is not an institution",[4] and its word "is present whenever a convinced Christian, in his own spoken testimony, hands on the message which he has received".[5] Does this mean that only a believer can bring other persons to the faith? If so, it is very doubtful, for may not belief be induced by the reading of a book or by

[1] op. cit. p. 136.
[2,3] op. cit. p. 122.
[4] op. cit. p. 139.
[5] op. cit. p. 142.

impartation of Christian truth by someone not in the full sense a believer himself? If it be replied that this brings us into relation with believers at some point, if only with the 'apostolic witness', or that, as Brunner stresses, there would be no continuity of Christian teaching, no Bible even, without a community of believers, then we must answer that this is hardly the way we expect to interpret the emphatic assertion that "personal fellowship with God is only possible . . . within the fellowship of the Church".[1] Nor will it help to add that, as Christ 'is present' to all believers, they enter also into a special relation with each other. For this, besides being almost a tautology, is hardly what we normally understand by the Church, especially in the sense in which (although 'not an institution'!) it needs, as Brunner tells us, "concrete arrangements, ordinances, forms of organisation, offices, laws".[2] Consider, again, the assertion that "the divinely present Word cannot be tied to a correct doctrine",[3] flatly opposed as it seems to be to the equally definite insistence that "the preaching of the Word which demands obedience can never take place without correct theological doctrine, nor without correct doctrinal ideas".[4] Here also there is much side-tracking of the issue— for example, by insisting that correct doctrine is not everything,[5] or that knowledge of doctrine may be incomplete.[6] Nor does it help the reader when the claims made on behalf of sound doctrine (in spite of the fact that 'no doctrinal formulation' is the 'infallibly correct doctrine'[7]) is watered down by regarding doctrine as saying "something definite about God",[8] even such as might be found "in the simplest prayer which a mother offers at the bedside of her child".[9] The real question is whether 'purity of doctrine', in the sense in which doctrine would include Brunner's idea of human sinfulness and the atonement, whether in abstract formulation, or implicit in a simple prayer, is essential to Christian experience—what, for example, of the efficacy

[1] op. cit. p. 148.
[2] op. cit. p. 139.
[3] op. cit. p. 145.
[4] op. cit. p. 154.
[5] op. cit. p. 152.
[6] op. cit. pp. 157-160.
[7] op. cit. p. 153.
[8][9] op. cit. p. 151.

of the simple prayer, if, as might well happen, the 'doctrinal content' is doubtful? But there is no explicit answer to these and many other similar questions, the general impression being conveyed that Brunner adheres very rigidly to the main traditionalist theories, but in a vague disembodied form, the shape but not the substance of orthodoxy. But there is no resting place here, and one wonders whether the followers of Brunner will eventually find their way back to the much denounced Roman Church, of which they are in many ways true, if somewhat turbulent, children, or whether they will follow their own better insight and break more frankly and fully. They can not subsist long on equivocation.

There is less ambiguity in Brunner's treatment of the position of other religions than Christianity. For he rejects outright any claim to revelation that may be made on their behalf, except to the extent that all forms of idolatry are made possible by the original 'revelation in Creation'. Were it not for this latter factor, naturalistic accounts of 'other religions', in terms of fear and wishful thinking, etc., would be quite adequate, and Brunner makes concessions to this way of viewing religious phenomena (and to naturalism in general) much more extensive than seem to be warranted, thereby making plainer what his view of the exclusiveness of the Christian revelation carries with it. It is because there is contained within various forms of paganism this 'relic of the original total *imago*' that, although lacking anything further in the way of *revelation,* "none is without its impressive truth" to which the more 'transcendental' and 'idealistic' accounts bear witness. These latter, however, err both by being too abstract in their approach to what is after all *revelation* and by not taking due account of the distortion of the *imago* through original sin, the inveterate tendency of man to set himself up as God which "breaks out first of all and mainly in his religion".[1]

That some forms of heathenism might at any rate stand in some relation to Christianity itself similar to that of the religion of Israel is also denied, it being noted that the only serious claimants for this role (conceived in the 'prophetic' way

[1] op. cit. p. 264.

described above), namely Judaism and Islam, far from pointing towards Christ have rejected him.

How then, we must finally ask, does the exclusive revelation in Christ stand in regard to our reason? Is reason so perverted that we must eschew it altogether? By no means, according to Brunner, although there seem to be some theologians who do not shrink from this strange conclusion. Brunner insists, against Barth in particular, that it is equally important to understand that the divine image has not been lost altogether as it is to realise that it has been marred. Reason is the sign of our inalienable 'likeness to God'. "God himself thinks", and he has created a world, an ordered reality which we are meant to understand and use by the exercise of reason. It is only when man seeks to fathom the mystery of God by his reason that he sins. It is only in this reference that reason is corrupt, and even here it does not wholly mislead. There is much to be said, for example, in favour of, as well as against, the traditional proofs of the existence of God, and Brunner shows much partiality for the ontological argument as showing that "in the human mind we come upon something that points beyond man to the dimension of God".[1] There is also much truth in 'rational theology' in general, whether, in the form of atheism (!), it points to the falsity of religious systems dominant at a particular time, of pantheism, to our creaturely dependence (albeit conceived 'in a one-sided manner'), or of idealism, to the way the divine "pierces directly into human consciousness"[2] which thus cannot "be severed from the divine self-revelation".[3] But it is not possible in these ways to come to know the Living Creator God. What we have at best is the 'abstract *ens realissimum*', a formal distorted impression of the true nature of God as Person—the God of Faith, Father and Redeemer. 'The Logos of Reason' (thought of very much as the *philosophia perennis* thinks of meaning and value—'a principle of the cosmos as well as of humanity') is derived from God, is a "reflection of his own Being" which is its 'hidden form', but we do not know God himself by it, but by the 'Logos of

[1] op. cit. p. 344.
[2] op. cit. p. 260.
[3] op. cit. p. 354.

Revelation' in which a mystery is 'mysteriously revealed'. The 'rational doctrine of God', while thus never wholly illusory, is a perversion of the Christian idea, it gives us neither the content nor the certainty of the knowledge of faith, and is at some essential points "irreconcilably opposed to it".[1] The same imperfection infects all other uses of reason as they bear on the relation of man and of the world to God, but the more we draw away from this relation the more we can rely on our reason. "In so far as the knowledge of things as they are in the world, and its order, is concerned, reason alone is quite competent to deal with them".[2] "For the claim of faith does not summon the rational man to suspend his intellectual habit of control and examination of facts; all that faith claims is that he must not try to exercise it in a sphere where it has no function".[3] It "leaves man his freedom and ability to carry on research, to classify, to make profound studies".[4] We have not thus to suppose that there is a 'Christian multiplication table', 'a Christian grammar' or a 'Christian logic'. The Bible tells us nothing about 'the making of machines', 'about counterpoint', or 'the principle of the division of power in the State'. But the position is, none the less, not one of straightforward dualism. For there are many matters in which it is evident that both faith and 'mere reason' are involved. There is 'an interpenetration of the two spheres', and we "cannot indicate the state of affairs by drawing a line of demarcation between them, but only by a proportional statement. The nearer anything lies to that centre of existence where we are concerned with the whole, that is, with man's relation to God and the being of the person, the greater is the disturbance of rational knowledge by sin .... This disturbance reaches its maximum in theology and its minimum in the exact sciences, and zero in the sphere of the formal".[5] This 'law of the closeness of relation', to which Brunner has elsewhere also attached the greatest importance, leaves us with the task of correcting rational knowledge in the spheres where faith and reason intermingle, such as are all

[1] op. cit. p. 361.
[2] op. cit. p. 381.
[3] op. cit. p. 208.
[4] op. cit. p. 217.
[5] op. cit. p. 383.

questions 'that concern human beings as persons', questions of law, politics, appreciation of literature, etc. It also sets us the problem of Christian philosophy. For although knowledge of faith is not grasped by reason, there is the need to integrate what is given in this way with experience as a whole, a 'process of thinking' about 'the act of faith' which begins in theology with "direct reflection upon the divine revelation", but is 'carried further' when Christian philosophy enables the faith "to penetrate into and influence every sphere of human life", giving all culture "a Christian foundation".[1]

Brunner makes an eloquent plea for a Christian philosophy of this kind, challenging Christian thought "to emerge from its fatal theological isolation".[2] The Barthian view that we have no need to step outside of revelation but can find in the word of revelation 'the sufficient source of all truth' is shown to be quite untenable and out of accord with all our practice even when dealing with the Bible. But the complementary aspect of this matter for Brunner is that only when account is taken of the Christian faith can there be truly 'critical' and realistic thinking.

In his criticism of rational theology Brunner, in common with other Protestants of his school to-day, makes considerable play with the number and diversity of metaphysical systems which confront us.[3] This is an old and by no means unimportant objection. But it must be pointed out, in lieu of the full discussion which cannot be attempted here, that disagreements do not normally invalidate the pursuit of truth, and that differences deep and disconcerting also in their way might arise in the practice of Christian philosophy as conceived by Brunner.

But Brunner's main objection to rational theology, and the nerve of his arguments here as elsewhere, is that it fails to take account of the truth that has to be *given*. All rational knowledge is "truth that I acquire for myself";[4] even when it has to do, not merely with things and formal relations, but with persons, and when it arises from exchanges between persons, it is yet

[1] op. cit. p. 395.
[2] op. cit. p. 395.
[3] op. cit. p. 361.
[4] op. cit. p. 365.

something which I could, in principle, have learnt for myself. It comes from another person 'accidentally', for "nowhere in the sphere of rational knowledge does there emerge truth for such a kind that *essentially*, of *necessity*, it could reach me only by way of the 'other' ".[1] Rational knowledge leaves me isolated. Even when I think of God, and think of him as 'Absolute Subject', he is yet the object of my knowledge. "I introduce God into the world of my thought", and what I know of him is a "truth that already lay in the depths of reason".[2] "All the transcendence that I think out for myself is only transcendence within immanence".[3] But the ring of this 'self-isolation' can be broken by the 'true self-impartation' of love. Such love is, however, not possible at the human level. "The human love which we experience is 'all too human', tainted with egoism, falsified by self-love, and is precisely *not* unconditional self-surrender",[4] it has to bring 'the other within the sphere of which the self is the centre, making it object for me, not a subject, 'a thou'. It is love within the medium of reason, and reason knows nothing of unconditional love, for it "cannot conceive that which transcends it, which breaks through that ring of immanence of the self-world in which the rational self is the centre".[5] That can happen 'only as the love of God', the forgiveness that knows 'no must', the 'folly and scandal' which comes 'too close', and 'offends' just because it cannot be rationalized and made part of our own world.

But there is much to query here. For apart from questions concerning the ultimacy of the Subject-Object relation, and without enquiring here into the nature of our knowledge of other selves—is it direct, or, as I incline to think, inferential?— it seems evident that, however subjectively conditioned, there is nothing in the nature of this knowledge of others as such to preclude our having a genuine interest in them. My neighbour is not a chimaera; I can know enough of him to love him—and to hate him. And both these are feelings which, however intermingled, it seems to me that we do entertain. Could we know the Love of God if accents of love and goodwill were altogether

[1] op. cit. p. 366.
[2] and [3] op. cit. p. 367.
[4] op. cit. p. 368.
[5] op. cit. p. 369.

alien to our mutual dealings? But even if they were, if in all our relations, as involving reason, the self had perforce to be the centre of interest, then this predicament would not be one to be conceived in an ethical way. It would be an incident of our rationality by which sin would be erased as effectively as virtue —neither being possible. But none of this follows in fact from what Brunner says about reason (if it did could reason be regarded as the mark of our being made in the image of God, and of original innocence?) And this fact provides the true basis for estimating Brunner's success.

For much that he has to say in criticism of rationalism (in spite of a proneness to include under that description views to which it is not quite appropriate), the insistence on the need for revelation as something which has to be 'given', and involves some kind of encounter, together with more detailed matters in Brunner's account of the general nature of revelation, are of very great importance and show him at his best. The insistence, for example, that, although revelation is some kind of miracle, it happens within a context which it does not annul or disrupt (much as superior forms of determination—those which involve life and mind, for example—do not suspend, but rather use, physical or material processes) is exceptionally instructive. So also is the view that, in these ways, religion itself should be regarded as a 'miracle within a miracle' (Chapter XIV). But this in itself suggests a continuity of revelation at various levels, and is not this just what Brunner overlooks? There is revelation in art, and in 'other religions', as well as in Christianity, and these are understood best in relation to each other. There is more than one way in which God breaks into the circle of our loneliness. He speaks to us in 'divers manners', and to be aware of this is to be more open to what Christianity in particular has to give. Brunner denies this, and he does so, I submit, because, in spite of all that he himself says about the 'given', 'supra-rational' nature of revelation, *he has an inveterate impulse to rationalise it.* This he does in terms of traditionalist dogma, the procedure being facilitated by certain affinities which subsist between the desolation of man when he feels himself imprisoned within his own thought and the peculiar lostness of sin and guilt. This leads to grave confusion in ethics; and, in other ways also, as we have seen in dealing with Brunner's account of the Church and of doctrine, the attempt to contain revelation within the restricted confines of a highly rationalistic dogma leads to the strangest shifts and evasions. There is need thus for much bolder thinking about the whole problem of reason and revelation, for being more resolute than Brunner in interpreting dogma in terms of revelation rather than *vice versa*, and for relating these matters to what seems most certain in the moral life. Only in these ways can religion recover its significance for us today.

Chapter III

OBEDIENCE TO CONSCIENCE[1]

I

THERE are many ways in which the hold of a people on the ultimacy of ethical conceptions is apt to be undermined in an age of transition. One of the most insidious, because it presupposes much that is true, is the following. It is urged that, even if there is an objective truth and an ultimate right or wrong to the alternatives that confront us in practice, yet every individual must be guided by his fallible conscience and, therefore, so the argument goes, a duty is always for everyone that which he takes to be his duty. The final answer for all practical purposes in ethics is subjectivism. Every age and every society must abide by its own standards and never presume to claim any inherent superiority to any other. Into the support which this attitude derives from other assumptions about ethical principles, and from the circumstances of the present time, we shall not attempt to enquire. My aim will be the limited one of considering what is involved in the principle that everyone must obey his own conscience, and it will be urged that many confusions into which we are apt to fall can be dispelled when we view this principle in the right perspective.

II

We must begin by noting an obvious condition of moral responsibility, namely that the agent should be aware of the distinction between right and wrong. It has not always been so apparent that a failure to discover what is required of him in a particular case exonerates the agent in the same way. But there does not seem to be any valid reason for making a radical distinction between these two forms of ethical blindness. Nor is it very common today to suppose that ignorance or error in regard to the nature of our duties, or the defection that is due to such ignorance or error, is itself an instance of the kind of

[1] *Mind*, July 1945.

imperfection for which we are morally responsible. Censure is withheld more especially where defective judgment arises from ignorance of facts, but even where there is a faulty ethical judgment, we do not, as a rule, count that in itself a fault of the agent in the properly moral sense. Our ignorance may, of course, be due to neglect in the past, for, as has often been pointed out by moral philosophers, ethical insight requires to be cultivated—the conscience which is little regarded is blunted and distorted. But, in that case, it is for our neglect in the past, or the failure to take sufficient pains to find out what is our duty, and not for the failure to discharge that duty here and now, that we are accountable. Insensitiveness in regard to ethical standards, as in aesthetic matters, is indeed to be deeply deplored; but we can hardly be blamed for it, and if anyone is able to assure us in regard to an act which we consider it wrong for him to have done, that he did not know (or think) it was wrong, then we consider him to have produced as valid an excuse as if he had shown that he could not have avoided the act. In neither case was there a defection which he 'could help'. The former plea is as firmly established as the latter. We forgive, "for they know not what they do".

The adoption of this attitude is one mark of an enlightened or civilised community. A primitive people looks to the outward effects of action, or, at any rate, it draws no distinction between the effects and the intention, an attitude for which there is much evidence in parts of the Old Testament. Indeed, we sometimes read of a visitation of the God of Israel on his people because of a blindness which he himself, in his wrath, has accentuated. And it is a not unimportant sign of a lapse into more primitive attitudes in much of our religious thought in these recent years of tumult and confusion that influential religious thinkers should revert so readily, and with such lack of discrimination, to the more naïvely fatalistic parts of the teaching of the post-exilic writers.

It is not, indeed, usual to allow the plea of ignorance in law. This is mainly because it is presumed that the citizen has the means of ascertaining what the law of his country requires of him. And where, in some circumstances, that is not ensured, even if expediency requires that the law be allowed to take its course, we do not think one whit the worse of persons who fall foul of the law through unavoidable ignorance of its nature. Normally, the law itself underlines the fact that it is for 'malice' that is 'aforethought' and 'wilful' misconduct that men are accountable.

This is not peculiar to modern times. Little though the idea of obligation had impressed itself upon the mind of the Greeks, they were not unaware that ignorance exonerates. This is evidenced in Aristotle's celebrated account of deliberate action, notwithstanding the difficulty he found in reconciling the admission with other features of his theory of conduct. For us who have been taught, by notable individual thinkers like Kant as well as by the general ethical and religious tradition of the West, how fundamental is the idea of obligation for the moral life, there will be less reluctance to accept its implications.

III

It is one of these implications that the moral worth of a person does not depend on the rightness or value of the end at which he aims, much less on the actual effects of his actions. It depends on his determination to do the best he can 'according to his lights': if he sets himself to do what is 'subjectively right', in the technical term of today, and does so 'because it is right', his worth as a moral agent is assured. By 'subjectively right act' we mean the act which appears right to any particular person. In strictness we should distinguish between (A) the act which is really right, 'the objectively right act', (B) the act which is right relatively to the situation as the agent conceives it, and (C) the act which seems right to the agent. B and C are distinctions we must draw because the agent may be mistaken about the ethical significance of the facts before him. We do not, however, require to consider these distinctions very closely for our purpose.[1] It will be enough to bear in mind the general distinction between the act which seems right and the one which really is so.

The need for a distinction of this kind is brought home to us especially by the ethical disputes and perplexities which we

[1] They are very fully discussed by Sir David Ross in *The Foundations of Ethics*. See especially Chapter VII.

meet almost every day, and which, in their acuter forms, lead to the most agonising, if also, in some ways, the most ennobling, experiences. Since, with the best will in the world, we are often bewildered and baffled, it must often happen that we shall have done our duty to the full, in one sense, namely, that of obeying the dictate of our own conscience, but, at the same time, shall also have done what, in another sense, a sense that does not directly affect the estimation of moral worth, is altogether wrong.

There seems to be no escape from this conclusion. The clear enunciation of the principles in question by some recent ethical writers opens the way for the solution of many dilemmas, and the adoption of a more reasonable attitude in practice. It is, however, a principle viewed with the greatest suspicion by a great many other writers.

An excellent instance of the kind of situation which calls for the distinction we are stressing is supplied by Professor Laird in an article entitled, 'On doing one's best'.[1] But the article also illustrates the reluctance of writers to bring the issue to a head. Professor Laird admits that "we commonly hold that the persons we call wrong-headed but honest fanatics are to be admired for doing what seems to them best". But they may also require to be restrained if "their action is very mischievous", and "the manifest consequence is that we do not believe that everyone ought to do what seems to him probably best according to the best of his lights".[2] But it is hardly satisfactory to leave the matter there. What I believe should be said is that, in one sense, everyone ought to act according to his lights, in another sense, the sense in which the deluded fanatic is doing what is wrong, he ought not. It will not do to say, as some have suggested, that the admiration we have for the fanatic is divorced from his doing what is right. That would lead to an embarrassing divorce of moral worth from obligation. What we require is a subsidiary meaning of 'ought'.

IV

There have been several attempts to avoid this conclusion. Professor Laird himself returns to the topic in his article

[1] *Philosophy*, January 1931.
[2] op. cit. p. 65.

'"Subjective" and "Objective" in Morals'.[1] But he does not substantially modify his original view. He declares: "I agree with Sidgwick that 'no act can be absolutely right which is believed by the agent to be wrong'". Also: "his conscientious action cannot be right if his conscience errs".[2] It is admitted, however, that "conscientious action may always be better than the contra-conscientious", "better" here meaning "more highly commendable from a moral point of view".[3] But do we not consider it better because it is a case of doing one's duty? It may be linguistically awkward to have to say that it may be our duty (in one sense) to do what is wrong. But we cannot avoid this unless we are prepared to deny that it is significant in every situation to tell a person that he ought to obey his conscience. To put the matter otherwise, there must be some sense in which it is always and essentially right to do what our conscience requires. Most people would consider this the more important use of 'ought' and 'right', and this is why it is so hard to persuade them that we can also be said to have a duty without being aware of it.[4]

A somewhat bolder attempt to deal with the problem is that of the late Professor de Burgh. He has given the repudiation of our principle a position of central importance in the elaboration of his own metaphysical views.[5] Briefly the argument is this. There can be no doubt of the absolute character of the obligation to obey our conscience. But "we can never know, in any particular situation, what it is *really* right to do. We know indeed that it is always right, really and absolutely right, to do what we believe to be right . . . . But this knowledge is purely formal and gives no clue to the matter of moral obligation. . . . Our beliefs and judgments as to material rightness . . . . are notoriously liable to error . . . . We never get beyond what we, or other persons, judge to be right . . . . Once again, to put the paradox in its most glaring form, if we are never able

[1] *Mind*, January 1941.
[2] op. cit. p. 55.
[3] op. cit. p. 56.
[4] See below, Section VII.
[5] A short statement of the view developed in Professor de Burgh's books will be found in his articles on "Right and Good," in *Philosophy*, Vols. V and VI.

to know our duty how can we perform it? And if we are never able to perform it, what meaning is there in calling it our duty?"[1] No attempt is made to avoid this paradox. Morality is boldly asserted to depend on the command to will "what can neither be willed nor known",[2] it is the "endeavour to achieve the impossible".[3] For the solution of this and "analogous antinomies" we must go "beyond the confines of ethics into the field of religion".[4]

Now whether there are, or at not, antinomies that point to religion as their solution will not be considered here. Neither shall we consider what is the significance for a final view of reality of the imperfection in our ethical knowledge, and the obvious limitations that beset us in practice. But I think we may well raise our voice against the exploitation of a 'paradox' for which there is a simple solution. The defectiveness of ethical knowledge, and the obstacles that stand in the way of outward achievement, have nothing to do with the properly moral worth of the agent. It only gives point to the need to distinguish between the 'inner' and 'outer' meanings of 'doing our duty'. The procedure of de Burgh savours strongly of the artificial way in which Kant sought grounds for belief in immortality by looking, not to actual ethical achievement, but to an insurmountable defect in the moral life—or what appeared so to him.

The paradox to which de Burgh attached so much importance is discussed in some detail by H. Osborne in his *The Philosophy of Value,* Chapter XI. He offers a rather unusual solution. Proceeding on the assumption "that conscience is on the whole a veridical faculty", he maintains that the fundamental moral rule is that a person should act in a way that ensures the fullest discharge of duty on the part of men generally. Obeying one's conscience will be the best means of fulfilling this aim. Therefore, for the maxim "I ought always to do the best practicable act" we substitute the "wider maxim 'I ought to adopt that rule of conduct which is most likely to ensure that I and all men, present and to come, will produce a

[1] *Philosophy,* October 1930, p. 582.
[2] op. cit. p. 583.
[3] op. cit. p. 588.
[4] op. cit. p. 588.

greater amount of positive value throughout our lives than would be ensured by any alternative rule' ".[1] But this can only provide a solution of our paradox by disregarding the fact that it is the individual that can have a duty and that it is his duty to act in a particular situation. Osborne, in fact, gives his case away by admitting that his theory cannot take "the particular ethical situation or the single individual as its unit for discussion. It is necessary to take as the ultimate unit for ethics the notion of mankind as a single ethical substance . . . . " This appears to me to run counter to the clearest deliverances of the moral consciousness.

This would be readily admitted by Professor C. A. Campbell, whose criticism of the idea of 'objective duty' is of a very revealing kind, notwithstanding the sternness with which it is pressed. He brings much vehemence to his denunciation of "the whole conception of objective rightness" as "one of the most confused, and confusing, in the sphere of morals".[2] This is, in some ways, surprising. For Campbell dissociates himself altogether from a view such as that of de Burgh, he is in fact at the opposite extreme. Difficulties would never arise for him from the need to consider the 'material' (de Burgh) or content of obligation in our estimation of the agent's devotion to duty. Neither ignorance nor incapacity have any direct influence on the free effort of will in terms of which he would evaluate the moral worth of the agent. It would therefore appear that there is no obstacle to regarding the question of what we ought to do outwardly or 'objectively' as a separate one. Indeed, this appears to be especially required by the theory in question.

There need, of course, be no serious dispute about the terms which are most appropriate here. If it be thought less confusing to speak of a 'moral end' rather than an 'objective' obligation the issue would cause little stir. But the point is that Campbell will not allow that there can be a 'moral end' which is not directly a moral end to the agent. "There is only one end which we can say in strictness all men ought to strive to attain, and that is the end, be it what it may, which each individual agent presents to himself as morally the best".[3] If any persons could

---

[1] H. Osborne, *The Philosophy of Value*, p. 119.
[2] *Scepticism and Construction*, p. 252.
[3] op. cit. p. 250.

not present an end to themselves as 'morally right', "if the end in question could not be their moral end, it is nonsense to suggest that they 'ought' to be aiming at it" . . . . "It is the extremity of theory to hold that a man 'ought' to do what he believes to be wrong".[1] "It seems undeniable that that which each man ought to do is to pursue his own ideal".[2]

Now Campbell is especially concerned here with the problem of moral evaluation. And this, without doubt, may be allowed him; in any sense in which 'doing one's duty' involves the attainment of moral value, there can be no obligation other than that of following our own ideals whatever their nature. But it is precisely this which induces us to postulate another meaning of obligation. The ideals which we severally present to ourselves are, after all, ideals, claims that one course rather than another be followed; and there must be some sense in which it cannot be true, in the same situation, that more than one course should be finally adopted—or if not there is an end to all controversy, and ethics becomes a chaos. Campbell, in fact, speaks in the same breath of a man's ideal as undergoing "refinement, elaboration, or even reform".[3] But in that case there must be a sense in which we ought to do something which we do not now consider obligatory upon us; it is not thus so absurd "to hold that a man ought to do what he believes to be wrong".[4]

Yes, it will be answered, but in that case we are using this term ('moral end') as "signifying the most satisfying state of mankind, or something of the sort, without any direct implication of 'oughtness' ".[5] But are we? Do we not rather say 'We ought to seek the perfection of mankind' (if that is our ideal) and try to persuade our fellows, who do not agree, that this is what they ought to do? We cannot speak of the subsidiary question of morality, the question we put to ourselves when we are already resolved to do our duty, as anything other than the question 'What in particular ought I to do?' And this 'ought', while it does not directly affect moral evaluation, is none the less an ultimate ethical 'ought' — it can only be

[1] *Scepticism and Construction*, p. 250.
[2] op. cit. p. 252.
[3] op. cit. p. 252.
[4] op. cit. p. 251.
[5] op. cit. p. 253.

translated into terms that are really synonymous with itself, for example, 'ideal', 'moral end'. It is not a hypothetical 'ought' or the kind of 'ought' we have in arithmetic when we assert that some addition ought to give us a certain total, or, in day-to-day affairs, that it ought to be hot this afternoon, meaning that it will be hot if the conditions are as we take them.

We must, in short, press on our critic the situation described by Laird. The fanatic is deluded, but about what is he deluded? About the facts, it may be answered; but may there not also be an error of moral judgment? and even if the error in its substance is only about facts, it is responsible for an error about the duty of the fanatic. To put the matter otherwise—Conscience is fallible (that can hardly be denied), but about what is it fallible? Clearly our consciences claim to enlighten us about our duties. If, then, we can be mistaken about our duty, we can have a duty without knowing that we have that duty or, for that reason, being able to discharge it.

The arguments of Campbell, however, serve to make it very plain why there is such reluctance to allow that there can be a duty which we do not acknowledge or impose on ourselves. He wishes to safeguard especially the conditions of moral responsibility. And if we become very preoccupied with 'objective' rightness, or limit the term to this more outward reference, there may ensue such a divorce of morality from obligation as will much confuse us about the conditions of responsibility. The misgiving is not without a great deal of foundation.[1] But the matter cannot be pursued closely here. All that we require to note is that there is a serious pitfall into which the unwary may easily fall in making the distinction between various senses of obligation or rightness. But this does not convert the distinction into an "easy solvent"[2] to be summarily dismissed; it pro-

---

[1] For example, by thinking of rightness solely in terms of what ought to be done, several ethical writers come to an easy acquiescence in the view that moral freedom is merely the freedom to *do* what we will, whereas, if freedom is required by responsibility at all, if 'ought' implies 'can', it must be freedom to will. The question whether this is so and what it involves has been much neglected in many notable ethical discussions of recent years. This, I should contend, is a prime source of confusion in recent ethics, the more so since those who have brought the idea of obligation and rightness into especial prominence have, for the most part, been the worst offenders.

[2] *Scepticism and Construction*, p. 251.

vides no justification for refusing to acknowledge a distinction which seems so unavoidable. If the distinction holds, it holds, however hard it may be to present it without ambiguity.

V

It is in the light of this conclusion that we can form a reasonable view of the attitude that should be adopted by society towards those who find themselves unable, for reasons of conscience, to observe its rules, especially such as are embodied in the 'law of the land'. The issue has been clouded by much confusion which we can ascribe very largely to the failure to draw the distinctions we have stressed above. It takes this form. An individual, it is noted, ought always to obey his own conscience; but it must be his right to do what he ought to do, and, therefore, no other person can have a right to prevent him from doing so. This reasoning is implicit, but not always very clearly formulated, in much of the anarchist strain in our democratic traditions, especially that which derives directly, as do some of the most distinctive and influential factors in British democracy, from Puritan teaching in the time of the Commonwealth. But it is clearly very specious reasoning, and we have already shown that the conclusion hardly conforms to the attitude we generally adopt in practice. For there are few who will not be willing to restrain the deluded fanatic at some point. And the way we have to think of that procedure is evident when we distinguish clearly between the duty of every person to do what seems to him his duty, and what is 'really' or 'outwardly' his duty. When we restrain someone against his own conviction it is on the basis of what we consider to be 'outwardly' his duty. And it is important that this should be admitted without prevarication. For, otherwise, the plea for exemption on grounds of conscience is seriously prejudiced by being confused with the wholly untenable view that conscience exempts invariably and wholly.

Repudiating the latter view, then, we have now to ask whether a 'conscientious objection' has a bearing on the question whether the law should take its normal course in the case of persons who offend on 'conscientious' grounds? Should there be exemption or some similar suspension of legal proceedings?

Most persons in this country would give an affirmative answer. And the law endorses their view even in the grave matter of national service in time of war. What justifies this attitude?

One answer that can be given to this question is that usually denoted by the rather ambiguous term 'expediency'. It is this. Compulsion avails little in many cases of conscientious objection. The more sincere the objection the less likely is it to yield to threats and punishment. On the contrary it will often be sharpened by opposition of that kind. Persecution, moreover, ensures for the objector much sympathy and support; passions are apt to be inflamed by it. Conscientious objectors can, moreover, be set to useful work in ways which are not contrary to their principles. In many cases, as at present in the case of military service, the numbers concerned are few and their attitude not very infectious. While the exemptions allowed by the law may afford a cover for some malingering, the loss to national service is small in comparison with the trouble and confusion that would ensue from any attempt to enforce conscription on all of military age.

But is this all that can be said? That it represents the attitude of many people is, I think, plain. But is not tolerance in such cases very uncertain and watery? Can we not find for it a basis more respectful to the objector and more integral to the principles by which a democratic community lives?

This, as we have urged, cannot be found in the belief that conscience invariably exempts, but there is nothing here to preclude the possibility that conscientious scruples do, to some extent and in some matters, directly afford a ground for exemption. And it is for this reason that we can speak significantly of the 'sanctity of conscience'.

There is much confused thinking about the 'sanctity of conscience'. And many who would not be prepared to abide in practice by their principles continue to write and speak as if every scruple of conscience deserved the same respect and was never to be frustrated. Such excesses, as we have already stressed, must be avoided. But the term does denote something of the utmost importance. What is this?

The essential consideration here is the supreme inherent worth that attaches to the determination to do one's duty. This, of course, is not diminished where outward restraint is placed upon the agent or if he has to endure penalties and ostracism. The glory of the saint is not dimmed but brightened by his martyrdom. But it would be perverse indeed to seek therein an extenuation of the wrongfulness of persecution. We do not perpetuate privation because of the fortitude which may be exhibited in the face of it. On the contrary the greater the desert, the more urgent the need for alleviation. Similarly, there is a special wrongfulness in the imposition of a sanction on conscientious action, however much it may be required to avoid a greater wrong. This is because it involves treating with disrespect that which is deserving of the highest regard. We may not agree with Kant that nothing is good besides the good will, but we can certainly say that the good will shines with a radiance nowhere else seen in the life of man. We therefore owe it a respect which should always give us pause before we impose any penalty on the conscientious pursuit of mischievous ends (or such as seem so to us). Those who are sensitive to the supreme worth of moral goodness will always for this reason be reluctant to make the path of the honest man hard. Admittedly, it is not always possible to know when we are dealing with honest men, and there are certain forms of arrogance and stubbornness which masquerade as determined adherence to conviction. Nor is it a mark of respect never to put a conviction to the trial. Morality is not a plant of tender growth. Even so, when all allowance has been made for these and for kindred considerations, there remains a hard core of respect for conscience which should be a prime factor in the attitude of individuals and the community towards those whose conduct seems otherwise to warrant a sanction of some kind. This, I think, is what we have mainly in mind when we speak of the 'sanctity of conscience'.

But it has also to be remembered that, in addition to the respect we owe to the attitude of moral resolution, there is a duty to encourage the cultivation of it, both for its inherent worth and for its usefulness to society. Ill fares the community that produces not upright as well as enlightened citizens. But the atmosphere created by penalising conscientious scruples hardly conduces to a high regard for moral integrity. While in theory it is possible to distinguish between condemnation of outward conduct and censure of moral character, and while the distinction should always be kept before our minds, it would be too Utopian to expect the measures required for effective restraint not to bring the characters of persons against whom it is directed into some contempt, especially where sanctions take a legal form. Here, then, is a further reason why we should be mindful what we are about in dealing with 'matters of conscience'. And this is, I believe, also comprehended by the term 'sanctity of conscience'.

A further reason for toleration, but one that has been emphasised more in regard to the freedom to express opinions that seem mischievous or subversive than in the more difficult case of action in accordance with those opinions, is the presumption that the 'resister' may be witnessing to an important, if, possibly, a one-sided, truth upon which the health and prosperity of society depends. It is possible also that he may be found in due course to have been more right than his society.

The course which various forms of censorship have taken in the past, and the proneness of a people to stone its prophets more often that it welcomes the wise innovator, favour most the mature counsel of Gamaliel even in cases where there appears on the surface to be little likelihood that we are 'fighting against God'. There is, as indeed I have insisted, a limit to this freedom, but it is a limit less readily reached where its privileges are exercised with a due sense of responsibility. Much as an individual must hesitate more before resorting to unconstitutional actions in a democratic community which affords opportunity for persuasion and constitutional change—a matter to which we shall return—so the community ought to be more tolerant of the resister who normally shows due regard for orderly procedure and does not require the gravity of the measures he feels compelled to adopt brought home to him by the emphatic condemnation of society. But we cannot enter into these matters in detail here or allow ourselves to embark on a treatment of the general question of toleration. It must suffice for our present purpose to indicate in a general way how we must think of the 'right of conscience'. And if it be allowed that the 'appeal to conscience' is not to be lightly rejected we have also to note that it should not be lightly made. To this side of the matter we have now to turn.

VI

In the sense of obligation which we must regard as the most fundamental, at any rate in so far as it is the one directly relevant to the evaluation of the agent, an individual will have done his duty by obeying his own conscience. To that extent he is a law to himself. In other regards he is not. And this, as was intimated in the preceding section, affords us our clue to the problem what attitude should be adopted towards those whose convictions bring them into conflict with established practice. But we have now to consider whether our conclusion has any other significance for the individual agent. Can it affect a man's practice more directly to be told that there is a sense in which it may not be right for him to act as he thinks he ought to act? Is he not bound to follow his own convictions? Must we not be content to leave the matter there?

This point is sometimes put by urging that the idea of 'objective duty' resembles the notorious 'unknowable reality' of some metaphysical theories. Is it not too inaccessible to be significant? While it may be true, for theory, that there is an ultimate right and wrong, practice must be guided by fallible opinions.[1]

Now the first point to be made here is that ethics is not unique in this respect. We have, in fact, for most purposes to be content with fallible beliefs. But that does not mean that there is not a truth to be known; our opinions 'claim' truth—they are about the world as it really is, and if we lose sight of this fact our purpose in seeking the truth may become so confused as seriously to mar our chances of attaining the fullest probability for our opinions in the spheres where absolute knowledge is not possible.[2]

In day-to-day affairs this will not happen very often. If I want to measure a field or find my way about a new district, the

[1] From my experience in teaching moral philosophy I should be inclined to say that this consideration is one of the main reasons for the attractiveness of a relativist theory of morals.

[2] Whether it is possible, and in what regards, need not be considered for our purpose.

purpose in hand is sufficiently clear to keep me in pursuit of it. It is the real distance, the real way, that I want. But when our purpose is more complicated, and has not a fairly immediate practical aim, we do not always keep our objective so clearly before us.

This is especially true of ethics. For there is much in ethical matters to draw us away from a steady pursuit of the truth. This is where we must beware especially of prejudice and wishful thinking; and the variability of ethical opinions, far from inducing a greater exactitude of thought, has often the effect of discouraging effortful thinking about ethical questions. It is therefore all the more important to have it established that, in the sense that is important for practice, it may not be our duty to do what we think is our duty.

This will have the effect of inducing a greater readiness to take pains to ensure that the opinions we do form are as sound as we can make them. It will also help us to disentangle questions of outward duty from matters that are relevant only to the estimation of the moral worth of the agent. In this way our attention will be directed more effectively to the complicated features of the situations that confront us. We shall take a more objective and, thereby, a more comprehensive view of the problems of practice.

It would indeed be impossible for any moral agent to disavow wholly the duty to find out what is his duty. For this has some relevance to every situation that confronts us, and it is very closely related to the idea of obligation as such. The ordinary person may not present this duty to himself in abstract terms, or reflect upon it. He can hardly fail to be aware of it if he is accountable at all.

But while everyone will be aware, in some measure, of this duty, not many will appreciate the difficulties involved in the proper discharge of it. The average individual will content himself with the 'duties of his station', and, where these present difficulties, a summary solution will be found by simplifying the issue. This is what finds such substantial encouragement in the unadventurous shelving of responsibility by a one-sided insistence on the principle that a man must act according to the light which is given him. For the latter induces, or at any rate perpetuates an unthinking, uncompromising attitude of mind which makes the individual in every sense a law to himself—which has such a regard for the 'inner light' as to hide it under a bushel where it will never shine on the dreary, complicated and often unromantic facts of the world about us.

The supreme example of this procedure, in the more theoretical field, is the belief in inalienable rights; and the mischief for which this belief has been responsible in practice has been so fully and so frequently exposed that it would be idle to mention it further here were it not that it is, in fact, far from exhausted. When some particularly ugly business is afoot, when exploitation or obstructiveness has to be dignified by a theory, we may count on the resurrection of 'inalienable rights'. A moderately innocent, but hardly less mischievous, form which it assumes is the bare enumeration of abstract rights, often by the seemingly more progressive thinkers. Such are the 'right to happiness', the 'right to freedom' or the 'right to live'. Until they are given a specific content these avail little more than their prototypes, the celebrated 'bills of rights' and 'fundamental laws', to indicate something important to preserve. And while they appear to the unthinking to take us a long way, their main effect is to departmentalise our thought on ethical and social questions in such a way as to lead to boundless confusion when eventually we turn to the particular interconnected facts of the social situation.

The elaboration of general principles has, of course, the highest importance. Their absence is only another indication of a limited view. It is the presentation of one-sided principles, or principles so abstract as to be more confusing than helpful, that must be deplored. Nor can society lightly dispense with firmness of conviction amongst its members, as Plato showed so effectively in his account of the 'democratic' man,[1] so unfortunately named. But the price of firmness ought not to be a limited outlook. Communities may be well served on occasion by the blind adherents to a principle of limited application, but that usually betokens some unhealthy, or at any rate, abnormal state; their ruin is assured when fanaticisms prevail, for stability and the vitality that makes for continuous growth comes from

[1] *Republic*, Book VIII, 560.

the character that seeks the most comprehensive view of its duties.

VII

How much the failure to take a comprehensive view of our duties, and to acknowledge the perplexities that arise especially from the need to adjust one duty to another, is due to failure to make the distinctions we have stressed is shown very clearly by the course of modern ethical thought. For some of our profoundest and most influential thinkers have concluded that since we are morally responsible only for deliberate wrongdoing, it cannot be said that we ever have an obligation without being aware that we have it. The adoption of this view is facilitated in turn for the thinkers in question by their unawareness of the acuteness and extent of moral perplexity. If it is assumed that in fact there can be little doubt at any time what in particular we ought to do, then we shall not be much prompted to look beyond the supreme importance of doing what we take to be our duty, or realise how much that principle requires to be supplemented.

This, I believe, is how we must understand the position of Kant. He stressed more than any other moralist the principle of 'duty for duty's sake', and it is fully assumed in this paper that there is no ethical principle of greater importance than this. But such was the concern of Kant with the 'purity' of our devotion to duty that he thought of duty as standing in such a relation to the conscientious will of the agent that there could be no doubt about the course of action to be followed. The belief that there are duties of 'perfect obligation', indisputable and invariable and flowing from the nature of the moral will itself, together with the very meagre acceptance of duties of 'imperfect obligation', and the absence of serious reflection on the implications of the latter, is so related to the belief that our duty is 'the duty to do our duty' that it is very hard to determine which of the two beliefs is more responsible for the other.

This is thrown into high relief in the development of Kant's views by some of his idealist followers. T. H. Green affords us a particularly good example. The adherence of Green to Kantian views is full of significance but it has not been sufficiently remarked. Moral theory is essentially 'circular' for

Green because, for him, there is no criterion of duty that is not relative to the will to perform our duty. And since the 'articulation' or 'filling' of duty stands in this special relation to the agent, even though it may be said to be objective in the sense that it does not depend on the inclination of the individual, its nature can never be misconceived. This consequence Green was quite ready to accept. He repeatedly assures us that the conscientious man finds the path very clearly marked out for him.[1] The only kind of perplexity which Green allows, and that in a somewhat uncertain fashion, is that which concerns the discernment of some independent duty which does not complicate our acceptance of standards already established.[2] When the problem of perplexity is pressed on his notice he cuts the matter short by reaffirming the principle which precludes it. "There is no such thing really as a conflict of duties" for "a man's duty under any particular set of circumstances is always

[1] We are constantly assured in Green's *Prolegomena to Ethics* that "it is only to our limited vision that there can seem to be such a thing as good effects from an action that is bad in respect of the will which it represents ... The good or evil in the motive of an action is exactly measured by the good or evil in its consequences" (section 295). The only question of importance, then, is "will our hearts be pure?" (section 299). When we respond to the "challenge to purify the heart" (section 298) conscience "speaks without ambiguity" (section 221). Throughout his ethical writings Green adheres to this astounding confidence in the infallibility of conscience. See in particular *Prolegomena to Ethics*, Book IV, chapters I and II. Cf. my "Does the Good Will define its own content?" *Ethics*, April 1948.

[2] This is seen very clearly in the following passage: *Prolegomena to Ethics*, section 353—"We all recognise, and perhaps in some fragmentary way practise, virtues which both carry in themselves unfulfilled possibilities, and at the same time plainly point out the direction in which their own further development is to be sought for. It has already been sought in this treatise to trace the ideal of the cardinal virtues, as recognised by the conscience of Christendom. In none of these would the man who came nearest the ideal 'count himself to have attained', nor would he have any difficulty in defining the path of his further attainment. No one is eager *enough* to know what is true or make what is beautiful; no one ready *enough* to endure pain and forgo pleasure in the service of his fellows; no one impartial *enough* in treating the claims of another exactly as his own. Thus to have more 'intellectual excellence'; to be more brave, temperate and just, in the sense in which anyone capable of enquiring what it is to be more perfect would now understand these virtues, is a sufficient object for him to set before himself by way of answer to the question, so far as it concerns him individually; while the state of society in which these virtues shall be more generally attainable and attained, is a sufficient account of the more perfect life considered as a social good."

one." Having ascertained the course to be followed, "the one duty is to pursue that course".[1]

The implications of this attitude are many, and they cannot be fully exhibited in one paper. But it will be evident that the suppositions we have noted bring us to the view that the members of society will recognise clearly the nature of one another's duties. For the same reason our rights will always be 'conceded claims'. That universality of ethical conceptions which precludes our making claims on our own behalf without admitting that others are entitled to claim something from us, will require also that the particular nature or content of our claims, since they are bound up with the general duty of doing our duty, will be likewise admitted or 'recognised'. There is therefore 'no right but thinking makes it so' and the basis of rights is accordingly found in the 'general will' of society, against which there is therefore no appeal. Further confusions enter into the development of this view, for example that between the nature of 'positive' law and the nature of morality, but these confusions are themselves made possible for Green[2] by the persistence, in his celebrated theory of the 'general will', of presuppositions derived very directly from the Kantian view that nothing is good in itself besides the good will.

It has to be stressed here how little of substance there is in the collectivist aspect which the theories of the 'general will' and the 'common good' present to us in the first instance. The notable idealists who brought these theories into prominence in the last century had, indeed, a keen awareness of the dependence of man on society. But this was very largely misconceived, and the more extreme form which it took in some views about political absolutism is itself to be ascribed to the individualism which obscures the conflict of claims or evades its problems. Where the good 'does not admit of competition', where it is not unambiguously allowed that the welfare of one person is in many ways opposed to the welfare of another, maladjustments and the considerable admixture of justice with injustice will not

---

[1] *Prolegomena to Ethics*, section 324.

[2] And to some extent for Bosanquet and other idealists. The extent to which Bosanquet follows Green is very evident in Chapter VIII of *The Philosophical Theory of the State*.

be much noticed. Enactments which are just at all will be just throughout.

This is the nemesis of the individualism which has been so outstanding a feature of modern thought. Beginning in the assumption of 17th Century thinkers that all the citizens owe a 'like debt'[1] to the State, thinly disguised in Rousseau's conception of a common good;[2] it acquired a peculiarly significant form in the idealism of a later period. For in this final stage it exhibited more clearly that affinity with an attitude prevalent in popular thought which accounts for much of its attractiveness. That is the simplification, not unnatural where there is little reflection, whereby a duty is thought of as something complete in itself, and not in relation to other duties and the order of society. This, as we have stressed, is much helped by the view that duty is altogether bound up with the moral worth of the agent, and helps in turn to perpetuate that view.

VIII

It is only by making it plain that there is a sense in which duty is not 'self-imposed' that duty can also be seen not to have any other imponent. Moral duty is not set either by the individual or his society, which is composed of other individuals —both are fallible. And it is only when this is made clear that we can understand properly what sort of ethical guidance the individual agent can derive from the opinions and the purposes of others. For it can then be shown that while the individual must in the last analysis obey his own conscience, yet, as part of his duty to find out what is his duty, there is much in the mean-

---

[1] Hobbes, *Leviathan*, ch. 30. The criminal law is our nearest approach to an equality of treatment and the simplification that ensues. But even here it is apt to be a chimaera. The same punishment affects different persons in very different ways and degrees, and the commission of every crime has features peculiar to itself. Passing to the civil law and to matters of general public policy it is very clear that we are altogether removed from Rousseau's idea of a just law as something which affects all the citizens in the same way. This is still more the case in 'private' morality. And once we rid ourselves of these false simplifications, derived from an ill-founded analogy between morality and law as envisaged in a superficial analysis, we cannot fail to recognise the complexities alike of private and public morality. From this to the further admission of considerable perplexity and much variation in ethical opinions is but a short step.

[2] Compare C. E. Vaughan, *The Political Writings of Rousseau*, Introduction.

time that he requires to do to correct the limitations of his private point of view. The following are the main ways in which he must be careful not to arrogate undue importance to his own ethical judgment.

(A) We can hardly discover what is our duty independently of what has been thought about the matter by others. Principles that are widely acknowledged and have persisted through many changes deserve special respect. So do the opinions of a good man, as Aristotle taught us. The effort to live worthily brings a maturity of judgment. By regard to such opinions we may sharpen our own insight.

(B) Regard for the opinion of others has a further form arising especially from the fact that much that is relevant to ethical decisions is not accessible to each individual. Not only must we seek to modify our own opinions by consulting others, we must also defer to the opinions of others, in some measure, although our own opinion remains otherwise unaltered. The extent to which our convictions can be based in this way on authority is not easy to determine. There is a natural reluctance to act on principles which we have not made fully our own. But it seems probable that something of this nature enters into our ethical judgments at almost every point. This is partly because questions of fact and questions of value are so closely interconnected in practice. But it is also due to the fact that in ethics, as in art, our gifts are varied; different individuals have a special competence in some matters, especially in matters with which they have most acquaintance. Nor is this reducible to greater knowledge of facts. Some have more ethical insight than others, and insight can be sharpened. Whether this is sufficient ground for taking our ethical opinions generally from a particular teacher or institution is another question. It would at least be necessary for such 'authorities' to convince us directly of their credentials by producing immediate conviction in some fundamental matters. That appears to be the only way in which a case could be made for the complete submission to authority which we sometimes find in religion and politics. But even this attitude would still leave important problems unsolved, since principles require application to specific situations. And here there would again be room for deferring to the judgment of a great number of persons. It is this, however it presents itself, that I wish to stress here.

Deference to the judgment of others has a wide application outside the strictly ethical field. In regard to questions of health we usually defer to the opinion of an expert, even where we have sufficient knowledge to form a tolerably enlightened opinion of our own. And the function of the expert, in this as in a host of other matters, is heightened in a complicated civilization such as our own. Throughout our lives we are taking important opinions on trust. This is normally very evident. But there is a widespread tendency to make an exception of ethics, regardless of the fact, not merely that we are variously endowed with ethical insight, but also that those who know the facts best must also, to a great extent, evaluate them for us. And the reluctance to accept this limitation of our conscience is largely to be attributed to the misconceptions about the personal character of duty with which we have been especially concerned. This heightens for us the importance for practice of exhibiting the 'objective' meaning of duty in respect of which others will be better qualified, in some ways, to determine what is our duty than we are ourselves.

(C) There is a further way in which the opinions of others are relevant to the appraisement of our own duties. For not only may these opinions help us to form our own, they are also factors within the situation in which we have to act. This makes it meaningful, in some circumstances, to affirm that we ought to act as other persons think we ought to act even when we are assured that these others are mistaken and our own opinions sound; the 'weaker brother' has to be considered. But we have to be careful how we understand this matter, and it is less misleading to state that the opinion of others is one factor in the situation that confronts us.

(D) The course which our ethical judgment suggests in regard to the general nature of a situation may require to be modified in the light of the procedure adopted by others, whether or not this procedure is prompted by ethical considerations. This matter has special significance today and calls for some further comment.

The necessity to reckon with the attitude of other persons

arises, like the deference to the opinions of others which we have already noted, from the complexity of the situations in which we have to act; and, as there are other ways, such as the terms we normally employ in this reference, in which the second compromise, if such it may be called, resembles the first, it is not easy to keep them separate in our thought. But it is quite important to do so. For the situation which justifies the one does not necessarily warrant the other.

To describe the compromise which we are now considering a distinction must be drawn between the effects of our actions on other persons as agents and as patients. The distinction is indeed usually a relative one, for it is rarely that our conduct will not require some response from those it affects. But the distinction is not less important for that reason. And it is important. For while the effect of conduct on those it affects mainly as patients will rarely be disregarded, men have a very uncertain hold on their responsibility for the effect of their actions on those who are agents along with themselves in any situation. Where such agents are at variance with ourselves, the fact that the will of those agents enters into the matter, that it is their responsibility as well as ours, is often deemed a sufficient reason for conceiving our own responsibility in terms of strict adherence to our individual conviction. But when the matter is viewed 'objectively', as the term is used in our distinction of subjective and objective duty, we shall be much better prepared to take proper account of the attitudes and convictions of those who participate with us in joint undertakings.

Plentiful examples of this kind of compromise may be found in the sphere of professional duty. A surgeon, for example, may find himself committed to assist at an operation which he would not recommend himself. He cannot dissociate himself from the judgment of others that a certain course is necessary, although, of course, there will be cases where he feels that nothing is gained by co-operation.

A similar situation is found in the case of the eminent divine (mentioned by Professor Field in a valuable paper),[1] who

---

[1] "Some Reflections on Pacifism," *Proceedings of the Aristotelian Society* Vol. XLIV, cf. also *Pacifism and Conscientious Objection*. In this later work Professor Field gives an admirable account of confusions into which

announced himself 'pacifist up to the outbreak of war'. This was thought in some quarters to be a contemptible attitude. But it is, in fact, a very reasonable position to adopt. The fact that a certain policy has been endorsed and adopted by the country in general is a factor of first importance in coming to any conclusion about our own duty, although it is not always a decisive factor. A pacifist may, with equal consistency, hold that war is so wrongful an expedient as to warrant his continued opposition to it. What he cannot deny, if his judgment is to be open and impartial, is the relevance of the decision of other people to his own decision.

This is what makes it very hard in practice to distinguish between prevarication and compromise, both in regard to decisions we have to make on our own behalf and in our judgments on the conduct of others. When we prevaricate the decision is affected by some regard to our private advantage; and the desire to avoid that corruption of our motives, or, in some cases, the suspicion of corruption, will sometimes lead to a less flexible policy than the situation requires.

To a similar source may be traced the ambiguities that attach to the idea of 'expediency' as an ethical and political principle.

The case of the pacifist raises the problem of compromise in one of its most important forms, that is, in regard to our duty to maintain the general conditions of social order. Where our convictions come into conflict with the requirements of the State it is normally our duty to submit to the State. The judge, for example, does not follow his private opinion of the matter before him; he acts on his interpretation of the law, although the law itself may, of course, require of him to follow his private judgment in certain regards. Similarly, an individual who feels that he himself, or another, is wronged by legal enactments, does not usually seek redress by unconstitutional methods. To resist all measures of which we disapprove would be to open the door to anarchy. The normal instrument of reform and redress is persuasion, and where, as in democratic countries, there are

---

conscientious objectors are apt to fall. But I imagine that it would not be difficult to compile a list of similar confusions which beset the opponents of the pacifists, not excluding the arguments of some who sat on the Tribunals to settle their cases.

constitutional methods of making persuasion effective, the duty to conform is considerably heightened. Even here, indeed, circumstances may present themselves in which the individual feels that he must 'make a stand' on some particular issue. In that case he must decide whether the benefits accruing from such a course compensate for such evils as the weakening of public confidence and the break in the law-abiding habits of himself and others. In the last analysis each person must judge for himself when the point which justifies resistance has been reached, the point at which, in a celebrated phrase, he "can do no other". But he has always to remember, not only the bearing of his particular problem on other similar problems, but also its relation to the general duty of supporting the structure of an ordered society. Resistance is an extreme medicine.

This applies in all matters of public procedure, and in regard to other societies than the State. But it is more apparent, and usually more important, in the sphere of political obligation. This is because the activities of other societies can be departmentalized for purposes of public enactment, and we can withdraw from them. But the State has to do, in some way or another, with all our activities. For these activities, whether they concern the things of the 'spirit', or more 'material' things, overlap in a way that requires the 'device of government' to co-ordinate and regulate them.

It does not, of course, follow that the State should regulate all matters directly. To attempt that is the fault of totalitarian governments. But it is equally a mistake, and one that has disastrous effects in practice, to suppose, as the strict pluralist does, that decentralisation and the limitations of State interference follow strict demarcations of interest.

IX

It is important that the compromise we make when we conform to social enactments of which we do not approve should be viewed clearly as a case of subordinating a less important duty to a more important one. This is what St. Augustine had in mind in his justly celebrated distinction between 'relative' law and 'absolute' law. The early Christians found themselves members of a society which was far from acknowledging their principles, much less adopting them in practice. This left them two alternatives. One was to form an isolated self-subsistent community of their own—a procedure to which some Christians have been attracted in recent times as well as at various periods in the past. In addition to the practical difficulties of such a policy, it seems also to run counter to the express injunction of Christ that his followers should be at least 'in' the world even if they were not wholly 'of' it. The heathen had far-reaching claims upon the Christian, and since these entailed living together as members of the same society, a compromise had to be effected between the 'ideals of the Kingdom' and what could be achieved in a society where allegiance to those ideals was very imperfect. And it is in this spirit that Christians, in the main, have proceeded ever since.

This attitude is fraught with the greatest dangers. For once we have accepted the idea of compromise, it is easy to lapse into an uncritical acquiescence in accepted practice. This has been facilitated in Christian thought and attitudes by the acceptance of the doctrine of original sin; for this doctrine, in some of its forms at least, converts the limitations imposed upon us by unavoidable circumstances into radical defects of human nature which preclude the pursuit of the very ideals by which man is to be judged. But this is a topic in itself. It must suffice here to note that the uncritical acquiescence of the Christian Church in accepted practice has often required fanatical excesses to remind it of its own ideals and responsibilities. Against lapses of this kind a constant vigilance must therefore be maintained by various institutions as well as by individuals in their more private capacity. For this purpose, and also to ensure an appreciation of one another's difficulties, we require a proper understanding of the nature of legitimate compromise as an adjustment of one duty to another, and to distinguish between this and compromise in the bad sense, namely a concession to our own weakness. For the latter there is no excuse although the severity of a temptation may lighten the blame that attaches to our failures.

It is especially unfortunate that compromise in the good sense prepares the way so often for compromise in the bad sense. And it is therefore all the more important to distinguish between the two. We are justified in departing from what seems to us, after due regard to the views of others, to be right in a particular regard, only when some other matter, usually a social requirement, renders full adherence to the former impracticable in a certain situation. The belief that ideals must always be 'beyond our reach', that they would cease to be-ideals if we could fulfil them, is a mischievous confusion which is due very largely to failure to appreciate how a compromise is justified. An ideal is a standard to which we ought to conform, and if we are to say at the same time that we ought not to conform to it, unless we are referring to the case of honest adherence to a false ideal,[1] we must mean either that it conflicts with another more important ideal, or that it represents some duty in the future for which we can prepare by discharging some other duty now. In the main, to represent ideals as some kind of pattern which we may imperfectly copy leads to confusion of thought and laxity.

Similar strictures must be passed on the suggestion that compromise is to be understood in the light of 'two moralities' —the morality of 'duty' and the morality of 'grace'. The attractiveness of this view lies in the fact that a right does not always carry with it a right to insist on that right. Thus its recent advocate, the Master of Balliol, asserts that the morality of grace "is not something we take for granted; we do not demand it of other people".[2] On this basis he argues that even if it is "a duty to respond to the highest demands that we can hear, other people have not a corresponding right to such response in us".[3] On this plane, rights and duties are not, as the 'textbooks' maintain, reciprocal. But surely the fact that the effect of certain kindnesses upon us is spoiled where they are sought or demanded, does not make it nonsense to say that we owe such kindness to one another if we can render them without prejudice to more urgent duties? The importance of spontaneity and graciousness in our relationships may be readily admitted, but the fact that we cannot proceed by rule in these regards, and that much depends here on our individual gifts and

---

[1] Compare above, section IV.
[2] A. D. Lindsay, *The Two Moralities*, p. 42.
[3] op. cit. p. 43.

affections, does not remove these matters from the sphere of duty—and its correlative, right—for it is always a duty to cultivate these qualities and seek opportunities to display them. And apart from this there is no 'morality of grace'. The viciousness of the doctrine of a 'morality of grace', so it seems to me, lies in the suggestion that in some respects the discharge of our duties is an arbitrary matter, that, if we may so put it, there is sometimes 'a little extra' which does not present itself as something we are bound to do. This belief, which we often encounter in popular thought, is hardly compatible with the highest endeavour. As applied to the compromises that we have to make in respect of public enactments—and it is here, in fact, that it is thought to have the greatest importance—this principle defeats the expectation of its advocates by inducing too comfortable an acquiescence in the 'duties of my station'; whatever goes beyond this or calls for opposition to it will tend to lack the 'compelling' character of duty.

The idea of 'two moralities' also reminds us of the view of some pacifists who argue that they have a special duty to witness to a 'higher way' or to respond to the challenge of a higher morality than that which countenances war. Individuals may, indeed, have special obligations. In some circumstances celibacy may be such a duty; every obligation, in fact, has some element of uniqueness. But it cannot be anybody's special obligation to act in a way which he could not recommend to others similarly placed; nor could anyone with consistency adhere to an ideal which he himself considers to run counter to the discharge of more urgent duties. Since all men have to live in the world it cannot be the privilege of some to disregard the compromises that conscientious persons generally have to make. The 'challenge to perfection' cannot be a challenge to act otherwise than is compatible with the fullest discharge that is practicable of all the claims that confront us in any situation. To consider the war to be justified for the State and for the majority of citizens and yet believe it too evil for oneself to participate in it according to one's age and circumstances appears to be sheer inconsistency. What the consistent pacifist must hold is that the evils which it is hoped to arrest or eradicate by war can be more effectively and completely cured in the long run by passive resistance.[1] Whether or not it is so does not concern us here.

We affirm then, that a man's duty in any situation has a single definite nature. But it may be very hard to ascertain its precise character. For into its composition there will usually enter a great many factors between which a delicate adjustment requires to be made.

Adjustments of this kind, as well as deference to the views of others, will clearly have less importance in some spheres. These are the spheres sometimes designated by the term 'private morality', although this ambiguous term has other uses. In regard to his affections, pastimes and other 'personal' interests the individual must rely more completely on his own resources. The intrusion of others will be much resented here, and advice, if it is not solicited, will be treated as an imposition. The more cultured we become the more jealously shall we preserve this independence and privacy. But even in respect to these personal and private matters there will be required some regard for the beliefs and reactions of others, not merely in respect to general matters, as when an artist attends to the criticism of an expert, but also in regard to the moral quality of our conduct. Not even the highest gifts or the finest sensibilities entitle the agent to be in any sphere wholly a law to himself. For his conduct will certainly have some repercussions on the lives of others, and the opinions which other people hold as to what he should do may be relevant, and will almost invariably be so in some measure, to the decisions that he has to take about the course of his own conduct.

But it is in matters where our own conduct is most closely interlinked with that of others that compromise in its various forms has the greatest importance. Such, as we have seen, are public enactments, and the fact that there is no monopoly of truth in these matters is wisely acknowledged in democratic practices. One of the main problems of democracy is to find a means of consulting each individual about the matters into which he is likely to have special insight, such as the effect of public enactments on himself and his immediate community.

It is in public matters, also, that it is usually hardest to make

[1] But see also above, pp. 67 and 68.

substantial allowance for the attitude of others. For it is here that our conduct is most likely to have the appearance of prevarication. In fact it may often require considerable resolution, if only because it will seem to one's friends and associates as a refusal to face obloquy and persecution or, at any rate, as the absence of any depth of conviction. The enthusiast is apt to have little patience with refinements of the kind. Few paths are harder, and none, I imagine, more solitary, than that of the 'noncomformist' or objector, who continues to think, and who, being aware of his own fallibility, endeavours to allow for the insight and reactions of others. The support of those who march with him will often be an embarrassment, while the suspicions of his friends and the bitterness of the more uncompromising among them, proving in many cases more unrestrained than the antagonism of their joint opponent, will put on him a burden he had not reckoned to carry.

Moreover, the person who appreciates his own limitations, and endeavours to remedy the matter in the ways we have described, will usually be the one most disposed to consider all the factors of a complicated situation. For the same reasonableness is operative in both cases. But the conduct suggested will not always be the same. The fairness and comprehensiveness of his judgment may itself be the cause of divergence from accepted standards. This will be especially so in regard to the opinion prevailing at a particular time. For popular opinion, while it is the repository of much that has been searchingly thought and felt, is also notoriously variable and, when we pass from more fundamental principles to the complicated questions of policy, apt to be 'deaf and shortsighted', to borrow one of the less severe strictures of Plato. Reasonableness will, in these cases, be divided against itself. Anxious to allow for the wisdom of others and for aspects of experience obscure to him, the reflective person, when he finds himself in a minority on an important issue, may have experiences of an excruciating character of which the more dogmatic dissentient, often moving in the full tide of a fanatical faith, is quite unaware.

Much of the dignity of human existence comes from the fact that we have to make our way through an entanglement of ethical problems. The effort and adventure to which we are thereby challenged must not, however, be identified with moral effort in the strict sense. The responsibility we have for finding our way through the complications that confront us, so far as it refers to the fact that we are thrown on the resources of our own moral thinking in distinction from the effort to continue to think, is different from the properly moral responsibility to continue in the way when the path is hard. But both these matters have the highest significance for our final view of the meaning of human existence. How they are related in a religious view of the world is a question of first importance to which we can only allude here without any comment.

Chapter IV

THE PRESENT STATE OF ETHICS[1]

"ETHICS is essentially boring". Such was the declaration made, at a recent philosophical conference, by one of the most influential of British philosophers of the present time. I cannot give you his name, for the remark was made in the course of a general discussion, and not from a printed paper. For the same reason I cannot vouch for the strict verbal accuracy of my quotation. But it is a very significant one, for it expresses in downright terms what has often been vaguely suggested of late and what seems to be the prevailing view of the most vigorous, and especially the most assertive, thinkers in this country today, although there are few who would put it as bluntly as the speaker to whom I referred. It should be stressed that the words do not simply condemn a particular ethical trend or express dissatisfaction with the way ethics are handled today. It is not even a case of suggesting, as the late Professor H. A. Prichard did in a celebrated article, that moral philosophy as hitherto conceived is 'founded upon a mistake'.[2] It is not a case of simple ethical scepticism, although, heaven knows, there is plenty of that. Sceptics as a rule are quite ready for debate. But the phenomenon with which we are confronted today is that of a large and influential body of philosophers who find any sort of examination of ethical questions along the lines we traditionally know as moral philosophy tedious and little worthy of the attention of those who truly know what philosophers ought to be doing. To leave ethics alone, or to abandon it to those who have more taste for uplift than thought, and not even to trouble about refutations of established beliefs or explanations of their persistence, seems to be the proper course for those who would really be in the fashion. But this is not just a fashion. Nor is it merely reflective of a prevailing trend in philosophical thought.

[1] A paper read to the Modern Churchmen's Conference at Bristol, September, 1949. The general subject of the Conference was 'The Flight from Reason'. The paper was published in the *Cambridge Journal*, Feb. 1950.
[2] *Mind*, 1912. Reproduced in his *Moral Obligation*, Chapter I.

It expresses what is, in my opinion, a deep and especially significant aversion to turn the mind to the problems of ethics, amounting in some cases to positive nausea.

To appreciate fully the nature of this situation we need to remember how sharp a departure it is from the practice of philosophers hitherto. In the past ethics has usually been of the greatest concern to philosophers. In some celebrated cases, for example those of Socrates and Spinoza, its problems have provided the main incentive to reflection. Not that the major problems only appear in ethics. Far be it from me to suggest that. Nor should we expect all philosophers to be equally interested in all fields of philosophy. Nowadays especially we must be allowed, in this discipline as in others, our specialisms. But there is that in the nature of philosophy which precludes too rigid a demarcation of spheres, as Plato so insistently taught, and the greatest philosophers, even when their main interests have lain in metaphysics or theory of knowledge, have allowed their curiosity and concern to range in the same philosophical way over the fields of ethics and politics as well. Thus Locke, whom we know so well as the father of modern empiricism, has his assured place also as the author of a celebrated treatise on Civil Government than which few books have had a greater influence on practice. But today it seems possible for some of our ablest thinkers, even when they do not generally seal their thoughts off in watertight compartments, to keep their minds closed at least to ethics. Professor Price, for example, in an otherwise notable survey of the course of philosophy between the two wars,[1] includes no reference to ethics beyond the observation that the omission must not be itself taken to imply that nothing of importance happened in ethics during that period. And he is not by any means alone among philosophers of recent years in having been most productive in many fields without seeming ever to turn to ethics.

This is all the more surprising in view of the urgent practical problems which confront us today. But it certainly cannot be ascribed to any slack period in ethics itself. For those who have turned their minds to this subject in the first half of this century have made remarkable progress, notably in British philosophy.

[1] *Horizon*, January, 1949.

I need only instance the work of C. D. Broad, G. E. Moore, H. A. Prichard and W. D. Ross. Here alone we have a body of new and carefully thought out ethical teaching. It has indeed its ancestry, also mostly in British philosophy. But rarely has so much that has been but dimly apprehended in the past been set forth in such clear and exhaustive terms as in the discussion of moral objectivity and its implications by recent moralists such as those I have mentioned. Abroad we have the very solid work of Nicolai Hartmann, whose brief spell of popularity has already receded before the more spectacular work of far less discerning and strenuous thinkers. It has always seemed strange to me that so little is generally known about the important advances made of late in ethics. All the publicity seems to be given to debates with positivists of some brand or another, or to matters on the fringes of philosophy. And although serious philosophical work can hardly be expected to be very popular, but must on the contrary affect general opinion by slow and steady permeation, it is, I think, extremely regrettable that the public should be left under the impression that little of a constructive nature has been attempted in recent philosophy when in fact we have seen as lively a period in moral philosophy, and as substantial a positive achievement, as any in the history of the subject. It is also, as I have often stressed, singularly unfortunate that theology has been so little affected by the best ethical thought of today, for recent ethics is peculiarly relevant to just those questions which most agitate our theologians. The way out of many theological muddles has been very clearly pointed out to us—if only we could take it. But what is bewildering most of all is that the achievements of moral philosophers in this century, and the acute argumentation that has proceeded amongst themselves about their main contentions, should have created so little stir in the philosophical world at large, and is, at present, in real danger of being neglected altogether, so much has the tide of philosophical fashion left it high and dry.

The attitude of our younger philosophers in particular is well exemplified in the following quotation from a recent paper.

"As a fair example of contemporary academic moral philosophy let me take Sir David Ross's *Foundations of Ethics*. I fancy that I am not alone in finding this book thoroughly dissatisfying and depressing. Yet the reason is not that it is a bad book; on the contrary it is a book which it seems presumptuous to praise. It is the mature work of a very keen intellect, representing a lifetime devoted to its subject. It is sound and complete, in a sense in which even the great classics of moral philosophy, such as Kant's *Critique of Practical Reason,* are not. One is conscious that nothing relevant to its purpose has been neglected—everything has been considered and given its due weight. Why, then, are we still unsatisfied? The answer, I would suggest, is that its purpose does not interest us. We are looking for something else".[1]

But for what, then, are we looking when we find that moral philosophy, as we have known it, is not very relevant to our need? We are looking, I suggest, very largely for something which it is not the business of the most basic ethical principles, and those which are most amenable to philosophical treatment, to supply. The dissatisfaction with ethics is due in part to frustration arising in turn from a wrongful expectation. The expectation is that the moral philosopher should prove himself more immediately useful in the sphere of practice than he appears to be. We are faced today with urgent practical problems, in the sphere of public and private affairs, and many of these are of a nature to which there is little guidance in similar periods of stress and transition in the past. I need not dilate on this. We all know how completely the social and political scene has changed in the course of our own lifetime. There has been more change in a few years of late than in many centuries in the past, and it is all the sort of change which gives a novel character to many questions of right and wrong. The old standards are, in many cases, not so much false as irrelevant. And the younger generation in particular is apt to regard a continuation of the old ethical debate with extreme impatience as a symptom of the indifference and blindness of their elders to the chaotic and bewildering conditions in which younger folk in particular find themselves. Accusations of smugness and escapism are very common, and it is not surprising that these should be reflected in the attitude adopted towards basic ethical

---

[1] Towards a New Moral Philosophy. A. M. MacIver. *Proceedings of the Aristotelian Society,* 1945-46, p. 180.

principles and the philosophical study of them. The philosopher, we have been told by so many of late, must leave his ivory tower and prove his worth in the heat and dust of affairs. He must deal with real problems, he must be contemporary; and above all, if he is a moral philosopher and has to do with questions of practice, he must prove the relevance of what he has to say to urgent practical problems of the present if he is to deserve a hearing.

Now this is a reaction we easily understand, and there is a great deal more involved in it than the impatience of the man of affairs with those who are given to contemplation of what is more permanent and abiding. The last thing we can afford to do is to be patronizing and superior. Even so, it is well to bear in mind that this sort of impatience is not, in itself, a very new phenomenon. It made a very deep impression on Plato, much of whose thought is designed to counter it. Plato, no doubt, went to extremes in turn, and put too great a reliance on abstract philosophical thought as a guide to action. He underestimated, as Aristotle did not, the practical wisdom of the man of affairs and the wisdom enshrined in common experience. Hence his misinterpretation of democracy as the rule of the mass. Even so we cannot but side with him in his denunciation of those who courted cheap popular support and acclamation by offering deceptively attractive short-term solutions to questions which call for the greatest patience and breadth of vision in the study of their many-sided complications. The unusually passionate outburst of Plato in a famous passage of the *Theaetetus*, in spite of its extremism, and of the unfortunate, if understandable, dualism which led him so often astray, constitutes still to my mind one of the noblest defences of the supremacy of reason, and his words come echoing down the centuries to us today with an unusually poignant significance. It will be no waste of our time to repeat them.

Plato begins with an account of the rhetorician (in words reminiscent of that remarkable phrase in *The Republic* which speaks of 'the shrewd little eyes of the soul' of men reputed vicious but clever[1]) as one "always talking against time" and having thus acquired "a tense and bitter shrewdness", and as

[1] *Republic* 519.

one, "whose apprenticeship in slavery has dwarfed and twisted his growth and robbed him of his free spirit, driving him into devious ways, threatening him with fears and dangers which the tenderness of youth could not face with truth and honesty; so, turning from the first to lies and the requital of wrong with wrong, warped and stunted, he passes from youth to manhood with no soundness in him and turns out, in the end, a man of formidable intellect—as he imagines".[1] With this we are to contrast the philosophic nature:

"On the other hand, my friend, when the philosopher drags the other upwards to a height at which he may consent to drop the question 'What injustice have I done to you or you to me?' and to think about justice or injustice in themselves, what each is and how they differ from one another and from anything else; or to stop quoting poetry about the happiness of kings or of men with gold in store and think about the meaning of kingship and the whole question of human happiness and misery, what their nature is, and how humanity can gain the one and escape the other—in all this field, when that small shrewd legal mind has to render an account, then the situation is reversed. Now it is he who is dizzy from hanging at such an unaccustomed height and looking down from mid-air. Lost and dismayed and stammering, he will be laughed at, not by maid-servants or the uneducated—they will not see what is happening—but by everyone whose breeding has been the antithesis of a slave's".[2]

Plato concludes that when you get the slick rhetoricians alone "and make them explain their objections to philosophy, then, if they are men enough to face a long examination without running away, it is odd how they end by finding their own arguments unsatisfied; somehow their flow of eloquence runs dry, and they become as speechless as an infant".[3]

All this, together with Plato's continuous insistence that the philosopher has to take the long and toilsome route himself before he can return to 'the cave' to enlighten others, needs to be borne very carefully in mind at present. Alluring roads to an

---
[1] *Theaetetus* 173.
[2] op. cit., 175.
[3] op. cit., 177.

easy utopia and short-sighted policies of quick returns must not be allowed to blind us to the need for sustained and disciplined thought about questions that reach beyond our immediate situation. But there is, none the less, a great deal involved in the present impatience with the traditional approach to ethics, with its presupposition of abiding ethical truths, than the mere general impatience with the rather slow return which philosophy and the long-term consideration of practical questions are apt to yield. And it is, in my view, of the greatest importance to know what this is.

Let us be clear on one point. It may well be the case—I should certainly maintain that it is—that philosophers, and especially moral philosophers, ought to take greater part in public affairs than they usually do. The compulsion on many to do so during the war has shown how well their training suits them for the purpose. And it will, no doubt, be as much to their own advantage to do so, in the long run, as to that of the community, provided, in the case of professional philosophers, that the ever-growing burden of administration within their profession does not absorb all the energy and time they can spare from their studies. But whatever the advantages may be of setting philosophers to various tasks in public spheres, the main function which they have to discharge, and that for which they are most indispensable, is to uphold the general principles which they are specially trained to study. And in times of stress and confusion the need is especially acute. But here perhaps we shall encounter a major objection, namely that there are no abiding principles but only those which fluctuate with particular circumstances, and that the failure of moral philosophy to make itself relevant to present need is that philosophers are too slow to shift their principles with the changing conditions on which their principles must be based. They lag in this way behind the times and throw in their weight with old-fashioned and obstructionist forces.

This seems to me to be the main charge made against contemporary moral philosophy in the paper to which I have referred above. "Why," the writer asks, "is there even now no moral philosophy which is not Victorian, in the sense that it presupposes the Victorian moral code? Why have we left this subject, if not to old men, then to those who are by temperament or upbringing old-fashioned? The immediate answer is simple. We can produce no moral philosophy of our own because we have not settled our own morality. We reject the Victorian code, but we have found nothing to take its place, so that the moral philosophy based upon it, hopelessly unreal though it seems, still has no rival."[1] Now this seems to me to involve an entirely mistaken view of basic ethical principles, and of the function of moral philosophy. The question of objectivity and its alternatives in ethics has been much debated of late, and I do not wish to intervene in that debate more than I can help in this paper. My main purpose is something different. Nor has the article on which I have ventured to comment any solid arguments to offer against the views which, on the writer's own admission, have been set forth with surpassing skill. His charge is the general one of irrelevance and unreality, and I find the charge, and the prevalence of similar complaints, especially significant because it does, to my mind, point to something of great importance. But first of all it will be well to pause and make plain just in what way the rapid shift in social conditions, together with more comprehensive knowledge of similar changes in the past afforded by new advances in history and anthropology, bear upon ethical questions. In what way is history relevant to ethics, and how far must moral philosophy be contemporary?

We have here to distinguish between two types of ethical questions. First there are specific questions of practice—'What should be the terms of a peace treaty?' 'Should we have greater nationalisation?' 'Should we take part in war?' 'What should be the treatment of conscientious objectors?' 'What money should we contribute to a cause?' 'What time should we give to matters outside our strict professional duties?' Now all these questions depend very largely on matters of fact, whether we think of more personal problems like that of contributing to a charity, which plainly depends on the money available to us and on the extent of other claims upon us, or of more public questions like that of amending a treaty. The facts in question have, moreover, often to be viewed against a particular social environment, and the more we know of the relations of this environment to others,

[1] A. M. MacIver, *Proc. Arist. Soc.*, 1945-6, p. 185.

and especially to those most directly connected with it, the better. In public matters this is very plain. It has often been pointed out, for example, that the framers of the Treaty of Versailles could have avoided many mistakes had they, or their advisers, been better informed about the history and traditions of the peoples whose destinies they tried to settle, and had they paid more heed to such knowledge. I cannot argue here how far this is the case in the particular example in question. All we need allow is that it is a very reasonable view to take that history is, at any rate, relevant to such questions. The new knowledge provided today by anthropology, of which so much is heard in debates about the status of ethics, has an obvious bearing on the question of the treatment of backward peoples, and it is not without relevance to questions like marriage and divorce as they appear among civilised societies, much though students of this subject, as often happens in such matters in the first burst of enthusiasm, are apt to exaggerate its relevance to our problems.

It should be added that among the facts of which account should be taken in this way, we have to include the opinions current about ethical questions themselves. This is not, to my mind, because anything, whether action or experience, can acquire an ethical character of any kind, rightness or goodness, merely by being thought to have it. But our dealings with other people are bound to be affected by the opinions which both parties hold. Right action requires that we take account of susceptibilities we do not ourselves share, and consider the 'weaker brother', even when we think him wrong-headed. How much we should allow in this way is always a hard question which must be settled differently in particular cases as they arise. But the fact that we need to make allowance of this sort must not obscure the fact that it is only indirectly that opinions, of ourselves or of other persons, affect questions of right and duty, and that many other factors are involved.

There are also other, more indirect, ways in which history bears on questions of practice, although we need do little more than mention them here. Knowledge of what has been notably achieved or thought in the past will refine our own moral sensibility even when it does not bear explicitly on some particular issue. It will also help us to view our problem in a wider cultural setting. There are again 'the lessons of history' about which there has been so much debate. But it is of course a very serious travesty of this to suppose that history follows certain rigid patterns which will of themselves prescribe the course to be followed in particular times and situations. Idealist thinkers in the last century, fortified by metaphysical views which seem to me very mistaken, and made remarkably complacent by the tranquillity of the times, lent much support to this comfortable view. The Marxists adopt it as a dogma today. But we hardly need to look very closely at this strange supposition to see how readily it lends itself to the defence of any policy we choose, and most obviously of all to the view that might is right. Students of Croce's *Politics and Morals* can easily perceive how disastrous such a principle may prove even in the hands of a fairly liberally-minded writer.

But this is rather by the way, although it also has its not unimportant bearing on the general question of ethical relativism and the 'flight from reason' in ethics. The main point at the moment is that matters of fact, including changes in moral, social and political attitudes, are in various ways very closely relevant to specific ethical problems of practice. But whether they are so to the exclusion of further considerations depends on the view we take about rather different and more abstract questions which it is more peculiarly the business of moral philosophers to study. These are the questions, 'What is the general nature of goodness or of rightness, and what conditions do they presuppose?' And we must now ask how far consideration of facts is relevant to these more peculiarly philosophical questions.

The plausibility of the view that questions about the general nature of goodness or rightness can be settled by consideration of facts, such as those adduced by history or psychology, is superficially heightened by confusion of this sort of question with specific questions of practice. As we have seen, consideration of facts is highly relevant to the latter, and in a great many cases the only serious consideration, on any view, will be that of the particular facts of the situation. It is easy, for this reason, to conclude without further thought that no ethical problem can be settled in any way other than by examination of matters of fact. This is, however, extremely hasty. It begs the most important issue in ethics, namely, whether all ethical qualities can be described in naturalistic terms. This sort of question, the question whether it is by reference to some kind of natural facts or not that we define the main ethical conceptions, clearly cannot itself be settled by appeal to such facts. What we must do is to put it to ourselves whether or not we find in ethical ideas something not exhaustively reducible to naturalistic terms. In the last resort there can, in fact, be no kind of argument here. If there are non-naturalistic ethical principles we can only say that they are so; we cannot prove it, certainly not in any empirical way; for what we claim is that we know something to which empirical considerations are irrelevant. Advocates of non-naturalistic ethics are still, I fear, inclined to forget this. But their claims must finally rest on some kind of intuition or direct insight, and others must ask themselves whether or not, on reflection, they find that they share these intuitions. Much irrelevance on both sides of the issue has been caused of late by neglect of this. But it still does not follow that consideration of facts is entirely irrelevant to these more ultimate questions about the status of ethical principles.

It would be relevant in this way. Although the final appeal must be made to intuition (or the absence of it), intuition does not function altogether in a void, and if we are to retain an open mind, and in that way find really firm foundation for our beliefs and know them to be convictions and not prejudices, we must ask ourselves from time to time whether what seems to us to be clear intuition is not some kind of illusion and capable of a different explanation. And we must ask this especially when new facts come to light which might afford an explanation in empirical terms of what had formerly seemed to be immediate insight. Facts of this sort have recently been adduced by anthropologists and psychologists, especially of the psycho-analytical school. No moral philosopher can therefore afford to neglect these subjects, and the plea that he ought to be abreast of the times has particular force in matters of this kind and in respect of those general aspects of contemporary culture, such as modern art and literature, in which they are most plainly reflected. But while it is necessary for the advocate of non-empirical ethical principles to put his intuition to the test in this way, one must stress again that, when we have fairly reviewed the facts, the issue is not settled by arguments from the facts, but by direct reflection. And it is well to add a protest against the facile supposition that when a plausible alternative account of what had formerly been taken to be some distinctive ethical truth is available in terms of some new advance in psychology or general science, we must straightway accept it. I have not myself been much shaken in my conviction of the distinctiveness of ethical truth by anything I have read, for example, about recent psychoanalytical discoveries, important though the latter may be in themselves when properly set forth and critically appraised—a qualification which, incidentally, needs to be stressed.

A further matter which lends attractiveness to the view that recent studies in anthropology or kindred fields support some kind of relativism in ethics is the very mistaken assumption that belief in moral objectivity implies belief in principles about which all are agreed. Mr. MacIver, for example, declares: "It has often been observed—it is regularly quoted in proof of the objectivity of moral judgments — that, wherever moral judgments are made at all, the same types of action are generally considered in themselves right or wrong, the same dispositions virtues or vices".[1] I do not know where the writer has found this quoted. But so far as the most important advocates of moral objectivity (including Ross, since the writer refers to him) are concerned, the position is quite the reverse of what he envisages. These thinkers have gone out of their way to insist that moral objectivity is to be understood in terms of the independence of ethical truths of what we may feel and think about them ourselves. One of the main considerations they adduce is that we continue to adhere to our views even when we know that most other people think or feel differently; and although we cannot *prove* the objectivist case in this way, at any rate in a non-naturalistic sense, the crucial importance of this consideration shows it to be sheer misunderstanding of the points at issue to instance diversities in the opinions of individuals or societies in refutation of the objectivist.

[1] op. cit. 195.

Admittedly, the objectivists have pointed out, quite properly and with justification, that many apparent differences on ethical matters are really differences about matters of fact, and not about strictly ethical questions; and the most recent studies tend to suggest that the difference between different cultures in properly ethical matters is far less than was commonly thought.[1] It has also been stressed that, although ethical principles are independent of us in the sense that they are not made true by what we think or feel, we have often all the certainty we need for practice and, in cases of graver doubt, ways of making our opinions more probably true. But there is nothing here to suggest an equation of moral objectivity with unanimity, immediate or eventual.

It seems, therefore, plain that while the moral philosopher can ill afford to lose touch with advances in cognate fields, and with social changes, less so than ever today, this need not be straightway understood in the sense that his basic principles vary with changes of this sort, that the very nature of goodness and obligation are themselves different for us from what they were in the past because they take different specific forms. We may take different views from our fathers about what is obligatory, but that hardly alters the meaning of obligation. And it may well be the case—I should certainly maintain that it is so— that the main function of the moral philosopher in times of rapid and extensive change is to ensure that we do not fall under the lure of a superficially attractive relativism, and thereby lose hold of the principles to which we need most of all to cling. It is this, in my view, which makes the work of the thinkers to whom I referred above[2] especially important and relevant to present needs. And if it be admitted, as I think those who know their books would readily do, that their work lacks little in skilful presentation, then we must look further for any substantiation of the complaint that there is some peculiar air of unreality and irrelevance in our ethical thinking as it comes before the present generation.

We draw near the true explanation, I think, if we ponder the shrewd observation with which Professor H. B. Acton

---

[1] cf. C. A. Campbell, *Moral Intuition and the Principle of Self-Realization.*
[2] p. 80.

closes a recent survey of philosophy in France. He notes that Mademoiselle de Beauvoir (author of *Pour une Morale de l'Ambiguité*) "is led into what at first sight seems to be the paradoxical position of earnestly castigating 'earnest' people. She does not use the plain moral language, because if she does people will sarcastically murmur that that is the sort of thing they were taught at Sunday School. Existentialist moralists are endeavouring to restate, in a language of paradox, what the sophistication of the age prevents us from taking seriously when stated in the language of tradition."[1] But there is more involved here than the staleness which comes from mere repetition. Ethical terms have been bandied about in contexts that are not deeply charged with ethical significance, and have been much monopolised by those least entitled to use them. The coinage has thus been seriously debased, and many find themselves unable to think fairly about ethical questions because of *the dissociation of ethical ideas from ethical realities.*

This reflects itself in philosophical attitudes in the contemporary protest against an alleged excessively abstract nature of philosophical thinking in the past—and especially in what is now coming to be regarded, in theology as well as in philosophy, as the baleful influence of Descartes. More lies behind this change than can be indicated or examined here. But most of you will be familiar already with the attempts that are common today to be rid of any propositional element in ethics. This takes its boldest shape among out-and-out positivists, but subtler variations of the same determination to have an 'ethics without propositions' are found among writers too elusive for us to pin a definite label upon them. It is argued, for example, that the thinking involved in actual conduct is so different from theoretical thinking that it is best described as part of action itself—this being in some ways a reversal to a view current among the much derided idealists. Others urge that our use of ethical terms is in fact a form of doing rather than thinking—'doing things with words', in the familiar philosophical terms of today.

On a basis of this sort Professor Gilbert Ryle, in an extremely influential paper, arrives at the conclusion that moral impera-

[1] *Philosophy*, January, 1949, p. 81.

tives must be relegated to some stage of fumbling over-deliberate action and not to high ethical conduct. "They are bannisters for toddlers, i.e., they belong to the methodology and not to the methods of intelligent practices. What logicians have long half-realised about the venue and function of their rule-formulae has yet to be learned by moral philosophers about their imperatives and ought-statements. When they have learned this they will cease to ask such questions as whether conscience is an intuitive or discursive faculty. For knowing how to behave is not a sort of knowing that, so it is neither an intuitive nor a discursive sort of knowing that." Professor Ryle continues: "Now conscience is an old-fashioned faculty word, but if the assertion means that the conscientious man exercises his conscientiousness by issuing propositions or prescriptions, then this is false . . . . Moral imperatives and ought-statements have no place in the lives of saints or complete sinners. For saints are not still learning how to behave and complete sinners have not yet begun to learn. So neither experiences scruples. Neither experiences maxims".[1] It is not easy to determine just how far Professor Ryle desires to go with this,[2] nor is it plain what he would substitute for moral imperatives in normal ethical experience. Few desire to hold that we live our day-to-day lives in obedience to abstract rules, but it does not follow that we can think of moral experience in any way except as shot through with the consciousness of our confrontation with moral imperatives of a very different nature from the rules of grammar and more irreducible.

There is of course much in Professor Ryle's contentions, and in those of others of a like mind, which calls for a very different sort of scrutiny from that which can be attempted at this stage in a fairly non-technical paper. The distinction, for example, between 'knowing how' and 'knowing that' does not seem to me to be as ultimate as he suggests. But I refer to these matters at the moment mainly by way of illustration. There are however two points that I would like to take the opportunity of making. The first is that the familiar terms 'doing things with words' are highly ambiguous. Suppose I were to tell my friend "There

[1] *Proceedings of the Aristotelian Society*, 1945-46, pp. 12-14.
[2] Nor has the matter been subsequently clarified in his much-discussed book, *The Concept of Mind*.

is a puddle just ahead of you", what am I doing? I am preventing him from getting wet, but strictly I have done nothing more than convey my meaning to him; I have not forcibly held him back. So I might save my friend's life by telling him of a dangerous ledge. We are 'doing things with words' in this sense all the time. But this does not reduce the apprehension of meaning, as involved in such action, itself into some form of doing. The propositional factor remains. My second point is that I much suspect that the protagonists of 'ethics *with* propositions' may be giving too much away to their opponents by admitting that there may be some meaningful statements which do not assert anything. When it is urged that, if ethical statements assert nothing they can only be meaningless exclamations, the reply is often made—'But what of questions and commands, etc.; they affirm nothing; they are not true or false; but we understand them'. On the face of it this seems very true. If someone says 'Open the door' and I reply 'No it is not', it will be assumed that I have not understood. But may not this be simply because the appropriate response to an utterance of this sort is not affirmation or denial but action or refusal to act in some way, and that the utterance still remains an affirmation of some kind. I do not care now to attempt a translation of commands into assertions, for even if I were quite confident that I could do it, which I am not, it would require more detailed analysis than would be in order here (more being involved, I am certain, than mere expression of a desire coupled with a threat). But I cannot refrain from making the tentative suggestion that a resolute attack on the problem of questions and commands in this way may not only lead the way out of notorious logical difficulties, but also enable the defender of traditional ethics to turn the tables on some of his opponents.

But my main concern at the moment is not to argue the case with the positivists—that would require much space—but to suggest a general explanation of the prevalence of this sort of extreme empiricism, namely, in the first place, that the distrust of all non-empirical explanation is largely due to insensibility to the ethical truths which provide one of the major meanings of explanation which we would offer as alternatives to its strictly scientific meanings, and, secondly, that this insensitivity to ethical truth, and consequent attempts to argue its claims away, are due to an alienation of ethical thinking from crucial forms of ethical experience.

This was, in my view, already well advanced in the idealism which dominated European thought at the turn of the century. For not only did this sort of idealism fail to acknowledge the ultimacy of any kind of evil, having rather to explain it away as appearance or goodness out of its place, but it also proved peculiarly unable to accommodate the notions of the freedom and responsibility of the individual. For much though some of its votaries strained their theories to 'save the appearances', it seems to be quite impossible to regard the individual as properly accountable for his actions if he is himself determined in all his conduct as a 'phase' of the Absolute. Idealism thus imposed the rigidity of its monistic system on the living flow of experience.

This contains an especially significant warning to those, like most members of this Conference, who have a particular concern to uphold the claims of reason. For few things in the long run prove more to the detriment of the place of reason in our lives than the perpetuation of that misconception of the function of reason which supposes that it must absorb all things into itself, and that every truth can therefore be educed from the notion of rationality itself. For not only are there limits to the operation of reason in the transcendent character of reality, but the work of reason as co-ordinator within finite experience presupposes terms which subsist independently—moral intuitions for example. A narrow rationalism may do the very greatest injury to the just claims of reason and present a very distorted view of experience. This gives encouragement, by way of reaction in particular, to the various forms of irrationalism we encounter today, ranging from its subtler and more refined philosophical modes to crude and frenzied political dogmatism.

In recent ethics likewise, notwithstanding the important achievements that lie to its credit, there is one serious defect that tends to devitalise the whole, and this has also to do with the problem of freedom, or rather with the evasion of it. This I have discussed in some detail in a more technical paper.[1] I have

[1] See below, ch. VI.

argued there that, while there have been some notable discussions of this problem in recent years, they have been off the main lines of ethical controversy, and that some of our best and acutest ethical thinking has been seriously at odds with itself because the idea of obligation, on which so much attention has rightly been centred, has been discussed without much direct attack on its main postulate of freedom, and usually within a deterministic framework. We have thus heard much about 'right' and 'good', but little about guilt and remorse. And this has helped to a very great extent, in my opinion, to throw an air of unreality over discussions which are otherwise of the greatest merit and importance.

The neglect of the crucial ethical notions of guilt, freedom and responsibility has also led to their resuscitation in distorted forms in pseudo-philosophies which lack the equipment to deal with them carefully and critically, for example in certain forms of Existentialism. Credit must be given to this latter movement for the importance it has usually accorded to the idea of freedom, and for its protest, in the name of living experience, against the rigidities of abstract systems. But this has often led to little more than ridiculous travesties of genuine freedom in the shape of obscurantist metaphysical ideas of freedom as a choice which itself somehow establishes the standard which can give it meaning, and sometimes even as a bizarre "freedom for death". Few ideas can be so easily and viciously distorted as the idea of freedom, as is evidenced at many points in the long history of thought. And many of the present cults of irrationalism make it distressingly plain, in their treatment of freedom, how grim are the consequences of an abjuration of his function here by the philosopher. But they also help us to understand what it is in the nature of recent ethical thought which detracts from its interest by keeping it out of touch with genuine ethical experience at a vital point.

It is worth noting here that one recent detractor of moral philosophy, Mrs. Lan Freed, in a book which, if not always very thorough in its argumentation, is often very shrewd, finds the weaknesses of ethics exposed especially in inconsistent accounts of the freedom presupposed by moral obligation. Mrs. Freed voices very bluntly the dissatisfaction with ethics with which we are concerned in this paper. She holds that nothing but harm can come of our 'thinking ethically'. For ethics "is simply an age-long accumulation, a conglomeration of muddles piled up into one vast rubbish heap of tangled concepts and outworn consolation fictions, blocking the path to human happiness. It was this oppressive vision of ethics, as an obstructive rubbish heap",[1] Mrs. Freed continues, "which led me to write this study in the pragmatic approach to problems of conduct, which will give such deep offence even to some of the best kinds of people".[2] The persistence of ethics is ascribed to our love of 'posing as saints'[3] in spite of the fact that we cannot be properly disinterested, and to "the various advantages, both material and spiritual, accruing to the purveyors of moral doctrines. There are plenty of people who love preaching and exhorting, and who are far better equipped to talk uplift than to talk sense . . . . thus in our culture there is a quite considerable body of persons to whose advantage it is that the minds of our children should be deeply moulded to this way of thinking in their most impressionable years".[4] "Again, moral thinking, like Christianity, is conducive to humility in the less educated and intelligent members of our society before those exalted persons who claim to know more about what they ought to do than they know themselves".[5] But "only by appealing to prejudice, and securing the whole weight of traditional thought habits firmly on their side, can moralists maintain an appearance of rational integrity, and appear before the world, not as the apostles of mystery and obscurantism, but as the sturdy upholders of common sense against the crankiness and perversity of those outside the ethical fold".[6] From these insinuations we proceed again to violent denunciation: "So ethics thrives upon the mental disorder and the fatal thought muddle which it has itself created, rotting away at our desirability-concepts, and making us despair, not of our world of things, but of ourselves. Truly moralism exacts no mean

---

[1] *Social Pragmatism*, p. 256.
[2] op. cit. p. 257.
[3] op. cit. p. 214.
[4] op. cit. p. 208.
[5] op. cit. p. 209.
[6] op. cit. p. 103.

payment for the little personal consolations it affords us".[1] Such is Mrs. Freed's opinion of ethics, an opinion which not only reflects much that is popularly thought, but is itself reflected in some ways in more cautious and subtle philosophical thinking. But what is of interest especially to me in this particular indictment of the whole of ethics is that the main muddles which moralists are thought to perpetuate are located in their treatment of freedom.

Two main points are made. Firstly it is urged that the notion of a categorical imperative is compatible with any sort of conduct, since all it requires is adherence to whatever we take to be right. It is thus urged that ethics leaves us without any particular principle of conduct and at the mercy of any who care to exploit us. I will not comment on this, for it depends on the sort of misunderstanding which has been most fully exposed by recent moralists and provided against by careful distinctions —if only the detractors of ethics took some trouble to examine them at first hand. The second point is that 'ought' presupposes "the logical monstrosity"[2] of "absolute" or motiveless freedom. Now I think Mrs. Freed is altogether right in connecting obligation with wholly undetermined choice, and I think that a great many 'muddles' do arise from the attempt to retain this presupposition within various forms of determinism, as much today as in the past. But I am far from thinking that it is in itself absurd, and I am convinced that unless we turn our attention again to this crucial issue, and bring our ethical thinking into line with the moral reality which even the detractors of ethics indirectly elevate, namely freedom and responsibility, we have little hope of giving to ethics the depth of interest and significance it deserves.

The same lesson may be learnt from the study of theology, especially in the Neo-Protestant forms which have such a high vogue today. For here also we encounter violent denunciations of ethics on grounds very similar to those advanced by Mrs. Freed. On this I have commented elsewhere, and there is hardly space here for me to return to that attack. But there is one matter which emerges with particular forcefulness out of the

[1] op. cit. p. 230.
[2] op. cit. p. 57.

theological denunciation of ethics and which has a closer bearing on the unreality which surrounds our ethical discussions than anything I have mentioned hitherto. It is to this that I have been leading up.

When theologians argue that we have not in fact the freedom which ethics requires, and when, in making formal acknowledgment of freedom, they urge, in contradiction of this, that we are collectively guilty and steeped in original sin, they hold before us certain 'impossible ideals' under whose condemnation we stand, although we could not in fact obey them. The confusions involved in this view I shall not attempt to unfold further here. But the upshot of it is that extraordinary maxims are set before us, and powerful exhortations made, in the pulpit and out of it, without expectation that our conduct should in fact be substantially modified. Nothing could be more calculated to bring ethics into contempt, especially in view of our proneness, very properly, to look to religion for moral leadership. But much more is involved here than the need to purge our ethical and religious thinking of obscurantism and confusion. There is needed, most of all, an effort to reinvigorate the ethical life itself, and to bring our practice more into line with our professions. This is not because we have become peculiarly degenerate and insincere. I think that, so far as we can judge at all of such matters, there is more goodness in the world, in spite of wars and atrocities, than ever before. And the present dissatisfaction with ethics, misguided though it is, reflects a growing impatience with shams and hypocrisies. But the moral ideals of which most is heard amongst us, namely Christian standards, cut very much deeper than we commonly appreciate, both in what they require in the way of inward attitude and in outward practice. To bring this home to us is one of the outstanding merits of the gloomy theology which sets Christian practice altogether beyond the reach of corrupt human nature. We find thus that there is a certain hollowness about our professions which alienates those who are clear-sighted and honest about them, leaving them to smug and self-satisfied persons who bring ethics and religion into ill repute. High seriousness in particular has become suspect except when it is centred on politics or economics or art in ways which make no explicit confession of moral principles—and sometimes in repudiation of them. Leadership in matters of practice is not unambiguously moral, and for this reason also the opportunity is lost of the moral adventure which seems in other ways peculiarly suited to the needs and the temper of our times. It is only by putting ideals to the proof that we can recover respect for them, and it is the ideals which make a really stirring challenge that can count today. Petty undertakings will only heighten the prevailing impression of humbug and sententiousness which surrounds ethics. Christians in particular need to remember this, and to consider with far greater determination than hitherto the relevance of Christian ideals to present conditions. It may well be that we have a unique opportunity. But that is a theme in itself, and the most that I wish to do in coming to the close of my address this morning is to leave with you the suggestion that the main clue to the prevailing distrust of ethics, and the usurpation of its place by irrational pseudo-moralities of various kinds, may be found in the sphere of practice, and that it is in that sphere also that the battle must be waged for the lost prestige of ethical thought. In the stress of more ambitious ethical activity we may find that matters which are dim and uncertain to us now, and problems which barely touch us, may come to be of the greatest moment.

I cannot refrain from one further comment. For no sooner had I dropped my pen than my eye alighted on a newspaper report of observations made recently by the Archbishop of Canterbury in his *Diocesan Notes*. The Primate was making an appeal for honesty and charity in the conduct of the approaching general election, an appeal which all of us will readily endorse. But in the course of his remarks Dr. Fisher went on to say:

"One may also express the earnest hope that they will all refrain from quoting, in political speeches, the words of the New Testament and especially the words of our Lord."

This, it is added, does not imply that "the linking of political thought to Christian principles is out of place". But actual quotations from the Scriptures, it is feared, are certain to be "misapplied and their meaning more or less gravely distorted".

One can understand well what lies behind this attitude. Few things are more irritating to those who have the truth of the Scriptures at heart than to find them quoted irresponsibly for partisan purposes and often without regard to their context or in sheer ignorance of it, by those who show no deep allegiance themselves to religion. One often met this in tribunals for conscientious objectors during the war, and not least from the side of the bench. It was peculiarly galling to find educated persons of much social standing, who would scorn to misapply a quotation from some ordinary classic, frequently distorting the meaning of the Scriptures in casual and ill-informed references to them. Even so one never thought that the remedy for this was to ban the Bible from the tribunals. Where could explicit reference to the Bible be more relevant? Abuse should clearly be countered by more honest and more careful use of the Scriptures, and will not this be the eventual result of encouraging greater recourse to them? The case of freedom of speech presents an instructive parallel. This right is often flagrantly abused, but one does not conclude that the right should straightway be suspended. The remedy normally is to set out the truth, as it appears to us, as persuasively and vigorously as we can, trusting the truth to do its own battle and giving as good an example as we can of a combination of strong conviction and openness of mind. So also in the case of politics and the Bible. The more we refer expressly to the Bible the better, however many abuses we may have to tolerate in the meantime. And the point of my present allusion to the Archbishop's views is that they afford a good illustration of that misguided zeal which so shelters religion as to leave it feeble and ineffectual. Throughout the ages this has been the ill fortune of religion. In mediaeval times the Bible was a closed book to the mass of the people, and even the priests read it, when they could do so, only as interpreted by their superiors and under their direction. Protestantism made an end of this, but we still suffer from the same general timidity, and there seems to me to be no more important or more distressing cause of the prevailing indifference to religion than the reluctance of its adherents to affirm it more boldly in all spheres of activity, and to have greater faith in its natural virility. Latterly suspicion and contempt have extended, as we have seen, to ethics as such, and my submission in closing this paper is that this is mainly due to lack of faith in supreme ideals on the part of those who, as professing Christians, are their accredited upholders. Can we not bestir ourselves now to go forth with greater boldness to meet the intriguing opportunities of the present time?

Chapter V

COLLECTIVE RESPONSIBILITY[1]

I

IF I were asked to put forward an ethical principle which I considered to be especially certain, it would be that no one can be responsible, in the properly ethical sense, for the conduct of another. Responsibility belongs essentially to the individual. The implications of this principle are much more far-reaching than is evident at first, and reflection upon them may lead many to withdraw the assent which they might otherwise be very ready to accord to this view of responsibility. But if the difficulties do appear to be insurmountable, and that, very certainly, does not seem to me to be the case, then the proper procedure will be, not to revert to the barbarous notion of collective or group responsibility, but to give up altogether the view that we are accountable in any distinctively moral sense.

On this matter more will be said below. In the meantime I should like to insist that the belief in 'individual', as against any form of 'collective', responsibility is quite fundamental to our ordinary ethical attitudes. For if we believe that responsibility is literally shared, it becomes very hard to maintain that there are any properly moral distinctions to be drawn between one course of action and another. All will be equally good, or equally evil, as the case may be. For we shall be directly implicated in one another's actions, and the praise or blame for them must fall upon us all without discrimination. This, in fact, is what many persons do believe, and it is very hard to uphold any form of traditionalist theology on any other basis. Of late this has been very openly affirmed by noted theologians who, if they seem to do very great violence to common sense, have, at any rate, the courage and consistency to acknowledge the implications of their view, and do not seek to disguise them by half-hearted and confused formulations. We have thus witnessed recently some very uncompromising affirmations of the belief

[1] *Philosophy*, January, 1948.

in 'universal sin' or the 'collective guilt of man'. This does not imply that there are no ethical distinctions of any kind which we may draw. Judgments may be passed upon the outward course of our conduct without prejudice to the view that guilt itself is 'universal', and this is why Reinhold Niebuhr, whose influence on religious thinking today is very pronounced, is able to combine with his assertion of the doctrine of universal sin an account of the "relative moral achievements of history".[1] One action may be much more regrettable than another, it may be uglier in some ways, or it may do much more harm to our fellows, and thus we have 'the less and more' of our day-to-day judgments, but where proper moral estimation is concerned there is not 'a big sinner and a little sinner'. We are all involved in the sins of all.

But this is not at all what we normally think. The distinction between what is outwardly right and the proper estimation of the worth of persons is not, one must admit, always very clearly drawn in our ordinary ethical thinking. And this is very frequently a source of great confusion. There is less excuse for this confusion today than in the past, since ethical writers have thrown the distinction in question into much prominence and stressed its extensive bearing on matters of practice. It has been shown, for example, that the facts of moral perplexity, and the diversities in our views about the problems of practice, admit of no reasonable explanation unless we allow that a person may do what is wrong in some outward sense without being morally to blame, and *vice versa*. For moral ignorance is not itself a moral defect. But while this shows that Niebuhr is perfectly justified in arguing that the 'historical' judgments we pass on the effects of actions have little direct bearing on questions of properly moral worth, it gives no solid support to his view that there is 'no less and more' where the latter are concerned. On the contrary, the more plainly we draw the distinction between the rightness of the act and the worth of the agent, the more will it also be evident that the main reason for stressing this distinction, and the main consideration by which men may be induced to draw it, is that in *addition* to the distinctions we draw between the ethical qualities of actions in their 'material' or outward

[1] *The Nature and Destiny of Man*, p. 234.
H

aspect there are even more important distinctions to be drawn in respect of their moral value. We want to be sure that our estimation of moral worth is not prejudiced by considerations relating only to outward action, and it is the former that is usually uppermost in our ordinary ethical judgments. It seems, therefore, plain that, however prone we may be to confuse the two sorts of ethical judgments which have just been distinguished, we normally have little doubt that some of our actions are better than others, not merely in their effects, or in some other material regard, but in themselves and morally. All our usual ethical thinking presupposes this. And if it is to be argued that, in respect of properly moral worth, there is nothing to choose between the lives of various individuals, then it must be made very plain that this is diametrically opposed to all that we normally think, to the attitudes we adopt from day to day, and to the main body of philosophical reflection on ethical questions; for the latter has been mainly concerned with the problem under what conditions may distinctions between the strictly moral qualities of conduct be drawn. If there are no such distinctions, if the questions we ask about them are without substance, then the greater part of ethical controversy has been a peculiarly vain pursuit of a will-o'-the-wisp.

II

This may be affirmed without prejudice to the further question of whether it is possible in practice to form reliable estimates of one another's moral worth. Subject to certain limitations, it seems to me not impossible to assess the moral worth of another person's conduct, and there appear to be some occasions where censure is in order, not merely as directed to outward conduct, or as a means of inducing reconsideration of the rightfulness of the course pursued, but as directed to the moral choice itself. But if this is denied, and if it is also held that the difficulties attending the attempt to appraise one another's moral qualities rule out every prospect of success, it by no means follows that the distinctions themselves are suspect. We can know in a general way under what conditions moral censure is incurred without needing to determine how far those conditions apply in particular cases. There is nothing very disconcerting to ethical theory in having to admit, should that appear necessary, that we have no appreciable insight into the strictly moral struggles of other persons, even in the cases of our friends and acquaintances, or such understanding of the factors involved as would lead to reasonably certain conclusions. It may even be urged that the injunction of the Scriptures, 'Judge not, that ye be not judged', holds without exception, and that it is none of our business to determine how any man fares in his inner moral life. For these are matters about which we may hold various opinions without seriously affecting the question whether there really *are* differences of value between different kinds of life. And what we need most to uphold is the reality of the moral distinctions themselves, not our ability to penetrate to the substance of them in particular cases.

Some comment may be added here on the reliability of the estimates we form of our own moral worth. Is fallibility in this regard also irrelevant to the question whether there really are moral qualities of conduct? This appears to me to be a most important question, but I will only venture here to make two observations. Firstly, the view which is commonly held, namely that we are usually wide of the mark in attempts to assess our own worth, seems to me very mistaken. To substantiate this in detail I should have to consider the main ways in which moral worth has been conceived. But it must suffice to note the two main alternatives. We may hold that moral distinctions depend mainly on our motives and characters. or we may relate them to some choice or free effort of will not determined by character. If we adopt the latter alternative it seems impossible that anyone should be in doubt about his own moral worth, for no one can really doubt whether he is making an effort to follow the course which his conscience requires. But if we adopt the former alternative there is room for deception of oneself in so far as we may be deluded about our own motives. But how far is such delusion possible, how far may a person persuade himself that he is contributing to a hospital from benevolent motives when he is really more concerned to ensure the esteem and gratitude of his fellows? It is often thought that we may be seriously mistaken about our motives in such cases, and that it is the business of the preacher and moral mentor to induce a deeper searching of heart and ensure a better understanding of our own characters. Literature seems to bear this out, but I am not sure that an alternative account of the facts usually adduced in this connection would not be possible if the matter were carefully investigated. But if this is denied, and if it is held that we can be widely astray in our grasp of the motives which move us to action, it seems to me that we have here a very formidable argument to advance against the first of the two main alternatives noted above, namely the view that moral worth qualifies character and motives. For, and here I come to my *second* observation, the nature of properly moral value seems to be such that it would be very strange to ascribe it to features of our conduct which we do not fully understand and bring within our control. To affirm that there can be serious delusion about our own moral attachments is thus in effect to cast very serious doubt on the validity of moral distinctions and the reality of moral responsibility.

The belief that we can be mistaken about our own moral worth owes its prevalence in no small measure to failure to distinguish effectively between questions about the 'material' rightness of action and the question of the worth of the agent. In respect of the former we are indeed frequently subject to much error and perplexity, and persons of sensitive conscience have often incurred a great deal of mental pain because the very proper concern which they have felt about the 'rightness of their act' became the cause of misgiving also about their own moral worth. But when the issue is clearly confronted, and it is understood that unavoidable ignorance cannot be imputed to the agent, it is hard to see how we can entertain doubts about our own culpability or blamelessness in respect to conduct sufficiently recent for us to retain a clear impression of the way we responded to what seemed to be a duty. Nor is our own impression in matters of this sort easily dimmed in the course of time.

It is in respect of other persons that appraisement of moral worth is difficult. For the factors involved are not easily accessible to the outside observer. But there is no cause for misgiving here. For even if we never knew how others fared, our assurance that their actions, like our own, are subject to moral distinctions, would not be a whit affected. But if we surrender the view that there are such distinctions, and substitute for it the notion of some uniform moral quality pervading the whole of humanity, or even the whole of a particular group, we are left with nothing which we can recognise as our workaday ethical ideas; morality has suffered a complete transformation. We seem, in fact, to have, not morality at all, but the repudiation of it.

III

How then, does this come about? Partly as a result of confusions which affect our ideas about value in general. We hypostatise abstractions and make them the bearers of value, forgetting that linguistic devices which make for succinctness of expression or poetic and rhetorical effect are not to be divested of their metaphysical and elliptical meanings, and taken as literal truth. We speak, for example, of sharing in the greatness of a nation, or we take pride in belonging to a musical or scholarly family even where we have no conspicuous claims to distinction in those regards ourselves. No objection can be taken to this provided we are clear what we are about. For the excellence generally attained by members of our nation or family warrants the presumption that we ourselves, having been subjected to the same influences, are not without a measure of the qualities for which others of our group are noted. The achievements of a relative, and especially of a son or daughter, may again reflect credit upon us, even when we have no part in what they have actually accomplished, to the extent that their success may be attributed to the devotion and discernment with which we have furthered their efforts. There is also the presumption that close association with persons of outstanding parts will have developed our own propensities, especially where general qualities of character are concerned. Men take legitimate pride in this way in their association with the great, or in erstwhile membership of a famous school or college. Our interest in those with whom we have special ties of affection will also enable us to follow their success with a glow of satisfaction as if it were our own. In these, and other ways, we participate in the excellence of others. But this does not mean that we can ever take credit directly for what others have become or accomplished. The worthwhileness of music does not become mine by my being the brother or parent of a gifted musician if I have no ear for music myself. What we are or achieve is affected by our relations to others, and we are emotionally involved in their lives, but what worth our actions and experiences have depends directly on their own nature. So that although we may be proud or ashamed of others, we add not a cubit to our stature; neither do we shrink through our association with them, except in the measure that we ourselves change under their influence.

This holds of all values. But it is peculiarly evident in the case of moral value. For failure or achievement may here be brought home to the individual in a very special way in blame and remorse. And this brings us to a further way in which men are apt to lose sight of the dependence of moral value on the individual.

IV

This turns on the definition of responsibility. The etymology of this word suggests that it means 'liability to answer', this being, of course, liability to answer to a charge, with the implication that if the answer is not satisfactory a penalty will be incurred. This is certainly the meaning of responsibility in the legal sense, and there can be little doubt that the original meaning of the word must be sought along similar lines, for men have not always distinguished clearly between law and morality—in primitive life both are merged in communal custom. But we do distinguish sharply today between law and morality. It is possible to be legally guilty and morally innocent, and *vice versa*. The question arises, therefore, whether the legal meaning of responsibility provides any analogy to the meaning of the term in the ethical sense. I do not think that it does. It would, no doubt, be easy to point to sanctions which societies impose on their members outside the sphere of State enactment, some of them, for example certain kinds of ostracism, taking very subtle forms, and there are also penalties which individuals are apt to impose on themselves, as recent psychology has shown so well. But these may also be out of accord with ethical requirements. No enactment is morally foolproof. A man may thus be morally guilty in respect of conduct to which no sort of penalty attaches. And this only helps to bring out in an indirect way what is in fact equally evident in cases where legal or quasi-legal requirements coincide with the moral law, namely that the mere fact of our liability to suffer a penalty is far too incidental a feature of conduct to constitute moral responsibility. Even if we hold, as do the advocates of the retributive theory of punishment, that wickedness calls for infliction of pain on the guilty agent, this is something *further* which we affirm about moral evil and responsibility, and not the essence of them. Such punishment presupposes the evil to which it is appropriate. We may thus reject the retributive theory of punishment, as I would certainly do, without impugning the validity of moral distinctions. What, then, does responsibility mean? It means simply to be a moral agent, and this means to be an agent capable of acting rightly or wrongly in the sense in which such conduct is immediately morally good or morally bad, as the case may be. But what do we mean by 'rightness', 'moral worth', and their correlatives? To this no answer is possible. For here we are dealing with ultimate ethical conceptions not reducible to natural fact. And the sum of this is that responsibility is an ethical conception not to be defined by reference to ideas which are not themselves distinctively ethical. It cannot therefore be conceived in naturalistic terms such as a threat of punishment and our liability to suffer it. But if we overlook this, and come to conceive of moral responsibility in ways not substantially different from our accountability before the law of our State, then it is easy to see how we come also to hold that there are some occasions, at any rate, when we share our responsibility with others and are immediately implicated in their wrongdoing.

This happens in the following way. Normally, the purpose served by the imposition of penalties requires the penalties to be inflicted on persons presumed to have offended, and on no others. For if punishment were meted out without discrimination, its deterrent effect would be substantially lessened and sometimes reversed. For punishment would then have to be regarded as 'an act of God' unrelated to our own volitions, and, while thus little able to hinder crimes, it would often provoke them. But there are, however, exceptional cases where expediency requires proceedings to be taken against a group as if it were an individual entity. No account will then be taken of the guilt or innocence of individual members of the group. It is in this way that a teacher punishes a class of unruly children when he is not able to discover the real offenders or when a meticulous apportionment of blame is not practicable. Such procedure may have effect in two ways, either (a) by directly deterring the main offenders or (b) by inducing the class to deal with them in ways not feasible for the teacher himself. The less recourse is had to such measures the better, both from the point of view of effective discipline and from regard to the ill-effects of a lingering sense of injustice. But there may also be some compensating factors, such as a deepening of the sense of community, which we might profitably investigate if we were concerned with educational problems or the general question of punishment. Suffice it for the present to note that, as a device for the achievement of certain practical ends, we have sometimes to accept collective responsibility. This is fully acknowledged in law, where a parent may in some respects be held to account for the conduct of children, or where a society or corporation may be proceeded against as a single entity or person. Extending our canvass still wider, we have the imposition of sanctions against a whole nation in the interest of international order, although it is plain that this involves quite as much suffering for the innocent as for the guilty, the former, in a case of this sort, being probably in a very great majority. Reparations and similar measures adopted against an aggressor among nations may also be mentioned here. Such measures may be needed both in the interest of immediate discipline, and as a part of political education, and they may provide means of redress to victims of aggression. But they will involve a great deal of suffering for persons who could not, by any streak of imagination, be held accountable for the culpable acts of the nation, most obviously in the case of infants and babes unborn. Something of this nature is, in fact, unavoidable in most forms of punishment and presents us with some of its most formidable problems. Locke, in consistency with his individualism, tried to show[1] that it could

[1] *Of Civil Government.* Part II, section 182.

be avoided. He urged that, while the participants in an unjust war could fairly be punished with death, there should be no interference with their property, for that would involve a loss to their wives and dependents. But apart from the well-nigh impossible question of apportioning guilt for participation in an unjust war, once the leaders and authors of atrocities have been reckoned with (and that in itself is a notoriously complicated matter), it is obvious that a man's family may be much more seriously affected, even at the economic level, to say nothing of the deeper personal loss, by the death of a parent or husband than by confiscation of property. Punishment is therefore very likely, in most cases, to fall, in some measure, on the innocent as well as the guilty. But this unfortunate feature of punishment, and the fact that punishment has, in some instances, such as those mentioned above, to be deliberately inflicted, without discrimination, upon a whole group, serves only to show the limitations of the expedients by which society furthers its ends. Perfect justice is not attainable in practice, and even if measures which we normally consider expedient and just in spite of their involving the innocent in the fate of the guilty, prove more easily avoidable than we are usually disposed to think, there will always be some intermingling of justice with injustice in human relations under any conditions we can anticipate. But what does this prove? Does it prove that the innocent share in the wickedness of the guilty, that the former are morally answerable for the ill deeds of the latter? Surely not. The question needs only to be stated plainly for us to see how foolish it is to allow our view of *moral* responsibility to be affected by imperfections in the ways in which members of society must deal with one another. And yet that is precisely what happens in a great many writings on ethics and jurisprudence, where the ideas of social and collective responsibility are put forward as properly ethical notions under cover of a false analogy with social enactments such as the enforcement of law.

An excellent instance of this may be found in two papers[1] by

[1] 'Some simple thoughts on freedom and responsibility' (*Philosophy*, January, 1937) and 'Individual, Collective, and Social Responsibility (*Ethics*, Vol. XLIX).

Professor Gomperz where the writer comes very frankly to the defence of the idea of collective responsibility along the lines just described. But Gomperz is only bringing out what is implicit in most accounts of responsibility in recent times. From Bradley's celebrated chapter on 'The Vulgar Notion of Responsibility' in *Ethical Studies* to the symposium on the problem of responsibility at a recent Joint Session of the Mind and Aristotelian Societies,[1] by far the most predominant tendency is to define responsibility in terms of a 'liability to answer' and to incur blame or punishment. This is how Bradley, like Rashdall and other thinkers, is able to reconcile responsibility with determinism. For blame and punishment would have significance even if our conduct could not be other than it is in the last resort, provided it conformed to certain other conditions. And in the symposium to which I have referred, while the first and second contributors eschew an unambiguously naturalistic theory of ethics, they both pass easily from the view that a man is responsible because "he can be called upon to answer" (the second writer adding, "by incurring blame or moral disapproval"[2]—a view which, even if it avoids being naturalistic, reverses the proper relation of blame and responsibility, for the latter is prior to the former)—to cases where one person takes responsibility for the action of another, in Mr. Falk's example[3] the case of a Prime Minister taking responsibility for the actions of his Chief of Staff by declaring his "readiness to take the blame". But this particular example serves to show very well on what a misleading course we are set when we conceive responsibility in the way described. For a Prime Minister can never be *morally* responsible for the act of a colleague, he simply cannot 'take the blame' *morally*. It may be necessary for the conduct of a war, or for the normal functioning of Parliamentary government where, in our country at least, joint Cabinet responsibility seems to be established, for a minister to allow the action of another to be treated as if it were his own. But his willingness to share the blame in this sense, especially if he puts his own position and career in serious

[1] *Proceedings of the Aristotelian Society, Supplementary Volume XIX.*
[2] op. cit. p. 249.
[3] op. cit. p. 249.

jeopardy, induces us to esteem him highly as a moral person even if it is also a reason for seeking to overthrow his administration. For his 'implication' in the follies or misdeeds of his colleagues is not a moral one, but a requirement of certain governmental procedures, and his loyal acceptance of it, at personal inconvenience, redounds to his credit. It would, of course, be a different matter if he had encouraged or condoned the wrongful policy himself, or if he were sheltering a colleague for personal reasons or were retaining him against the interest of the public. He would then be morally responsible, but in respect of his own action. But to accept responsibility for others for practical purposes, to incur certain consequences for what another person has done, is one thing, to be morally accountable is another; and in this last regard we cannot answer for one another or share each other's guilt (or merit), for that would imply that we could become directly worse (or better) persons morally by what others elect to do—and that seems plainly preposterous.

v

The belief that guilt may be shared derives some plausibility also from the loose expressions which normally serve our turn when we need to refer to the contributions of several persons to a joint undertaking. Take a case of burglary. We have first the thieves who actually carried it out. One of these may be the prime mover, a confirmed criminal perhaps, another a novice pressed somewhat reluctantly to be his accomplice. The temptation may have been put in the way of these two, and the opportunity provided, by an acquaintance who bears the victim a grudge but takes no part in the actual robbery beyond supplying useful information. Yet another person may have covered the escape of the criminals or, by hindering the work of detection, have become an accessory after the fact. Finally, we may have a 'receiver' who disposed of the stolen goods. Each of these persons is in some way implicated in the crime, and they may thus be said to share the responsibility for it. But it would be a great mistake to suppose that we have here a single criminal operation the blame for which rests equally on all concerned. Even the law would discriminate sharply in such a case, imposing the heaviest penalty on the habitual criminal, but, in his own case as well as that of the others, reviewing the judgment in the light of extenuating circumstances, previous convictions, etc. The instigator who provided the original inducement might easily escape the toils of the law altogether. But at the properly moral level many further factors must be taken into account, several of them, as has been stressed, not easily accessible to the outside observer. And in this reckoning many roles may be reversed, the instigator, possibly, proving the worst offender. What has to be stressed is that the guilt of each is strictly proportionate to his part in the joint undertaking. It is not one crime that we have but many.

This seems very evident in the simple case described. It is just as true, however, in respect of complicated matters, such as social and economic injustices, where the lure of vague collectivist explanations is stronger. Reformers have often reminded us that we need, not merely to hinder the criminal, but also to remove the causes of crime, and, in this connection, it is frequently maintained that society shares the guilt of the criminal. Gomperz instances the case of a poor woman who steals a loaf to feed her starving children, and he contends that society is really as responsible as she herself, inasmuch as society failed to provide for her needs. He even goes so far as to speak of blaming the social 'structure'. But that, it seems evident, is only meaningful in a figurative sense and as a rhetorical device when concern is to be aroused at distressful social conditions. If taken in the literal sense, as Gomperz appears to intend, it is very misleading. For a 'structure' cannot be the bearer of moral responsibility; neither can 'society in general', for these are both abstractions which we must be careful not to hypostatise. What should be said, if we are to speak exactly, is this. The guilt of the poor woman is lessened, if not eliminated altogether, by her circumstances. But she alone is to blame, if blame there is to be, for what she herself has done. Others are also to blame, but *for something else*, that is for their part in allowing her to remain in desperate need. But they are responsible for this as individuals, and strictly in proportion to what each might have done, directly or indirectly, to ameliorate her lot.

It has also to be emphasised here that there are severe limitations on the power of the individual to modify social conditions, for normally he can only do so by concerted action, and concerted action, moreover, which requires a consensus of opinion on highly complicated social and economic questions. It is thus very foolish simply to look about us, as we are prone to do, and, having noted grave and persistent social ills, such as poverty, waste, unemployment, war, straightway to take these as a measure of human wickedness. For ills of this sort, while they do in some ways reflect the moral life of a community, and provide the basis for *some* generalisations, cannot be regarded as an indication of intentional evil until we have considered carefully just what could have been expected of the average individual when confronted with them. Allowance must be made for ignorance, for the need for leadership, and for the peculiar difficulties which attend the corporate effort required for effective social reform. This does not imply that the individual must simply surrender to the drift of events, or acquiesce passively in the policies of a handful of leaders. There is much that he can do, but ultimate success will depend on a great many factors wholly outside his control, no less in a democratic than in a totalitarian country. And therefore we need to be careful not to form exaggerated conceptions of human depravity by looking, not to what could reasonably be expected of the individual, but to society as a corporate entity directly accountable for social and economic ills.

This has a close bearing on the problem of war guilt. This question, it should be stressed, is only one aspect of the general question of the treatment of aggressor nations. For many factors besides that of moral guilt enter into the latter problem. But so far as the properly moral issue is concerned, we do very serious damage to the prospect of eventual reconciliation if we allow a distorted conception of moral guilt to complicate questions which are already bewildering enough, the more especially as we shall not merely form a wrong estimate of the course we should pursue ourselves, but also encourage those pathological conditions to which vanquished peoples are prone, and which, however they may accord with our mood and the immediate requirements of a situation, are certain, if only by being an unhealthy condition unrelated to any rational assurance, to emerge at a later date in ways very little amenable to rational control—whatever the precise direction they take. What we need to ask, in the case, for example, of Germany, is not what is the record of Germany as a nation in the inter-war period or later—or our own for the matter of that—but just what could have been expected of the average German citizen in the swirling tide of the events which engulfed him and others eventually in the deep vortex of war. This is not to suggest that he was helpless and must be exonerated altogether, and that questions of guilt concern only those who were in positions of power and authority. There were undoubtedly many things which the ordinary citizen might have done, and I can only leave it here for the historian in due course to attempt to determine what they were. But allowance must clearly be made for tradition, outlook, and environment, for the difficulty of anticipating the course of events (and it is easy for us afterwards, and from outside, to be wise about these), for the very limited influence which the individual, even if he is of a heroic mould, can normally have on the policies of a ruthless totalitarian government, and for the determined opposition to warlike and despotic measures which a certain proportion, at any rate, of the German people showed. Let us seek, by all means, to extend the influence of democratic principles which will enable the individual to give of his best to his State. But in the meantime, let us be fair to him, wherever he is found, by relating the question of guilt, not to some abstract entity in which he and all other individuals are merged, but to what we can reasonably estimate could have been expected of the individual, who is the sole bearer of guilt and merit, in the particular situation confronting him.

I should like to stress again what has already been noted, that no one is morally guilty except in relation to some conduct which he himself considered to be wrong. This seems plain enough in our ordinary encounter with one another from day to day, for circumstances force it more sharply upon us in close and immediate relationships. But it needs to be borne in mind very carefully when seeking to form ethical judgments about a vast concourse of people with whom individual and personal ties are slight. Otherwise we shall be inclined to arraign other peoples for follies and misunderstandings which, whatever the measures they may warrant in practice, are, I repeat, no direct indication of *moral* culpability. Again I do not imply that 'to understand all is to excuse all'. But I insist that we must first understand, and then we can have some indication of guilt. But to understand is very much harder, it calls for more wisdom and patience, when dealing with men in the mass than when we have to do with individuals in relative isolation, the more especially as the normal working of our imagination presents us with a simplified picture in which the nation or group is personified, and, having been given a mind and will of its own, is set to act on a stage very much simpler than the actual stage of history.

We are most prone to these false simplifications of complicated issues in times of confusion and change such as the present. For in such times there is apt to be a recrudescence of primitive ethical attitudes, as the recent history of Europe shows so well. And primitive peoples pay little heed to the individual; the unit is for them the tribe or the family. But reflection upon the affinity between the doctrine of collective responsibility and the undiscriminating 'ethic of the tribe' should go a long way to discredit the former.

Failure to reckon with these considerations will not only distort our vision in this or that particular regard, and poison our relationships. It will also give us in general an utterly misleading picture of man and 'the human situation'. Of this there is ample evidence already in the prevailing fashion of gloomy denunciation of all human endeavour, an indulgence which may show itself before long to be a more serious business than we are inclined to realise. Its immediate progeny are despair and its twin, irresponsibility. But worse may follow.

VI

How far these reactionary estimates of human activity owe their persistence to mistaken philosophical views is not easy to determine. But they have obviously derived much support from 'organic' theories of society, such as the celebrated Idealist Theory of the State and the cruder forms of totalitarian theories which prevail today. These latter have not yet taken very deep root in democratic countries, and although the idealist doctrines, whose authoritarian aspect was, incidentally, qualified in important ways, were in the ascendant towards the close of the 19th century in Western thought, they do not accord well with the main tendencies in European culture and civilization, much less with the temper and traditions of the British people. They have been very extensively discredited today so far as philosophical thought is concerned. It is therefore well to remind ourselves that the ideas of a pervasive communal guilt and of collective responsibility are simply the obverse of the tendency to set some abstract good of the community above the well-being of its individual members, a tendency whose natural terminus is the ruthless oppression and totalitarianism against which our face is so resolutely set in democratic countries. Most of the arguments which have recently been used so effectively to demolish the ideas of a 'common good' and a 'general will', as those terms are usually understood in philosophy, hold with undiminished force, *mutatis mutandis*, against any theory of communal guilt.

The advocates of collectivist theories of society, whether they be theories of human good or of human evil, are apt to hold their opponents in contempt on the score of an alleged individualism. But this is very largely a case of hitting at random, and making play with the meaning of a highly ambiguous word. 'Individualism' may mean several things. It may mean that the good which human beings ought to pursue is always a private one, or it may mean, again, that individuals have unlimited and inalienable rights, this latter being, I think, its main meaning in Western philosophy, or it may indicate the general failure to appreciate the dependence of the individual on his social environment. In all these meanings the term stands for mistaken theories, and theories which have also, unfortunately, wrought very serious havoc in our thought and practice in the past, and which continue at the present time to obstruct very necessary positive reforms. But individualism in these reprehensible senses has no necessary connection with the view that the individual is the sole bearer of value. We may insist, and the need to do so is as great in many regards today as in the past, that no one can have proper interests of his own unless he has also interests in others, that we are 'members of one another' even with regard to properly moral struggles in so far as the attainment or failure of one person is a matter of concern to his neighbours who are *to that extent* involved in his moral attainment or failure. No one lives in a vacuum, no one is, or should be, unaffected by the destinies of others. And where natural sympathies reach their limit, or where the welfare of one is opposed, as in many ways it may be, to the welfare of others, there yet remain our duties to further the wellbeing of others independently of any advantage to ourselves. Although no one is 'responsible for' others in the sense that he is answerable for the conduct of others, we are all extensively 'responsible for' our fellows in the sense that we have duties towards them—most of our duties are of this sort. But all this may be fully allowed without affecting the principle that value belongs to the individual and that it is the individual who is the sole bearer of moral responsibility. This principle is not individualistic in any way which is incompatible with a true estimate of our essential social relationships. It is not 'atomic' in any objectionable sense.

VII

The point at which the problem of 'individual' versus 'collective' responsibility acquires the greatest significance for moral philosophy is in connection with the general question of moral freedom. For any attempt to reconcile moral responsibility with determinism seems to lead inevitably to the extension of responsibility to agents which have combined with ourselves in the shaping of our conduct. To bring this out fully would require discussion of matters which can hardly be brought within the scope of this paper. We should have to investigate closely the uniqueness of moral value and the significance of the ideas of guilt and merit which throw into sharpest relief the distinction between moral and non-moral goods; and we should have to examine the libertarian theory that some of our actions could have been other than they are although everything else in the universe had remained the same. But it must suffice here to note that the doctrine of freedom as 'self-determination' makes no substantial difference to the present issue. For the fact that the determinism is of a special kind, and involves a peculiar assimilation into the character of the agent of the forces which affect him, still leaves the determinist with the view that factors from outside ourselves have gone to the shaping of conduct. And if the notion of responsibility is to be retained at all in such case, it is hard to see how we can avoid extending it to these further factors,[1] an embarrassment which does not arise in connection with non-moral values which do not carry with them the notion of guilt and a correlative merit. The determinist thus finds himself extending the blame for wrongful actions to our environment, and eventually to the whole of reality. There arises in this way the notion of a principle of evil in the universe at large; and this notion has a wide currency at the present time. It derives much support from uncritical accounts of the findings of recent psychology, and it also encourages capricious play with the mythologies of primitive religion. This also contributes to the dissemination of irrational and despondent estimates of human attainment. But it seems evident that the quietus to such reactionary tendencies cannot be finally given until moral philosophers turn with much greater resolution than at present to the much neglected problem of moral freedom. This is a crucial problem today for religion as well as for ethics and politics. But here again I am touching on matters which cannot be effectively brought within the compass of this paper. Neither has it been possible to comment on the more specifically religious aspects of the problem of collective guilt, although these are in many ways the most important.

---

[1] It is in this way that Sir David Ross is forced to what seems to me the astonishing conclusion that "responsibility is always divided. Obviously responsibility for *results of action* can never be assigned to one person alone; there are always circumstances (and these will usually include acts by other people) which co-operate to produce the result, of whose complete cause one person's act is merely the most striking part. But it is also true that responsibility for *acts* is divided. It is never right to assign to one person the sole credit or the sole discredit for any of his acts. Other people by teaching and example, the writers of the books he has read, and so on, have all helped to mould his character into that form of which his action is the expression" *Foundations of Ethics*, p. 247-8.

Chapter VI

MORAL FREEDOM IN RECENT ETHICS[1]

I

THE problem of moral freedom has not been conspicuous in recent ethics. This is surprising. For the ideas which present it in its most formidable shape, the ideas of ought, responsibility, and of ultimate praise or blame, have been given much prominence in recent ethical controversy.

There have, it is true, been some notable discussions of moral freedom. Among these are Volume III of the *Ethics* of Nicolai Hartmann, Professor Broad's inaugural lecture, *Determinism, Indeterminism, and Libertarianism*, the middle chapters of Professor C. A. Campbell's *Scepticism and Construction* and the same author's inaugural lecture, *In Defence of Free Will*. Some papers on the same topic, such as Professor A. K. Stout's *Free Will and Responsibility*,[2] and Mr. R. E. Hobart's *Free Will as Involving Determination*,[3] both incidentally putting the case for determinism, have appeared from time to time. But these are exceptions, and they seem right off the main lines of recent ethical controversy.

More truly indicative of the present position is the fact that the problem of freedom is barely mentioned in two of the most influential ethical books of recent years, Professor G. E. Moore's *Principia Ethica*[4] and Sir David Ross's *The Right and the Good*. The lack is not felt very sharply in the former case. For Moore is much more concerned with the idea of value than with that of rightness or obligation. In this work he takes it that right can be defined in terms of a relation to goodness,[5] and the values which seem to impress him most are those of aesthetic enjoy-

---
[1] *Proceedings of the Aristotelian Society*, Vol. XLVII.
[2] *Proceedings of the Aristotelian Society*, Vol. XXXVIII.
[3] *Mind*, 1934.
[4] The problem of freedom is touched upon in the course of discussing Kant's view of the "autonomy of the Practical Reason" on page 127 of *Principia Ethica*. It is not discussed at all in *The Right and the Good*.
[5] *Principia Ethica*, p. 18, cf. p. 147.

ment and personal affection.[1] But *The Right and The Good*, stressing the uniqueness and ultimacy of duty, seems to call especially for a discussion of freedom which is not forthcoming.

In his later book, *Ethics*, Moore gives the ideas of right and wrong a more independent status; in support of his view that the acts which *are* right are those which produce most good, although this is not what we *mean* by calling them right, Moore is also induced to insist that the judgments which we pass upon motives are a different sort from those in which actions are pronounced right or wrong,[2] and that moral praise or blame may turn upon the worth of the motive in a way that leaves the rightness of an action unaffected. But Moore does not draw a perfectly sharp distinction here. All that he maintains is that a man's praiseworthiness does not depend "*entirely* or *always* upon his motive",[3] this being, furthermore, apparently due to the fact that moral praise and condemnation are regarded as utilitarian devices for ensuring right conduct.[4] In consequence, although the positions we have noted lead in the *Ethics* to a short chapter on freedom, it is not strange that the author is uncertain whether freedom of choice is required in ethics,[5] and believes in the main that, if it is, it must be compatible with "the principle that everything has a cause".[6] The ideas of responsibility and obligation do not stand out very distinctly as unique ethical conceptions. But the matter is far otherwise in the case of Ross. He is concerned especially with the ideas of rightness and obligation, and, setting himself to oppose any utilitarian

[1] op. cit. p. 188.
[2] *Ethics*, p. 184-185.
[3] *Ethics*, p. 189.
[4] Stressing the distinction between "what is right or wrong, on the one hand, and what is morally praiseworthy or blameworthy on the other", Moore declares: "What we should naturally say of a man whose action turns out badly owing to some unforeseen accident when he had every reason to expect that it would turn out well, is not that his action was right, but rather that he *is not to blame*. And it may be fully admitted that in such a case he really *ought* not to be blamed; *since blame cannot possibly serve any good purpose, and would be likely to do harm*" (*Ethics*, p. 193—last italics mine). Compare p. 189: we ought to blame a man less when there is "less need to deter him by blame". See also pp. 215 and 216.
[5] The uncertainty has since been removed. See G. E. Moore's "Reply to my Critics" in *The Philosophy of G. E. Moore*, p. 624.
[6] Moore's admission of perplexity as to the sense in which this is possible (*Ethics*, p. 221) is repeated in *The Philosophy of G. E. Moore*, p. 626.

account of either rightness or moral worth, he contends strongly for the ultimacy of both these ethical conceptions. We should therefore expect his arguments to take a very close account of the problem of freedom. But this is not in fact the case.

In his more recent volume, *The Foundations of Ethics,* Ross does indeed devote a chapter to this topic. But he turns to the task with obvious reluctance. "No discussion of fundamental questions of ethics", he declares, "would be complete without some discussion of the problem of free will; and I must therefore say something about the subject, even if I do not feel that I have anything very new to contribute".[1] The problem, we are told, "has been once more brought to the front by the appearance among physicists of the doctrine known as that of indeterminacy".[2] But surely the problem should have been brought to the front for Ross by the prominence to which he himself has helped to bring the idea of obligation in recent ethics. He finds it easy to show that the doctrine of indeterminacy in physics has little relevance to any ethical question.[3] The rest of the chapter is mainly concerned with the alleged "intuition of freedom" and does not bear very closely on strictly ethical matters.[4] The crucial question of freedom and *responsibility* is put off to a few pages at the end,[5] and they bring us to the confession:

"In remorse we are acutely aware that, whatever our outward circumstances may have been, we have ourselves been to blame for giving way to them where a person of better character would not have done so. I cannot pretend that this satisfies the whole of our natural thought about responsibility, but I think that in claiming more, in claiming that a moral agent can act independently of his character, we should be claiming a metaphysical impossibility.

"A philosophical genius may some day arise who will succeed in reconciling our natural thought about freedom and responsibility with acceptance of the law of causality; but I must admit

[1] *Foundations of Ethics,* p. 208.
[2] op. cit. p. 208.
[3] He also shows that it is fraught with much confusion.
[4] See below, section III.
[5] Even these are mainly concerned with a view that Ross rejects, namely, Mr. Wisdom's view that the idea of pre-existence affects the problem.

that no existing discussion seems to be very successful in doing so."[1]

No passage could typify better the attitude usually adopted today towards the problem of freedom. This, it is thought, is the problem which offers least prospect of solution, it is here that we are most prone to "argue about it and about" to no purpose; the deadlock is complete. In the meantime there are other fields where our labours will not go unrewarded, there are problems which will repay discussion. Such are the problems of "the nature of goodness", of "rightness and obligation", of "the relation of the morality of actions to their rightness" or of "motive to intention", of "*prima facie* rightness to one's full obligation", the problem of "subjective" and "objective" duty, and of utilitarian versus intuitionist views of duty. These are problems which have been very keenly discussed of late, not only in such books as those I have instanced, but also in a spate of most acute papers in philosophical journals. In the meantime the problem of freedom is postponed or, at best, set aside for quite separate treatment, often very perfunctory. But this, I submit, and it is the main contention of this paper, is just what we cannot do. It would be foolish to complain that philosophers do not provide a solution of the problem of freedom; on the contrary one admires the frankness with which they confess themselves bewildered by it; if they see no way to mitigate our perplexity, then we must say: "It is unfortunate but there is no help for it". But what does seem equally plain is that if there is uncertainty as to what we should think about moral freedom, if we remain on the horns of the dilemma, then it is equally impossible to make progress with many other fundamental ethical problems. In particular, some view about freedom is presupposed in any attitude we adopt towards the question of obligation; if we suspend judgment in the one case we should do so in the other. The problem of freedom is not one we can

[1] *Foundations of Ethics*, p. 251. It is significant also that the volume closes with the following words: "It seems to me that something like half of our ordinary thinking on moral questions implies a belief in the indetermination of the will, and something like half a belief in its determination; and I have neither found elsewhere nor discovered by my own reflections any adequate solution of this difficulty. But the truth can never be inconsistent with itself, and we may hope that better thinking will in the long run remove this apparent contradiction, as sound thinking has already removed many others".

isolate, it is essentially bound up with others; and this is, I think, a prime source of confusion in recent ethics. For while there is little direct attack on the problem of freedom, the problem itself winds itself subtly in and out of arguments which take little clear cognisance of it. These prove on examination to be essentially attempts to fit the idea of moral choice into a view of conduct which, as I hope to show, does not admit of choice in the way required by a "categorical imperative". This will be evident if we now turn to a topic which has been much discussed in recent years.

II

This is the celebrated distinction between "the morality of the action and the rightness of the act". And the first point that I should like to make is that, in one sense or other, a distinction of this kind seems to me unavoidable. One crucial factor here is that of the fallibility of ethical judgments. It seems beyond all reasonable controversy that we may be mistaken as to what is our duty.[1] All cases of moral perplexity and all attempts to educate and enlighten our own consciences or those of other persons presuppose this. There is therefore clearly some sense in which it is possible for us to be fully conscientious, to be loyal to our duty and worthy of the highest praise, and at the same time to be acting in a way that is wrong. May we not also do what is "materially" right for "the wrong reason"? What is altogether involved in loyalty to duty is another matter; we need not decide that issue to see that moral worth must be divorced from doing what is right in some sense of those terms. This paradox, as Moore shows so well,[2] is not in the least vicious; and it is quite ineradicable.

But as we have also suggested, the present argument commits us to no special view of the criterion of moral worth. Does this depend on our motives or on some free and "unmotived" willing? The issue remains open so far as the independence of moral worth on "material" or outward rightness is concerned. For what this mainly establishes is that moral ignorance is not a moral defect.

[1] There is, however, much reluctance to admit this without ambiguity. See Ch. III.
[2] *Ethics*, Chapter V.

But there is a further argument that is used in support of the distinction between moral worth and rightness. And it is this that touches our present discussion closely. It is the argument that we cannot control our motives and that, therefore, we are only under an obligation to do a certain act, not to do it from a particular motive. Ross has much recourse to this argument, both in *The Right and The Good*[1] where the distinction we are considering now finds its most celebrated statement, and in *The Foundations of Ethics*.[2]

Before indicating what I think is the real implication of this argument I should like to turn first to the question whether it is true that we cannot control a motive.

It seems plain to me that Ross has the best of it here. Is it not quite certain, as he says, that we cannot feel sorrow at will or summon up a feeling of benevolence as required? We do feel sorrow or we don't, we feel amiably disposed or we do not; there is nothing to be done in the matter at the moment of acting. Our feelings and desires are what they are, that is all we can say. Admittedly a person may set himself in the way of having certain feelings in the future, although this, as we shall see, is not quite so straightforward a matter as it seems. But there is clearly some sense in which a feeling can be cultivated, the way I act now will affect my character and modify my motives in the future. But it seems plain to me that I cannot command a certain feeling immediately; much less am I able "at a moment's notice to make it effective in stimulating me to act".[3]

This matter has not, however, been so plain to others, and several writers have joined issue with Ross at this point. One of the best known of his opponents is H. W. B. Joseph in his *Some Problems in Ethics,* a book completed before the actual publication of *The Right and The Good*. The position which Joseph takes up is not easy to grasp. The substance of it, if I understand aright, is as follows. If I perform an act to which I am prompted by a motive such as "gratitude, affection, or benevolence" there is "a kind of goodness"[4] in the act which can also be regarded as the ground of its rightness. This is not the

[1] p. 5.
[2] pp. 45-46, cf. Chapter VI, especially p. 116.
[3] *The Right and The Good*, p. 5.
[4] *Some Problems in Ethics*, p. 47.

only way in which an act may be right. Usually the ground of rightness is productivity of good results.[1] But rightness may sometimes be due to motives in the way described. Certain acts ought to be done because of the motives from which, if done, they will be done. There is, moreover, one very special kind of motive always available here. It is "a sort of urgency" to act in a certain way arising from "the consciousness of a determinate obligation to do this in this situation".[2] This consciousness need not be very explicit, it may prompt a man to do something, "even without his saying to himself that he ought to do it",[3] and it must not be confused with "the consciousness of duty in general".[4] When therefore we review the possibilities before us in some situation, or seek to resolve some case of perplexity, we may find that a certain course should be followed because the special feeling of "urgency" to take it is being "preferred to or prevails over the contrary inclination".[5] Motive here makes the act right, but if we do that act because of the rightness which belongs to it in this way there will be moral worth as well as rightness in our action. "I shall have acted morally as well as rightly."[6] It seems therefore that I do control my motives to the extent of choosing to do (or not to do) the act which will have the right (or shall we say the right-making?) motive, and thus, in maintaining that we have duties to do certain acts from certain motives, we need not be deterred by the objection that "it is not in my power to feel a particular motive which I am not feeling, nor therefore to act from it".[7]

There is much here that calls for comment.[8] But what concerns us at the moment is the contention that, in choosing to

[1] op. cit. p. 28.
[2] op. cit. p. 50.
[3] op. cit. p. 50.
[4] op. cit. p. 50.
[5] op. cit. p. 51.
[6] op. cit. p. 48.
[7] op. cit. p. 46.
[8] For example, the question whether the "sort of urgency" envisaged by Joseph can mislead. If it cannot, and if it is bound up with the general sense of obligation, how can we ever be in moral perplexity—as we often are? Ross seems to me to put matters very conclusively when he observes, in his reply to Joseph, that the "urgency" he describes presupposes the belief that the act is right and cannot therefore be regarded as the ground of its rightness (*Foundations of Ethics*, p. 132).

do one act rather than another, the motive from which the act is done can be regarded as part of what I choose. If 'motive' is given its usual meaning of some desire or feeling which moves us to act, the position is flatly contradictory.[1] It puts the cart before the horse in very shameless fashion. And this is indeed brought out by Joseph's own argument. For if I am to choose to do a certain act from a certain motive there must be some other motive which determines that choice; this, on Joseph's view, would be the "motive of duty". Now it is possible for an act to proceed from a combination of motives. But in that case we either think of one motive reinforcing another or of a number of desires pointing to the same conduct at the same time, any one of these being in itself stronger than any elements in my character which prompt me to a contrary action. We could then say that, if one of these desires were absent, the act would still be necessitated by one or more other desires which point to it. But in that case the desires in question would need to be independent of one another. And this is just what Joseph's account does not provide. Neither, clearly, is he thinking of cases where devotion to duty is not effective without support from some other motive. The agent is presumed to have resolved to do his duty once its nature is plain to him. And so what we have, on Joseph's view, is a very curious double determination of the same act. For a person to be determined to do act "A" by the motive of duty, one has to presuppose his being already determined to do it by the motive of benevolence or "urgency". And this seems to me an altogether impossible position.

The downright inconsistency of Joseph's theory is somewhat obscured by a proneness of the author to speak of motive, on occasion (but on occasion only), not as a feeling or desire moving an agent to act in a certain way, but as a "feeling expressed" in action. So conceived, motive may well be the justification of right conduct. For a suitable expression of a feeling of affection, to take Joseph's instance,[2] may lead to a deepening of the feeling itself and enhance a close personal relationship in many ways. But here we are looking to the effects of actions. And the fact

[1] This was one of the main points stressed by Professor H. A. Prichard in his much-discussed article, "Does Moral Philosophy Rest on a Mistake"? *Mind*, 1912, p. 27.
[2] *Some Problems in Ethics*, p. 47.

that an act may become a duty on account of its motive in the present unusual sense gives no justification for the very different view, but one which Joseph seems mainly anxious to hold, that it may be our duty to act from a certain motive in the normal meaning of the term. Against *this* view Ross's objection seems unanswerable. We cannot, in the moment of action, alter the balance of our feelings and desires.

The same point must be stressed in answer to a more recent critic of Ross, Mr. George Hughes. He takes up the subject in his paper on *Motive and Duty*[1] where he stresses especially the distinction between an impulsive or "involuntary act" and a willed or "fully deliberate act". In the latter case the self is aware of a number of desires or "potential motives" together, and "identifies itself with" one of them. The relation of act to motive is not therefore, in rational conduct, a simple example of efficient causation. It is not "diadic" but "triadic", for the self intervenes to "adopt" or "sanction" a motive and "give it its act". And if we leave out for the present, as I wish to do, the strictly libertarian view that there may be actions not determined by motives at all, the substance of Hughes's contention seems beyond dispute. It was a major contribution of the maligned idealists to the metaphysics of morals to show that the desires of a rational being oppose one another, not as isolated impulses with an independent force of their own, but as taken up into the unity of the self as a whole. But however important we regard this matter in itself, and however appropriate the terms "selection", "adoption", etc. may be in this context, the fact remains that I cannot, in any final sense, will my desires to be other than they are at a particular moment. They are as they are, and those which prevail, prevail. When, therefore, I choose to do act "A" rather than act "B" to which I am also drawn, whatever else may be said of this choice, and we shall return to its difficulties shortly, it is plain that the motive which leads to the act has an ascendancy which I cannot alter at the moment of acting. It does not come immediately within the control of my will, however the self, *in other ways*, may be involved in its victory.

In addition to the general claim that the "adoption" of a desire

[1] *Mind*, October, 1944, pp. 314-332.

by the self, in the process noted, provides the control required for responsibility, Mr. Hughes gives several examples of the way a suitable direction of attention may alter the balance of "potential motives". A dentist who has to perform a painful operation on a patient against whom he has a grudge may tell himself that it would be shameful to be moved to act by a desire to cause pain. He comes thus to act from the more worthy motive of doing what the case in hand requires, the amount of pain inflicted remaining the same. There seems thus to be a change in motive only. In other examples the agent is thought to evoke a new motive by suitable reflections. But there is nothing here which Ross would deny, for the examples afford nothing different from the cultivation of motives which he admits. That the cultivation may be almost instantaneous in some cases does not affect the main issue. What the dentist does is not directly to summon up a motive but to direct his thought in a way that brings about a rapid change of motive. And this is admitted by Hughes himself when he notes that, in this case, "two acts are involved",[1] the self-admonition of the dentist and the subsequent operation. The problem of evoking motives also draws attention from the main issue, for the question is not whether I can summon up a motive which I do not feel at all, but whether, with the aid of new motives or without them, I can alter the balance of my desires in the moment of action. The words "summon up" may be misleading here. But there can be no serious doubt about Ross's intention. The important point is that there is never a direct control of desire. We are thus more likely to find the weak point in Ross's defences if we concentrate on the relation between the predominant motive and the alleged choice of action.

And here the arguments of Hughes and Joseph and others who take a similar view, although not successful in their immediate aim of showing that the motives of actions can be controlled in a way which admits of there being duties to act from certain motives, have none the less an ominous bearing on Ross's position as a whole. The thought behind the positions we have noted is that motive and act stand in a peculiarly intimate relation. Joseph goes so far as to deny that they can be

[1] *Mind*, 1944, p. 320.

considered apart,[1] action being for him a "self-realising process".[2] This is, no doubt, an extreme view. And Ross has not found it difficult to meet the criticism as it stands. In his reply to Joseph he observes, first, that an act, considered in abstraction from the motive, is not a mere physical change: "Besides motive and a physical change there is a third thing—the setting oneself to bring about a change".[3] But this never happens, on Ross's view, except as we are moved by some motive: "all intentional acts are motived acts".[4] The real question is then whether we can "*consider* the act independently of the motive".[5] Ross maintains emphatically that we can, just as the shape of a body may be considered apart from its size, although the one would not exist without the other. And we have ourselves endorsed one important reason for adjudging rightness independently of motive. But it still seems true that the relation of a motive to an act is of such a peculiarly intimate kind that, if I could not have willed "at a moment's notice" to have another motive, *my act could not be other than it is either*. In so far as I cannot finally control the one I cannot control the other. Ross's argument thus proves too much—for his theory. For if he is to argue that "ought" has no application to motives because "we cannot desire a certain end at will"[6] it seems to follow also that "ought" has no application to conduct in any regard.

As an *argumentum ad hominem* the contentions of the writers we have noted have therefore considerable force. As Professor Field observes, also writing in criticism of Ross, "In any sense in which we can choose what action we shall do, we can choose what motive we shall act from".[7] In his reply, Ross contends that we choose to do an act "on the assumption" that the motive for doing it will be forthcoming when the time comes to do the act, as we may choose to walk down the High Street

---

[1] "But no act exists except in the doing of it, and in the doing of it there is a motive; and you cannot separate the doing of it from the motive without substituting for action in the moral sense action in the physical, mere movements of bodies." *Some Problems in Ethics*, p. 38.
[2] op. cit, p. 55.
[3] *Foundations of Ethics*, p. 128.
[4] op. cit. p. 127.
[5] op. cit. p. 127.
[6] op. cit. p. 46.
[7] "Kant's First Moral Principle", *Mind*, 1932, p. 33.

on the assumption that the High Street will still exist "when the time comes at which I mean to take the walk".[1] This argument I find very unconvincing. For how can we be thought to make a choice at all except in so far as, and at the time when, we are moved by the motive to do the act? Of course we do speak in a rough way of deciding to do something some time in advance of doing it. But this is a way of speaking which requires very careful analysis. As long as it is open to me not to do something, and it must be so on the present assumption until the motive is forthcoming, I cannot strictly be said to have chosen to do it. What does happen, however, is that I am so certain that I shall continue to desire to do something when the time comes that I take certain steps beforehand to facilitate the execution of it. I may also put the issue out of my mind on the assumption that it will be plain to me when the time comes. But to say more than this, to speak as if one could actually choose to perform a certain act beforehand on the assumption that the motive will be forthcoming, involves the same sort of distortion of the relation of act to motive as that which speaks of choosing to act from a certain motive. How can there be a choice except in so far as the motive moves us to make it?

Field's contention then stands. From it he draws the conclusion that we *can* act from one motive rather than another, and that therefore we may (and do) have a duty to do so. But it seems to me quite certain that Ross is right in holding that we cannot choose to act from a certain motive, and that, therefore, we must draw a very different conclusion from Field, and one that Ross himself is very far from drawing. It is that the idea of obligation cannot be fitted at any point into the normal view of conduct as the expression of motive and character. When, therefore, moral philosophers debate as to whether rightness qualifies "acts" or "actions from certain motives", they are bound to drive one another round in an endless circuit. Both sides to the controversy appeal to a postulate which has no bearing on conduct as conceived in terms of their problem. It would thus have been better *to ask at the start* in what way the idea of obligation presupposes freedom. A great deal of ingenious but misplaced argumentation might then have been avoided.

[1] *Foundations of Ethics*, p. 138.

III

This is, indeed, evident without going outside the writings of Sir David Ross himself. For the difficulties which beset his side of the controversy we have just discussed seem to be emphasised by his own account of the alleged "intuition of freedom". The view which he presents as adequate both to a determinist view of conduct and to the sense of freedom which we have in the moment of action, is the common view of freedom as "self-determination". The distinction between mental and physical causation is stressed, and we are shown that "what choice depends upon, and reveals, is not the strength of isolated desires but the trend of the whole character, of the whole system of more or less permanent desires".[1] "It is the universe of my desires that determines my action, and not the strongest single desire".[2] This is of great importance for the understanding of desire and character. But if it also gives us the freedom that is most distinctive of human action we should expect this to be the freedom which makes us morally accountable. In that case the freedom required by responsibility, and presupposed in the maxim "I ought, therefore I can", concerns the inner determination of conduct in the way of motive and character, and not the more outward aspect of actions to which Ross restricts the ideas of "ought" and "rightness" when the problem of "I ought, therefore I can" becomes insistent.

This suggests a much closer relation between the idea of obligation and the idea of moral worth than Ross is normally prepared to allow. Admittedly there must be *a* sense of obligation in which the discharge of it is independent of the worth of the will. For, as we have noted, it is possible to do what is "materially" wrong with the best intention. And in this sense also rightness presupposes freedom of a sort. For we never ask of any act whether it is right except on the assumption that it is an act which it is possible for us to do; no one asks "is it right to swim the Atlantic?"[3] But if the idea of obligation is to be

[1] *Foundations of Ethics*, p. 228.
[2] op. cit. p. 229.
[3] Some critics of Ross have assumed that he regards rightness as standing in no relation whatsoever to the agent. I think it is for this reason that Mr. Falk, in his "Obligation and Rightness" in *Philosophy*, July, 1945, wonders whether "fittingness of acts to situations" is "the description of anything real at all", p. 146.

retained in any ultimate sense, if there is to be a true "categorical imperative", it seems plain that there must also be a sense in which doing what is right is immediately tantamount to having moral value, there must be an internal loyalty to duty (or betrayal of it) on which the worth of the will directly depends. This is the common presumption of ordinary thought, and the conviction that ordinary thought is thoroughly justified here, has been the main cause of the dissatisfaction felt at Ross's divorce of obligation from moral goodness.

The point at which Ross asserts most emphatically that the conditions of moral worth are other than the conditions of doing one's duty—in any sense—is in regard to the much-discussed "infinite regress argument".[1] He holds that it is contradictory to say "You ought to act from the sense of duty" because this must mean "It is my duty to do act 'A' from the sense that it is my duty to do Act 'A'". But as has been pointed out by Professor L. A. Reid[2] and Mr. George Hughes[3] there is no contradiction here except on the supposition that we are using the term duty in the same sense in both parts of the proposition. That the meaning of duty which will resolve the paradox is a duty to act from a certain motive—in Hughes's version to do the act which seems to the agent right (the subjectively right act) "from the belief (or sense) that it is objectively right"[4]—seems to me also much mistaken for the reasons adduced above. But it seems none the less plain that if we are to speak of duty at all there is a sense of doing one's duty, and that much the most important, which is distinct from any form of rightness described by Ross, including one sense of doing what seems to us right; and that is the doing of what is right *qua* right. And it is the freedom involved here, that is, in that resolution to do one's duty *as such* on which moral worth depends directly, that mainly matters in ethics. The problem of freedom thus arises directly from the fact that we are subject to moral praise or blame. It is a postulate of moral worth (if that carries with it genuine praise or blame) *in precisely the same way* as it is a postulate of duty, and it must, therefore, qualify conduct *directly in that aspect of it in respect*

---
[1] *Foundations of Ethics*, p. 119. *The Right and The Good*, p. 5.
[2] *Creative Morality*, p. 46.
[3] *Mind*, 1944, p. 332.
[4] op. cit. p 324.

of which we hold ourselves open to blame. But, according to Ross, our "actions are morally good when and because they proceed from certain motives"[1] or as "manifestations of character"—"the larger and grander bearer of moral goodness".[2] It is character and desire, therefore, that should be free. By suggesting this and turning attention to the inner determination of the will, the view of freedom as self-determination affords a corrective to Ross's general account of obligation. But it also tosses us on to another horn of a dilemma. For Ross has also argued, quite convincingly as it seems to me, that we are not able to control our motives in the way required by moral obligation.

We are brought to a similar impasse when we consider two other main considerations adduced by Ross in his account of the intuition of freedom.

First he stresses the power that we have to "cause any one of two or more changes in the state of affairs".[3] This will sometimes be a "change in the condition of our own mind; but far more often a change of something in the physical world", such changes being "caused by first causing a change in the state of one's own body".[4] It seems beyond dispute that we have this power, whatever the final account to be given of the relation between mind and body. We find from experience that we are able to move about and to lift and carry various objects. Such powers are of course very limited, and illness or death may immediately deprive us of them. But life would not be possible at all, it would not be recognisable for the thing it is, if our actions never produced the effects we intended. So much is plain. It may also be allowed that the control of mind over body involves genuine activity as distinct from mere necessary connection, it is "immanent" and not "transeunt" causation. But does this explain the supposed intuition of freedom? If it does should we not conclude that the intuition is illusory in the extreme? For it gives us no sort of freedom which is distinctive of human action. It has no bearing on the inner springs of volition, and if it were the decisive factor in our assurance of

[1]*Foundations of Ethics*, p. 290.
[2]op. cit. p. 293.
[3]op. cit. p. 231.
[4]op. cit. p. 231.

freedom, then, incidentally, it would be hard to see what need there is to stress the unity of desire and character, etc., in connection with the problem. The freedom to "effect changes in the state of affairs" belongs in fact to irrational creatures as well as to human beings. But any freedom in which we are seriously interested when considering the nature of man must be freedom which characterises distinctively human activities. This is especially the case when we consider moral freedom. For the power to do what we purpose can have little significance here.[1] It seems quite an elementary principle in ethics that conduct is not to be appraised in terms of its actual consequences. This principle is, moreover, quite fundamental to Ross's account of moral goodness and rightness, and he himself insists that "the question whether the mind can control the body is irrelevant to the question of the freedom of the will. . . . Suppose that a man had, without knowing it, lost the power of speech. He could still set himself, or make the effort, to tell the truth, or alternatively set himself to tell a lie. . . . Morally, both the act and the decision to act are just the same as they would be if the control over the body still existed".[2] It seems, therefore, that the real issue is whether we are free in "setting ourselves" to do one thing or the other, but once the enquiry proceeds in this way to the more distinctive features of action which make it what it is for human beings, is it not also plain that we cannot omit the inner determination of choice in considering whether or not it is free?

Ross, finally, assures us that "possibility is always related to a judger, and that to say 'so and so may happen' is just to say 'I don't know that it won't' ".[3] Here again there would normally be little to dispute. For when we make judgments such as "It may rain tomorrow', we do not for a moment think that there is here an open possibility in *rerum natura*. What we mean is that the conditions, so far as we have been able to ascertain them, do not preclude rain. As a psychological, in distinction from the merely logical, condition of making such a judgment

---

[1] But compare A. E. Taylor, *Elements of Metaphysics*, Bk. IV, ch. iv., and H. Gomperz, "Individual, Collective and Social Responsibility", *International Journal of Ethics*, Vol. XLIX, p. 329.
[2] *Foundations of Ethics*, p. 234.
[3] op. cit. p. 235.

of possibility we must also be aware of conditions which make it likely that it will rain; the possibility must be a "real" one. But both these conditions are assured in the case of character and conduct without recourse to libertarian views. For even in anticipating immediate actions of our own there is always some possibility of error. "The situation is never *exactly* like any in which we have been in the past",[1] and hidden elements in our character may reveal themselves without warning. "Thus so long as *any* interval, however short, separates the present moment from that at which the act will be done, we do not *know* what the relative strength of the different motives will be when the latter moment arrives; and therefore do not *know* what we shall do, though we may of course think it highly probable that we shall do a certain act rather than any other".[2]

About this there need be no argument. We may also allow that possibility in this sense is of much practical importance in certain regards. No one is likely to put out his best effort in some undertaking if he is either too confident or too despondent about the prospect of success. To quote Ross's analogy, "Of the candidates in an examination, those who are most likely to make the needed effort are neither those who feel sure that they will pass nor those who feel sure that they will fail, but those who know that they do not know whether they will pass or fail".[3] This has its parallel in most spheres of interest. And the determinist can, with complete consistency, urge that possibility in the present sense is "just that which is needed to induce us to keep our moral armour in the best possible repair".[4]

But can this be the possibility that makes us responsible, is it in this way that we are to interpret the maxim "I ought, therefore I can"? Surely not, for that is not a possibility which actions share with any and every event. It is a possibility required in a special manner by moral praise or blame, and are we to say that the *rationale* of praise or blame is mainly to be found in unavoidable limits of finite knowledge? Does responsibility rest on no foundation more secure than ignorance? It would be more dignified to repudiate our responsibility altogether than to cling

[1] *Foundations of Ethics*, p. 236.
[2] op. cit. p. 236.
[3] and [4] op. cit. p. 239.

to so unsubstantial a replica of it as that. Moreover, we hold ourselves accountable, if at all, quite as much for our actions in the past, where the outcome is no longer in doubt, as for those we have yet to perform and whose nature is uncertain. In other words, the freedom for which we have a serious concern, especially where ultimate ethical questions are at issue, must be a genuine attribute of conduct itself, not a relation to a judger.

So much so that it is extremely surprising to find so doughty and clear-sighted a champion of objectivist ethics as Sir David Ross so willing to capitulate to the relativist on what seems the most vital point of his theory as a whole.

Nor is he very happy about it himself. He adds: "But the phrase 'it is possible that I shall do what is right, and possible that I shall do what is wrong' does not do full justice to our actual thought when it takes its usual form 'I can do what is right', though it expresses part of what that thought involves".[1] For a man is not the 'mere spectator of the play of forces' within him. "We say not merely 'I may do right, and I may do wrong', but 'I *can* do right and I *can* do wrong'. What exactly does this mean?"[2]

It means, we are told, that "if a certain condition is added to conditions already present in me, I shall do so and so",[3] and the unfulfilled condition "consists of my wishing to do this".[4] " 'I can do this or that' means 'I shall do this if I want, and I shall do that if I want'—'want' being here a brachylogy for 'want predominantly' ".[5] But if this is to add anything at all to the view that we are free in so far as we can execute a purpose, a view we have already found to be quite unsatisfactory, it must somehow represent freedom as turning on the fact that conduct is an expression of want or desire. We are thus again driven back on the inner determination of conduct in the way of desires or motives. But we have also seen, as very apt pupils of Ross himself, that the process of being moved to act by a certain motive is not free in the way required by the idea of 'ought' or 'duty'. So the deadlock seems complete.

To examine other arguments by which it is attempted to

[1] *Foundations of Ethics*, p. 239.
[2] op. cit. p. 240.
[3] [4] and [5] op. cit. p. 241.

reconcile freedom with determinism would take us farther afield than we can venture in this paper. It must suffice for the present to show how the critic of determinist views of moral responsibility finds support in recent arguments about obligation and rightness which take little account directly of the problem of freedom. But I should like to conclude with some comments on the position that faces us in ethics if the main contentions of this paper are sound.

IV

In the first place we seem to be committed to a much more serious and sympathetic consideration of the alternative presented by the libertarian than is usually accorded to it by philosophers. For it is very hard to rid ourselves of the conviction that there is ultimate moral responsibility. Much that is of supreme worth in the life of man, and especially in religion, seems to turn upon it. If thus there prove to be insuperable difficulties in the way of accommodating this conviction to any form of determinism, and on that score I, for one, have little doubt, the indeterminist has a very strong *prima facie* case to be considered—a great deal stronger than would appear from the cursory treatment of the position in ethical writings.

To go exhaustively into this matter would, however, require considerable space. The following comments must suffice for the present.

(a) A great many who call themselves indeterminists and libertarians, especially among the protagonists of Liberal Theology, turn out on examination to be no more than qualified determinists. This seriously confuses the issue. If the libertarian is to be heard, let it be on the claim that there is an unambiguous "open possibility", and that some of our actions at least could have been other than they are although everything else in the universe was the same. Mere rebuttal of the cruder forms of determinism is quite another matter, and makes no substantial difference to the present issue.

(b) It seems to be inordinately easy to travesty the libertarian view. Some, for example, ascribe to the libertarian the belief in a mysterious 'once for all' choice, or a choice at birth. This is the view subjected to criticism by a recent contributor to *Mind*.[1] The libertarian, it is urged, proceeds in the following way. He insists that we cannot be considered responsible for a particular action because it is due to our character at the time, and this is, in part at least, the result of our own actions in the past. If, therefore, I am to be praised or blamed, it must be for the past conduct that made me the sort of person I am today. But what I did in the past was also the result of the sort of person I was then, and this I could not help, because it was, in turn, the result of past actions on my part and that of others. And it is here, the writer concludes, "that the temptation to invoke a metaphysical *deus ex machina* becomes inviting. If we proceed on the assumption that, to be moral, an action must be uncaused, either we shall find a genuinely uncaused action at the beginning of the chain or we shall not. If we do not, then, according to the libertarian, there can be no moral praise and blame at all (and it was to account for these that Libertarianism was invented); and, if we do, then we must suppose that, while almost all our actions are caused, and therefore amoral, there was in the distant past some one action that was not caused and for which we can justly be praised or blamed. This bizarre theory has in fact been held; but the objections to it are clear. We praise and blame people for what they do now, not for what they might have done as babies, and any theory of moral responsibility must account for this".[2] But, we must reply, does any philosopher of repute today hold the preposterous theory discussed in this passage? It may be that the theory 'has in fact been held'. Support in some quarter or other can be found for the most fantastic views; and religious thinkers come perilously near the notion of a 'once for all choice' when they ascribe the wickedness of man to a 'fall' which is prior to his history on earth. But this is hardly a view to which the supporters of indeterminism would normally subscribe. What they hold is that there are *several* choices made from time to time in the course of our lives as mature human beings. And it is to this view, in the form in which it is held by philosophers whose work commands respect, that criticism should be directed, not to the caricature of it in the notion of an

---

[1] P. Nowell Smith, *Mind*, January, 1948.
[2] op. cit. p. 51.

'infantile choice'. The failure to appreciate this is all the more inexcusable because statements of the libertarian view are easily available in recent ethical books by philosophers of considerable standing such as E. F. Carritt and C. A. Campbell. There may not be many who agree with these thinkers. But if it is considered worth while at all to criticise the libertarian view, one should at least take the trouble to refer to the form in which it appears in the work of its most worthy exponents. This brings me to a point of much importance.

(c) On some counts, at least, such indeterminists as have ventured to take the field in recent years seem to have been very successful. They have answered some criticisms quite conclusively. Among these is the objection, usually considered the most formidable of all, that the libertarian view is incompatible with the observed continuity of conduct. It is taken to imply that "any action could come from any person at any time", that so far as his character is concerned a man can entirely "trammel up the consequences" of his action. And if it were the case that the libertarian did hold that belief, or if he were in consistency committed to it, his position would indeed be quite preposterous. All his conduct would belie his theory, for we can hardly act at all apart from the presumption that other persons and ourselves will behave in certain ascertainable ways in particular circumstances. We do rely on one another in practice, and a world in which we did not do so would be a world of madmen. In so far, therefore, as it is assumed that the indeterminist repudiates all connection between conduct and a continuous character, it is most understandable that he should usually be dismissed with contempt. But he need not hold anything so foolish, and he rarely does so today. His position only requires that there should be genuine choice *within limits,* the limits prescribed by conscience and character. To the extent that moral convictions summon us to courses of action opposed to the predominant trend of our characters, the libertarian holds that there is a free choice before us. We may make an "effort of will" to defeat the weakness of our character as formed at a particular time; but not otherwise. It is not suggested that we can disregard both conviction and character. When therefore I rest assured that my friend X will not cheat at cards, this will be, on the libertarian view, because I know him well enough to be reasonably certain that such conduct will not be in accordance either with his nature or his principles. In *this* regard there will be no occasion for moral choice where he is concerned. In the same way we rule out preposterous actions by persons whose sanity we have no reason to doubt. This leaves ample room for moral choice, and however severe the other difficulties which confront the libertarian, he seems thus to have a perfectly adequate answer to those who accuse him of absurd violations of the obvious continuity of conduct. So complete and so final is the answer, and so well has it been stated by recent writers,[1] that it is indeed surprising we have not heard the last of the objection. In fact it is still very prominent in discussions of moral freedom.[2]

(d) But if we are to follow the libertarian here, a clear distinction will need to be drawn between the properly moral worth (or badness, as the case may be) of genuine acts of choice and good or bad qualities of character. A kindly disposition does not lose its importance by being no longer regarded as the subject of distinctively moral praise. It may in fact indirectly reflect moral worth, since we have a duty to cultivate a good character. But in itself it must be classed with non-moral values, and as such it will lose nothing of its real lustre.

In consistency with this view the libertarian will also require to insist that moral worth must be appraised, not in terms of the end achieved in our actions or even of the content willed, but in terms of the effort required to obey our own consciences. For the end at which we aim, the content willed, can only reflect directly certain qualities of character. The aims of Gandhi were much nobler than those of most persons, but this was probably due in great measure to natural endowment and environment. His circumstances helped to make him the sort of person he was, he was naturally more tenacious of purpose than most men and more attracted to great ends. This may entitle us to say that he was a supremely virtuous or saintly person, but that will still have to be discounted by the libertarian in appraisement of *strictly moral worth*. For the latter would only be exhibited on those occasions when Gandhi's natural strength of character

[1] e.g., by C. A. Campbell, *Scepticism and Construction*, Chapter V.
[2] cf. Ross's *Foundations of Ethics*, p. 230.

proved insufficient to the demands made upon him by his ideals. No one can be certain what those occasions were. For however firm and heroic Gandhi's resolution may have been, no one could judge from anything in the overt nature of his conduct whether, in relation to his formed character as a whole at the time, he was not really acting in the line of least resistance. Only he himself, or God, could know that, although there is the presumption that no one is so richly endowed by nature as to rise to the heroic triumphs of a Gandhi without having at some stages to reinforce the natural bent of his character by free efforts of will. This latter need would arise more often perhaps in his case, not in the matter of sustained physical endurance, but on the occasions when he had to incur the obloquy and distrust of his own friends and followers by calling off campaigns which he himself had originally inspired (as happened especially when the non-violent campaign of 1922 seemed unlikely to take the course Gandhi himself expected). It is, among other reasons, because free efforts of will are presupposed in this way, that 'saintliness' has its especial appropriateness in describing a nature such as that of Gandhi. But one has always to remember that, if we are to adhere consistently to the libertarian view, a high degree of moral worth may be attained by persons of more ordinary qualities of character for actions which would cost Gandhi nothing in the way of strictly moral effort and thus reflect no strictly *moral* credit upon him. This makes properly *moral* censure or approval very unreliable; we can presume a measure of moral evil in actions which seem contrary to what we have every reason to regard as the agent's own convictions, these being, however, by no means so easy to ascertain as is commonly supposed—how far was Hitler morally wicked and how far the victim of absurd delusions? The injunction to 'judge not' is thus reinforced by the libertarian view, although there is nothing in that view to preclude strong expression of disapproval of outward action as likely to lead to more enlightened views or better characters.

Understood as involving these consequences, there can be no denying that there is something of a paradoxical nature in the libertarian view of moral worth. It does not altogether accord with our ordinary judgments and reactions, but may not the answer here be that there is much confusion in these latter which a sound moral analysis may help to remove; ethical reflection has certainly helped us in other respects to adopt more enlightened attitudes. Again, it may be felt that the cultivation of moral qualities is precluded on the libertarian view, and that this contradicts what we normally think about moral education and training. But again it may be answered that such training is not precluded where qualities of character are concerned, and there is no reason to be negligent of these when their importance in their own way is appreciated. It is not for us to create opportunities of moral triumph for ourselves by weakening our characters any more than we should rejoice over pain and privation because they afford opportunities of acquiring merit in relieving them. There will in any case be plenty of temptations for creatures situated as we are without inducing them artificially, especially since the conquest of certain kinds of temptation exposes us to others— the temptations of St. Paul or Gandhi may not be those of ordinary men, but they may be acute none-the-less. In these ways then, and by stressing the difference between properly moral effort and mere physical or intellectual effort or the effort involved when one strain in our nature subdues another, careful analysis of the libertarian view may show that in the long run it conforms more closely than is commonly supposed by philosophers to what we normally feel impelled to believe about the moral life.

But while the course for the libertarian is clear in these respects, his success is not so easily assured in other ways. In particular an especially formidable objection presents itself in the question, 'Is there not a metaphysical requirement that everything should be determined in some way?' The libertarian will not, any more than other moral philosophers who know their business, wish to deny the normal continuity of events, including most human actions. He only makes an exception of acts of moral choice. If he went beyond this his position would soon become absurd. For action is only possible in a stable world. But do the exceptions the libertarian makes jeopardise his faith in the continuity of other actions and events? The position is sharpened if it is believed that, outside the sphere of free choice there is *necessary* determination. I should certainly hold that there is such necessitation. Nor is this a matter that could be established empirically. For no observations can be relevant to the determination of a question about the relation of events in general. Our principle has to be known *a priori,* and I feel confident that it is known in that way. But to claim to know *a priori* that there is causal determination, and also to limit its operation, is certainly a bold undertaking. I think it is an undertaking in which the libertarian need not despair of success, and that a highly valuable clue to the procedure he ought to adopt may be found in Nicolai Hartmann's conception of a 'plus of determination' striking into other modes of determination without altogether suspending them. But to consider these matters properly would require, not only a careful examination of Hartmann's view, but also study of further formidable metaphysical issues. That can hardly be attempted here. And we are in any case concerned now with the ethical rather than the more metaphysical aspects of the problem of freedom. Not that the two can be divorced in a final account. But I think that the most that our present purpose requires is that acknowledgment be made of the formidable difficulties which confront the libertarian at the metaphysical level. If he feels that he has not the resources to meet them, he must have no illusions as to what he must eventually forfeit.

This brings me to the point I wish most to stress in closing this paper.

If we find that we have to reject the libertarian view, then we must also be ready to sacrifice much that is usually considered important in ethics, including the common conception of guilt and responsibility. Drastic changes will be needed at several points in our ethical thought, and to some extent also in practice. These changes must be carried out boldly and thoroughly. Otherwise we shall only perpetuate the sort of confusion in which, as we have contended above, some of the best ethical thinking is entangled today. There is hardly a greater need in ethics at present than this of considering closely what has to be sacrificed if we surrender the notion of ultimate responsibility. And if the task is neglected by those who do not despair of applying meaningful ethical distinctions to conduct, they may find it undertaken for them more ruthlessly and carelessly by others. The way will be open for the positivist, the Freudian or the advocate of "evolutionary", "scientific", ethics. Their pruning will be far too severe. For if we surrender the values that turn on final responsibility, it does not follow that all will be lost. There will still be important distinctions of value. Nor will these be confined to knowledge and aesthetics, although the latter will henceforth be more typical of values in general. Character and conduct of a certain kind will still have the highest worth and call for cultivation through training and environment. Among the best qualities of character, moreover, will be the desire to do what is fitting to the situation as a whole. And, if we are mindful what we are about, we may call this, if we please, the "sense of duty". Its worth will not depend directly on sound judgment, much less on correct information. The question what sort of conduct is "materially" correct will be a further one. In these ways ethical theory will wear much the same appearance as it usually presents today in such writings as we have mentioned in this paper. It will require no sacrifice of any of the main contentions of *Principia Ethica*. But it will have no room for guilt and remorse or for merit and demerit in any distinctive and ultimate sense not resembling, for example, the pride or despair of the artist. It must not embarrass itself with a "categorical imperative" or any of its preconditions.

Such ethics will approximate closely to the ethical thinking of the Greeks. And the problem of freedom will present itself in the same way, in essentials, as it appears in their theories. It will have much to try the mettle of philosophers. But it will not be altogether bewildering. The main values will depend largely, as in Greek thought, on harmony and adjustment, great goodness will go with enlightenment, and the supreme evil will be "the lie in the soul" as affecting personal relationships as well as understanding of nature. This may lack much we have usually held to be yet more important. That it is an ignoble view no one conversant with Greek thought will suppose.

Neither, incidentally, will it be very hard to accommodate it to certain modes of Christian thought. In some ways it will greatly simplify the procedure of traditional theology. For a great deal of the ethical thinking of traditional theology seems to the present writer to be a Socratic ethic into which there have been infused ideas of guilt and blame incompatible with it. "If a man could *see* evil as it is", says a prominent and very influential theologian of the present day, "he would not *really* be evil".[1] Unfortunately he proceeds, in the time-honoured way of theologians, to vilify man for his blindness (incurred through a "fall" in which each one is involved with the whole of his kind). This, as it stands, I submit, carries very little real conviction to anyone not committed to the perpetuation of a set of doctrines. But the general Christian view of man's blindness, and his salvation by "grace", present no special difficulty on a Socratic ethic from which we strictly exclude the notions of guilt and blame. On the contrary, they vastly deepen such an ethic. There is also much precedent for this course in traditional theology itself. For many theologians approximate it in the distinction between sin and guilt. This, again, will not do as it stands. For apart from the fact that "sin" is almost certain to convey the idea of guilt to the ordinary man, the latter notion is still accorded a place, and that within a system which does not allow of genuine freedom of choice, however prone theologians may be to persuade themselves that it does. Guilt, like the "categorical imperative", simply cannot be accommodated at all within a deterministic scheme.

To set these observations on religious thought in their proper context would however take us very far afield. The most that this paper attempts is a plea for the bolder consideration of the problem of freedom and obligation, together with more determination to follow the "wind of the argument" whithersoever it takes us. Sir David Ross expresses the hope "that a genius will some day arise who will succeed in reconciling our natural thought about freedom and responsibility with acceptance of the law of causation". But what if the task is plainly an impossible one? Would it not then be the wiser course to turn from it altogether, and set our house in order as best we can with what remains to us? That is considerable. But considerable also is the surrender to be made of ordinary ethical beliefs if we conclude that the law of causality holds universal sway.

---

[1] Emil Brunner, *Divine Imperative*, p. 75.

Chapter VII

GUILT AND FREEDOM[1]

MORAL philosophers do not seem to have had a great deal to say about guilt, and it would be easy to compile an impressive list of ethical treatises in which the subject is not mentioned at all. In recent ethics especially it has suffered much neglect. In theology, on the other hand, the problem of guilt has always remained to the fore, and of late it has also elicited the very lively interest of the psychologist. It is the moralist who remains aloof.

This is as regrettable as it is strange. For however important the problem of guilt may be, in some of its bearings, for religious thought or psychology, it is first and foremost an ethical problem. And when the moralists are reluctant to tackle some ethical question, and are content to hand it over to other disciplines, such as theology or psychology, which have an interest in it, the properly ethical features of that question are apt to be either overlaid altogether by extraneous considerations or distorted into some quasi-ethical religious or psychological form. Of this the treatment of the problem of guilt is an excellent example.

We have thus to insist at the start that our problem is essentially an ethical one. It is also a problem of first importance.

This is so for several reasons. (1) Some of the most crucial issues in theological controversy have turned on the nature of guilt, and the course which the discussion of these matters has taken has been such as would have been substantially improved by bolder intrusion into the field of theology by moral philosophers—especially in recent times. (2) The rapid advance of psychology in our time, and in particular the fascinating, if also somewhat uncritical, theories of the psycho-analysts, have added much to the plausibility of the view that a fully satisfactory account of guilt can be given in purely psychological terms;

[1] *Proceedings of the Aristotelian Society,* Supplementary Volume XXI. Also *Analysis,* Dec., 1947.

this alone would justify a fresh investigation. (3) Questions of penal reform and other matters of even more urgent and far-reaching importance, such as the problem of war-guilt and the treatment of "guilty nations", set our problem among the more pressing practical issues of this age. There is hardly another field where the philosopher, by close and impartial analysis can have a more immediate and beneficial influence on practice, nor any where the challenge to come out of the ivory tower is plainer. (4) Some of the matters most keenly debated in ethics today, and especially the question of rightness and moral worth on which so much ingenuity has been expended, could have been viewed more clearly from the start if the implications of guilt, as involved in the nature of moral evil, had been more carefully and boldly considered in connection with those matters. (This, although not taken up very fully in this paper—I have discussed it elsewhere—will, I hope, be plainer in due course).

We have thus a vast field of investigation before us, and it will only be possible to touch very briefly on some of the matters mentioned above. My aim will be to centre attention as far as possible on the strictly ethical nature of the problem of guilt. The crucial question here is that of freedom. In presenting it I beg your indulgence in traversing some rather familiar ground for a little.

I

The problem of moral freedom was never an acute one for the Greeks. This was because they thought of the moral life in terms of a goodness which men are by nature disposed to pursue. Aristotle typified well the attitude of his contemporaries when he made the conceptions which he had found useful in his study of natural life also fundamental for ethics. There is a growth which is natural to man, there is a certain capacity, to be thought of not merely as a power but also as a tendency, which it is his function to fulfil. The 'potential' stands in this relation to the 'actual', that the unorganised passions and impulses which constitute the raw material of goodness acquire a final form with an inevitability so inherent to the nature of man that it is not fundamentally different from the inevitability by which an acorn becomes an oak tree. Admittedly reason makes a difference, and no one would confuse the naturalism of Aristotle with that of Hobbes or Hume. Reason enters into the Supreme Good in the form of 'Contemplation' and the requirements of practical life are discerned by the exercise of Practical Wisdom in a way that makes reason the master much more than the 'slave of the passions'. Even so, the end that is proper to man remains one to which he is directed by his nature; and the problem of ethics is, therefore, the problem what is the nature of man and in what environment can he become most truly himself, most truly what he really wants to be.

This represents no substantial departure from the teaching of Plato. For although Plato does not set out like Aristotle to define the Supreme Good in terms of our own aspirations, but rather gives the Form of the Good a completeness and reality of its own, he is, none the less, convinced that man finds in the Form of the Good what is most akin to the distinctive constituent of his own nature—his reason. And in virtue of this likeness the 'Good' has an irresistible attraction for anyone who properly understands its nature.

This approach to ethical problems was facilitated for the Greeks by the absence of a sharp distinction between moral and non-moral values, such as we are familiar with today. They were indeed brought easily to the idea of one Supreme Good to be exhibited in the whole of life, and the fundamental principles of their ethical theories did not, therefore, deviate markedly from the principles implied in the attainment of estimable qualities and accomplishments generally. Analogies with some art or craft have a significant recurrence in the most important contexts of Greek moral philosophy. The pursuit of moral worth thus presented itself to the Greeks with at least such inevitability as we find in the cultivation of some gift in whose exercise a man is bound to take the greatest delight.

An obvious reflection of this view is the Socratic maxim 'Virtue is Knowledge'. But Plato and Aristotle understood well that this maxim could not be accepted without qualification. It did not accord altogether with experience. For very often we seem, at any rate, to choose the worse course knowing the better. For this problem Plato found an answer, satisfactory to him, in the distinction between genuine knowledge and opinion. It is only when we rely on uncertain opinions, on ideas derived at secondhand or conventions on whose purpose we have not ourselves reflected, that our conduct may not be in line with our principles. When we really understand, when the nature of the good is properly the possession of our own minds, then we are certain to model our conduct upon it. This did not satisfy Aristotle. He pointed out[1] that many persons hold their fallible beliefs with the same firmness and assurance as others their certain knowledge. But his own treatment of the subject does not take us very far. He observed, quite rightly, that passion or fear may induce a momentary blindness and that, again, we often fail to perceive the application of some general principle to our own case. But this is not the whole of the matter—far from it. There remain the much more important cases where we seem deliberately and calmly to do what we know to be wrong. And the fact that Aristotle manages only to touch the fringes of the problem shows that he did not concern himself deeply with it, notwithstanding the downright admission in one context that we do sometimes choose the worse course knowing the better. It is moreover hard to see what alternative to the Platonic solution is possible on Aristotle's theory of goodness.

We can still admit that Aristotle's principles fully allowed him to supply a very necessary corrective to the superficial views of the Sophists and their assumption that goodness, as well as intellectual excellence, could be produced by teaching alone. He was quite entitled to stress the importance of discipline and training. For he was not bound to regard this training of the will as a factor altogether apart from the process of ethical enlightenment. The value of the training and its perpetuation in the right sort of habit could be thought to lie in the deepening of Practical Wisdom to which it led, and the consequent fuller devotion to the good. This in the main seems to be the view that Aristotle does hold. At any rate there is no certain indication of the contrary such as would show a real appreciation of the issues involved in the problem of deliberate wrong-doing.

But whether or not it be held that the typical Greek view of the nature of goodness allows of some deviation from a 'Socratic ethics', there is certainly required by it the ascription of virtue

[1] *Ethics*, Book VII, 1146b.

and vice altogether to some combination of the factors of enlightenment, training, and environment. There is no room for genuine rebellion. On the contrary, as Professor A. E. Taylor reminds us, the principle "that goodness is in the soul what health and fitness are in the body" is "really at the bottom of all Greek thinking on morality."[1]

It has to be stressed that, to the extent that the Greeks were compelled to take some account of deliberate wrong-doing, they were driven to do so by the fact that experience seems to present us with instances of it. Men did apparently choose the worse course, and however perplexing the fact might be, it had to be accommodated somehow in ethical theories. But the thought that a power of making the wrongful choice may itself be a condition of virtue does not seem to have occasioned serious misgiving. Deliberate wickedness presented itself mainly as a fact of experience, not *as an ethical postulate*. And this is a most significant way in which the problem of freedom had not for the Greeks the acuteness which it usually has for us.

There would still be *a* problem of freedom. On its more theoretical side this would be the problem of deciding how we must understand and describe men's independence of their environment in so far as they are also clearly determined by their environment or, as it used to be put, not unfairly as it seems to me, 'organic to their world'. Art supplies an obvious illustration. The poet is in one sense the creature of his age, of his immediate environment, and of traditions that reach into remotest ages of the past, but he is also supremely free. The influences that affect him are assimilated by his mind with a completeness that makes his creations distinctively his own. The more sensitive he is the more are factors of the world about him brought into rich combinations and transformed as they become parts of a unique individuality. But just what can we mean by individuality here, and what can we say in a final sense about the distinctness of persons at this level? These are important questions, and they have been very fruitfully discussed by philosophers, not least in fairly recent times. They have the greatest importance for speculative thought, and they enter deeply into religious questions.

[1] *Aristotle*, p. 105.

On the practical side there are such problems as those of the statesman and the educator when they have to decide how far it is wise to interfere with the spontaneous development of mind and character if the finest qualities are to be elicited. How may instruction be effective without being mechanical or biased, how is society to give positive support to the arts and sciences without affecting the free play of the mind; in what measure should efficiency in matters of government be sacrificed when that seems necessary for the political education of a people; and again, a most acute problem at the moment, how far should we venture to influence one another in matters of religious belief? These are also questions of great moment, and here, as on the theoretical side, there is a great deal to be learnt from the Greeks.

For not only had the Greeks a distinctive feeling for the integration and harmony required for the development of persons in the present sense, and especially in those aspects of men's lives that are most easily assimilated to aesthetic pursuits, they also provided us with specific principles and conceptions of the greatest importance in this context. Plato's comparison of the education of the soul to the 'nurture' of a plant upon which we cannot impose a form of our own but which can be brought to its richest bloom by careful tending under suitable climatic conditions and in the right soil, the insistence upon the importance of general environment as well as direct instruction, and Aristotle's conception of 'the mean', of a fittingness to one's own nature and one's circumstances discerned by the insight that comes with experience and devotion to the good, are obvious indications of ways in which our grasp of the problem of freedom in the sense in question at the moment, in all its aspects, is enhanced by the study of Greek thought. But here we have, none the less, not at all the problem of freedom that men have in mind when they speak of freedom as a postulate of ethics, however much the latter may be intertwined in practice with such problems as confront the parent or the statesman.

II

The problem of moral freedom in the proper sense is one that arises when the idea of duty, obligation, law, of a 'categorical imperative', of guilt and remorse, of ultimate praise or blame, are made central to ethical thought. These are ideas we have derived mainly from Hebrew attitudes and habits of thought, deepened by Christian teaching, and preserved, with not unimportant distortions, in traditional theology. Their presupposition found classical expression in Kantian ethics and in the celebrated maxim, 'I ought, therefore I can'. It was unfortunate that certain beliefs about the life of man arrived at on independent epistemological and metaphysical grounds prejudiced the presentation of this principle, and its implications, by Kant himself. For he seems in some regards forced to the conclusion that only the good will is free, and even that its freedom consists in some timeless once for all act—whatever that may mean in relation to the conduct of men. This has helped to perpetuate those theological distortions of ethical principles at which I have hinted above. But Kant did distinguish between the 'holy will' and the 'good will' which, in spite of being 'objectively determined', is 'not necessarily in unison with the law'.[1] And it seems plain to me that, in spite of the unfortunate bifurcation of our nature into the 'pure' and the 'empirical' selves, Kant's conception of moral obligation turned essentially on a genuine conflict between duty and interest. What he was struggling to fit into his system, not always, it must be admitted, with conspicuous success, was the conviction of the ordinary man that if there be such a thing as duty, if there be genuine moral responsibility, then it must be the case, not only that we are able to perform certain actions, but also, as Professor Broad has stressed,[2] that we *need not* perform them.

Philosophers have not found it easy to determine how precisely we must conceive the freedom of choice which duty thus seems to require, and how far we can be said to enjoy it. During the last century it was common to seek a solution of the problem by combining the Greek view with that of Kant, a most unnatural yoking of principles which the idealists endeavoured to force upon ethics in other ways also—with much ingenuity and persistence, and to the great confusion of moral philosophy. Man, it was urged, is free because he is 'self-determined', his desires direct his conduct, not in isolation from

---

[1] *Principles of the Metaphysic of Ethics*, ed. Abbott, p. 37.
[2] In his *Determinism, Indeterminism, and Libertarianism*.

one another, but as taken up into the unity of 'the self as a whole'; influences from outside himself affect him only as they are assimilated into his own nature; his own past, as well as the environment to which he is organic, determines him only as brought to life anew in the continual shaping of character, and a motive takes its final form in the very process of issuing in action. There is thus no mechanical determination in the flow of conduct in accordance with character, a matter but little appreciated in Associationist psychology such as that of Bain and Mill which Bradley trounces so severely in his *Ethical Studies* and his *Logic*. But when every allowance has been made for the sounder psychology of the idealist view of character, are we much nearer a solution of the properly ethical problem of freedom? What we are offered is only a superior way of being determined, it is in essentials the same sort of freedom as is exhibited in knowledge or in art; it presents itself with greater completeness in good conduct than in bad, as the terms 'self-mastery' and 'consistency' as applied in the praise of conduct suggest. But the freedom which obligation seems to require is not itself in any way a part of the goodness of the action as symmetry would be an element in the beauty of a picture. It is the freedom to choose to do the action or not to do it, and it is not a whit affected when we choose the bad.

There is thus no solution of the problem of *moral* freedom by noting that there is usually a perfectly innocent paradox of freedom and necessity in rational experience. Admittedly freedom and necessity do meet wherever there is thought. We see the truth by making it our own in active thought, but the more we do so the more we are bound to think in a certain way, to submit to the structure of truth itself. Our freedom is also conformity to law. The artist is most creative when he sees that he *must* do just this and not that, when he is most held to his way; we love those to whom we are drawn, and give ourselves with most abandon when we are already in thrall; in religion there is also a 'service' which is 'perfect freedom', a 'perfect law of freedom', a 'law which is my delight'. But the necessity of duty is not of this order at all. It is not itself also freedom, but rather *presupposes* it, it is the 'must' of command, not of conformity, and it implies that we need not conform. It does not vary with attainment, as in art or knowledge. The wicked are fully as free as the good. Their freedom is in that regard absolute. It is a 'liberty of indifference', a liberty, not to go one way, the ideal way, but several.

Viewed in this way, moral evil is unlike any other; it is not a functional disorder or disease, it is not like our shortcomings in art or knowledge, for it can be brought home to the individual as his own disobedience or rebellion; it is guilt, a wilful violation of law, and thus reprehensible as no other evil can be. Moral value in turn is obedience, and calls for a distinctive sort of praise. But our terms are apt to confuse us here, for our usage of 'merit' is very ambiguous. A man may acquire merit as an athlete, a poet, or a statesman. But guilt, mainly because of its more strictly forensic origin, represents more truly that peculiar quality of moral distinctions which sets them in sharp opposition to other values because of the special way they rest on the will of the individual—hence we speak more of the problem of guilt than of merit. The Greeks had little consciousness of guilt, at least so far as the teaching of their main philosophers goes— Greek drama has a somewhat different tale to tell. And so there was no sharp distinction for them between aesthetic and moral good. But if we are to draw that distinction, and think of moral wickedness as violation of a law or imperative, we must not content ourselves with the freedom which matters most on a Greek view of ethics. And although this appears so plain it is not idle to stress it at some length. For the view of freedom as self-determination is still the view normally accepted by ethical writers, not excepting those who give prominence to the idea of obligation. But what we must presuppose for the latter purpose —and the word 'presuppose' is important here—is a freedom to go one way or the other, a freedom of open choice.

III

But here we may encounter the objection that, in the light of a better understanding of the nature of guilt, it will be seen that the postulate of freedom is no longer required, or that at any rate it comes in such a modest shape as to relieve the philosopher of the perplexities which this postulate has usually caused him in the past. This is thought to be especially the case when regard is had to the advances of recent psychology. At this point it behoves us therefore to consider more precisely how guilt must be understood.

Now the idea of guilt is one we most commonly encounter in a legal context; and here a person is guilty if he has contravened the 'law of the land' and incurred a penalty. But legal guilt and ethical guilt are by no means the same. It is possible to have the one without the other, as in the case of a person who breaks the law on conscientious grounds. How then must we conceive of guilt in the ethical sense?

There seems to be this at least in common to legal and ethical guilt, that a person is guilty when, in some way or another, he has done what is wrong. But there are several senses of 'doing what is wrong' in ethics. Sir David Ross distinguishes three.[1] (a) My act may be wrong by being out of accord with the actual requirements of a situation, or (b) by being out of accord with the requirements of the situation as I understand them, or (c) by being contrary to what I myself take to be my duty. These distinctions are required because we may be mistaken both about the facts of a situation and in our evaluation of them. Do we become guilty, then, by doing what is wrong in any of these senses? Not, it seems plain, in senses (a) and (b). And the reason seems to be that failure in these respects reflects no discredit directly on the agent, and that seems also, therefore, to be involved in the idea of guilt. What, then, of (c)? Here Ross's position is peculiar. For one of his main reasons for regarding (c) as the most important meaning of a failure to discharge our duty (and that in which "obligation" may be substituted for duty) is that it is the one in which blame is incurred, and blame is incurred because we *can* "set ourselves" or intend to do what we think is right, whereas we cannot guarantee the result. But Ross does not think that rightness or wrongness in the present sense is a direct indication of our moral quality. He argues that we may do what we think is right merely to suit our convenience or from thoroughly unworthy motives, and that our conduct would, then, be morally indifferent or bad, as the case may be. When we do what we think is *wrong* there is *some* evidence of

[1] *Foundations of Ethics*, Chapter VII. Ross speaks mainly of "right act" but what he says obviously holds *mutatis mutandis* of "wrong act."

moral wickedness, but motive must here also be taken into account in a complete evaluation. But it seems to me certain that conduct does not deserve blame except in strict proportion to moral disvalue, and that no one is guilty in the ethical sense except as he is also morally bad. I conclude, therefore, that guilt is some betrayal of what I take to be my duty by which my conduct becomes directly morally evil and blameworthy.

The conditions of guilt are therefore precisely the same as the conditions of moral evil, but we must not allow the notion of guilt to drop out in considering the nature and conditions of moral evil, for we shall then be inclined to overlook the peculiarity of moral evil, as so many moral philosophers have done, and assimilate it to other forms of evil which do not presuppose a special kind of wrong-doing and do not expose us to blame.

But the reference to the blameworthy nature of guilty conduct raises at once the question whether an exhaustive account of it may not be given—as in the case of legal guilt—in terms of the attitudes we closely associate with it, namely blame, condemnation, remorse, and righteous indignation. Some would include also overt punishment, but this raises some further rather complicated questions, and I leave it aside for the moment. But whether we have punishment into the picture or not, we can hardly think of guilt without thinking at the same time of blame and condemnation. And many have, therefore, concluded that what is most distinctive of guilt can be defined in terms of these reactions.

If that were in fact possible our ethical problems would be very much simplified. For it would follow that these reactions could themselves be exhaustively described in psychological terms, and this, in its turn, would give us the main indication of the nature of guilt which would also need to be naturalistic; from this, as we shall see below, would result a fairly easy solution of the problem of freedom. But this is not what we normally think. We think normally and, I believe, rightly, that blame and condemnation do not define guilt, but rather presuppose it. They are attitudes and reactions appropriate to guilt, but guilt comes first. This means that the latter is an ultimate ethical conception not to be wholly described in psychological terms. Moral blame and condemnation therefore derive their significance from it, not it from them. They are attitudes which have a peculiar irreducible ethical appropriateness to guilt. And as such they do not open up a possibility of defining guilt; but they aid our reflection about it, in particular by throwing into relief the contrast between guilt and other kinds of shortcomings which do not call for blame. And this, as we have noted, has special importance for the understanding of moral evil.

A vigorous protest must next be entered against the procedure of several eminent moral philosophers who, without any wish to put ethical ideas into jeopardy, but rather the reverse, have seriously prejudiced their case by defining responsibility as liability to punishment, and guilt as the meriting of it. Bradley is a good example. The position is in some ways redeemed by the fact that punishment is not itself conceived wholly, or even mainly, in utilitarian terms. There is retributive punishment, the appropriateness of which is distinctively ethical. But the case for retention of guilt as a properly ethical notion is made to depend on what seems to me, to say the least, a highly doubtful conception, namely that of retributive justice. I believe that something like the theory of retributive punishment may well be true, as I hope to suggest later, but I am certainly far from convinced that any situation is directly improved by infliction of pain on a guilty agent. But this does not vitally affect the problem of moral evil and guilt itself. The question of punishment is a separate issue for any account of moral evil which is not utilitarian. For punishment would have no special appropriateness (allowing for the moment that it has) were it not for the prior irreducible nature of moral evil.

If we overlook this, as Bradley and those who follow his lead are much inclined to do, we may find that we have moved unwittingly near to the naturalistic position, and it is because they have travelled further in that direction than they realised, I believe, that the thinkers in question find it so easy, as a rule, to reconcile freedom with determinism. This is why I think it important to keep the problems of responsibility and guilt distinct from the problem of punishment, except, of course, to the extent that punishment is bound to have a very central place in any naturalistic theory of guilt.

IV

But the view that guilt may be fully described in psychological terms, and that the representation of it as wrongfulness of a distinctively ethical character is an illusion—in the sense, for example, in which Freud regards religion as an illusion—may take a somewhat different form in the attempt to account for guilt, not so much in terms of the attitudes and reactions of other persons to our conduct, but in terms of certain states and reactions of the guilty person himself. This view of guilt has been given much prominence in recent attempts to account for ethical ideas exhaustively in psychological terms, but I do not think it is hard to show that it is only superficially attractive.

The first matter that falls to be emphasised here is the stubbornness of the belief that guilt is real, and that it is not to be described exhaustively in terms either of punishment or of the reactions of the agent himself. Illusion there may be, but it certainly dies very hard. The voice of vulgar opinion, whose prestige is rightly very high in ethics, speaks here in no unmistakable terms. The ordinary person, by no means so elusive a creature as is sometimes thought, draws a very sharp distinction between his shortcomings in art, or in matters of the intellect or good taste, and wrongdoing; and if it be suggested that the judgment to be passed on the latter is illusory, or can be exhaustively described in terms of fear and punishment or similar matters, he will be much offended, taking it as an affront to his dignity as a moral being. He believes that some conduct has an attribute of guilt which implies that it is evil in a deep and peculiarly revolting way. The "guilty" are not merely a menace, they are evil; and the evil nature of their actions is not at all on the level of some functional disorder or disease. It is deep and ultimate.

A reflection of this may be found in the procedure of some philosophers who, not themselves unsympathetic to subjectivist theories of non-moral good, have also held very firmly that moral good and moral evil are *sui generis* and ultimate! This may not be an easy position to defend. But at any rate it bears witness to the deep-rooted nature of the conviction that guilt and moral evil are ultimate and irreducible.

But someone may object here that the report of common experience is that, on occasion, we *feel* guilty or have a *sense* of guilt; and that might be taken to suggest that guilt is some feeling of uneasiness or fear due to anticipation—not very explicit perhaps—of some kind of punishment. This is, however, to ascribe far too great a significance to an ambiguous phrase. The consciousness of guilt will normally arouse some distressing emotion, of which remorse is by far the most distinctive and the most appropriate. And for the rough designations with which we are normally content the mere emotion may well give the best indication of the experience as a whole. But clearly we could not have guilty feelings unless, in the first place, we thought that we *were* guilty. This does not, of course, prove that guilt cannot itself be described, in the final account, in terms of our own emotions. But it does mean that such psychological accounts of guilt must have room for the distinction between the feelings consequent on guilt and the state which occasions them. And the fact that this distinction has to be drawn robs the popular expression "feeling of guilt" of any immediate support it might give to the notion that guilt can be exhaustively described in terms of our emotions.

Furthermore, "feeling" is itself a term notorious for its ambiguous usage in common parlance. We say "I have a feeling that the weather will clear", "I feel I ought to visit so and so", when clearly we mean primarily "I think that", etc., however much the thought may be prompted by feelings or accompanied by them.

V

It is not, therefore, so simple a matter to dispose of the belief that guilt is "a terrible reality,"—and a properly ethical one. But, it may be urged, it is just here that psychology, and especially recent psychology, comes to our aid. It can be shown that there are many hidden anxieties and fears whose subtle and elusive operations create the impression that there is some distinctive ethical guilt when in fact there is nothing that we cannot, on close analysis, reduce to some emotional reaction.

On this basis some thinkers, and especially followers of Freud, have maintained that guilt is to be conceived, in the last resort, as "a need for punishment" induced in part by "conditioning" when certain acts have come to be associated with punishment and we feel a doom hanging over us if punishment is not forthcoming, relieved when it has been administered. A subtler feature of the same phenomenon is the introjection into our "super-ego" of the relief experienced by those who punish us for offending against them by doing them some harm. This happens mainly in early years, and especially in the relations of children to their parents. It becomes in due course one of the most influential factors in our lives, and affords the clue to many social and pathological problems which we might be inclined to oversimplify if we overlooked the fundamental character of the "need for punishment" and the complicated forms which it takes, for example in the inhibitions resulting from the Polycrates complex,[1] or in the operation of vicarious punishment in cases where we have projected our own guilt on to others.

Now it cannot be denied that recent psychology has taught us a great deal in these ways about ourselves. Not that we must straightway endorse its main conclusions, even when presented without any ethical implications. For there is much to invite serious criticism in both the procedures and the findings of psychology, especially of the psycho-analytic type. An exaggerated and somewhat distorted importance is ascribed, for example, to the vicissitudes of our lives in infancy as a clue to later and more mature states. No doubt the formative influences of early years need to be carefully studied, and they can throw very special light on our subsequent history. But we must not overlook the fact that there is development; and that mature experiences remain opaque to inspection on the basis of early factors alone. Admittedly, the more elusive elements in the constitution of adult life will often be found in the experiences we are apt to forget most completely, and it is tempting to the psychologist to seek explanation of what he fails to understand in adult experience in matters which are least accessible to our consciousness. But he does so at his peril, however remarkable some of the discoveries obtained in this way may be. For apart

[1] Cf. Flügel: *Man, Morals and Society*, p. 151.

from the fact that conclusions about early years must be drawn with the greatest caution, there is a genuine re-forming of the main traits in our nature in the continual flow of life from infancy to maturity. Even in cases of grave maladjustment or mental disorder, the main clue may be found in some event of adolescence or maturity that does not involve the days of our infancy in any special way. Nor is the preoccupation with abnormal psychology, so noticeable among the Freudians, a help to the achievement of a balanced understanding of mature states. In addition there is a proneness to force the evidence into preconceived patterns, as well as some foolishness in the practice of psycho-analysis, resulting sometimes in no inconsiderable harm. But when objections of this sort have been pressed to the uttermost limit, there remain some truly impressive achievements to be put to the credit side of empirical psychology today. We have been shown as never before how to look below the surface for a better understanding of ourselves, and the rudiments at least of a new technique are being evolved. And this leaves us with the question whether, cured of its more extravagant and fanciful tendencies, psycho-analysis can provide an explanation of guilt along the lines suggested. While we cavil at much in the present formulation of the explanation, can we accept it in principle?

If we can, then we must be very clear what we are about. For the upshot of our conclusion will be that moral distinctions, as we normally think of them, will have to be adjudged to be quite without substance, and banned for the mischievous confusions they engender. About this there should be no prevarication. There will be no room for ethics in that aspect of it which we ordinarily regard as having most depth and importance, namely the study of obligation and moral good and evil. We must turn from these matters with the firmness, if also with something of the gentle sadness, with which Plato abandoned the poets. Our fondness for a noble illusion must not dim our eyes to the course we must take, for the brightest illusions are often potent of the greatest harm. And here the psychologists themselves must stand most rebuked. For they have not always understood their own procedures, and have written as though they were treating of properly ethical problems when in fact they were seriously impugning the validity of ethical ideas. Professor Flügel is a good example. His usurpation of the place of the moralist, in his recent *Man, Morals, and Society,* wears a most innocent appearance. For he gives no clear indication of the ethically barren land to which he proposes to lead us. One might often gather that his purpose was to treat of psychological matters subsidiary to distinctively ethical principles, and such expressions as "wrongdoing", "moral factors", "budding moral sentiments", "moral and social influences", "moral development", "a very genuine moral conflict", to select a few examples at random, appear in a disconcertingly normal shape in a context where they have suffered complete transformation. We are also disarmingly told at the start that, as psychology "is a positive, not a normative discipline", the author has "no concern with values as such",[1] but this does not deter him from asserting later, in much completer consistency with his main theme, that "we must substitute a cognitive and psychological approach for an emotional and a moral one".[2] Of the easy assimilation of Scriptural sayings into a context most incompatible with their true purport Hobbes himself might well be proud. But the result of this is most seriously to darken counsel, and prejudice fair estimation of the author's claims. If, therefore, we find that the notion of guilt is reducible to psychological terms, there must be the fullest and most unambiguous repudiation of its claims to strictly ethical significance, and of all that is associated with it in ethics. To waver in that matter is fatal.

But are we reduced to such a pass? Is that involved in the concessions we have made to the psychologist? By no means. We may freely admit that there are such fears and desires as he describes, and that they take shape through the complicated processes which psycho-analysis reveals; formative influences may be deeply hidden from us in aspects of our personal history which we have mostly forgotten. But this is no bar to there being *in addition* guilt of a genuinely ethical kind incurred in certain ways. Most of what the psychologist avers may be allowed without touching the properly ethical question. And, indeed, the significance of much that we are told about the

[1] op. cit. p. 11.
[2] op. cit. p. 255.

repression of guilt and its projection on to others, and similar processes, may be vastly deepened and extended if such operations are performed, not merely on desires and fears but, also, on a true consciousness of guilt and its accompanying emotions. It must be a more serious matter, and presumably one where subtler and more determined resistance would be offered to therapeutic treatment, to suppress real guilt and drive remorse itself underground to erupt elsewhere, than to treat the pseudo-guilt of the psychologist in similar fashion. Furthermore, one wonders whether pseudo-guilt, with its roots in fear and retaliation, would have quite the tone that it has were it not for resemblance to genuine guilt. But without pressing this attack too deeply into the ranks of the analysts, and remaining mainly on the defensive, we may at least insist that there is nothing conclusive in their teaching about introjected emotions and subsequent projection, etc., as it bears on the problem of whether guilt, in the properly ethical sense, is real or illusory. This question could never be finally settled by recourse to the psychologist alone, for the essence of the claim to be determined is that there is something not to be directly encompassed by psychology. To leave the final decision here to the psychologist himself is to beg the question in completest fashion. Our doubts can only be finally resolved by reflection on what we do mean when we think of guilt. This reflection is conducted fairly only when the facts adduced by psycho-analysis are kept steadily before us. But, for my own part, I must admit that the presence of a plausible alternative account in psychological terms avails little to shake my conviction that guilt is a distinctively ethical mode of wrongdoing to which blame and remorse have an appropriateness of an irreducible ethical nature.

VI

But if we are to think of guilt in this fashion there must be no illusions about the conditions which render it possible. For, as we have stressed, no conduct is open to blame unless it is free, and it is a fair rejoinder to an accusation to declare that we "could not help" what we did. But what sort of freedom is this? It would be easy to reply if we could think of the moral law as in some way analogous to the "law of the land", and, therefore, as having its sanction in the fact that we may be proceeded against or punished in some way, or if blame could be wholly described in psychological or naturalistic terms. For the most we would need on that view would be the sort of avoidability which would give point to the reactions in question. Its nature has been very clearly presented by several writers, including Mr. Charles Stevenson in his recent *Language and Ethics*. As he notes, an action need only be avoidable, for the present purpose, in the sense that we could have acted differently had we wished. It is folly to be angry with a man for not giving us the moon, or to punish him. Our action could not mend the matter at all. But we may well be angry with someone who strikes us a blow, and take measures against him; for that may prevent a recurrence. It will also deter others by affecting their wishes.

But this position is not quite as straightforward as it seems, and there are some aspects of it which its advocates would do well to ponder more closely than they commonly do. In particular we need to distinguish two meanings of the notion of freedom to act differently had we wished. For this may mean either (a) freedom to intend something other than what we do intend, or (b) freedom to carry our intention into effect. For the purpose of (a) we must, of course, take 'intention' in the strict sense in which it is equivalent to actually 'setting ourselves' to achieve some end, and not merely the forming of designs which we may or may not implement—intending in the sense in which 'hell is paved with good intentions'. But, taking intention in the strict sense, we have to ask whether it is meaningful to speak of freedom to intend. And it seems to me that it is not meaningful for anyone to do so if he also believes, as most philosophers do, that our conduct is invariably determined by our desires and feelings (strictly, of course, by our character as a whole). For in that case we can point to nothing over and above the fact that there are intentions (prompted by desire, etc.) which could be described as freedom to intend. Nothing need be said beyond the fact that we do intend. If it be objected that we need to distinguish between actions such as those of the kleptomaniac or the lunatic and the deliberate misdeeds of the thief, then we must answer that the former do not act or intend in the strict sense at all. If the kleptomaniac or the pervert have some strain in their nature which just makes it impossible for them to behave rationally in certain regards (and I suspect that the excuse is to be invoked with justice in fewer cases than is popularly supposed today), then they are, to that extent, in precisely the same position as the madman or the child, and their behaviour is not action in the proper sense at all. If anyone cavils at this, and prefers simply to speak of free as distinct from impulsive or non-voluntary action, then I have no serious quarrel with him. But what I do wish to insist upon is that, within action in the proper sense of the behaviour of rational beings, there is nothing which the determinist can describe as freedom to act or intend over and above the fact that we do intend certain things in particular states of mind, others in others. This does not directly invalidate the view of freedom we are now discussing. Intentions can be modified by punishment and rewards, and all that we need to do for the purpose of the present view, so far as intention is concerned, is to point this out. The question of a postulate of freedom just does not arise at this point for the determinist.

But it is otherwise when we turn to the 'freedom to do' in the sense of freedom to execute a purpose. And it is this freedom, it seems to me, which matters on the view that describes responsibility in terms of liability to punishment in the way indicated. It matters in two ways. Firstly, it might be held that certain intentions have such little likelihood of being fulfilled in practice that there would be little purpose in seeking to modify them. But it is not easy to provide examples of this, since the wicked intentions which we could wholly disregard would almost certainly be the behaviour of a madman and not of a sane human being. But the 'freedom to do' will have much importance in another way—an indirect way. It will be important as a clue to the outside observer as to what an agent really intends. It is plain that no one can intend to do what he considers impossible. And therefore, in respect to matters which there is a general presumption that they are not amenable to control by our will, the agent will at once be exonerated on the ground that he shares this general assumption. Let us suppose that a burglar breaks into a hotel and quickly overpowers and gags the night porter. If, then, the porter be reproached for not giving

M

the alarm, he can obviously reply, 'But I could not'. We normally accept this, but if we had reason to believe (possibly by having some 'psychic' knowledge of what was actually passing in the man's mind) that the porter was not really convinced that he was effectively gagged, but was remaining inactive out of fear of further attacks upon himself, the fact that in actual fact he was effectively silenced would not affect such censure as we might pass on his conduct. For, still keeping to the present view of responsibility, the porter's reluctance to risk his safety in the common interest might be modified in the future by our disapproval, and others, similarly placed, might be induced to show a bolder front. As Hobbes, taking substantially the present view of punishment, observed, it is "not only the unjust facts, but the designs and intentions to do them (though by accident hindered), are Injustice; which consisteth in the pravity of the will, as well as in the irregularity of the act".[1] It is intentions, and not outward action, that we can modify directly by punishment; and, for this purpose, all that we *strictly* need is knowledge of the precise nature of the intention. The law does not always allow this. The penalty for murder is different, in this country, from the penalty for 'attempted murder'. But there are various matters which help to account for this. Legal enactments have not yet rid themselves wholly of elements that have survived from primitive times. The morality of strict retribution, an eye for an eye, a life for a life, persists in some ways in the social codes of enlightened peoples. And the legislator has to take some account of this. Punishment, in matters of such seriousness as murder, may also need to be administered in part as a relief to public emotions which might otherwise find more sinister and unruly expression. It might also be pointed out, in the case of murder, that there is an element of doubt as to whether the criminal intended to maim or to kill, and that in being given a lighter sentence when the victim has not actually died, the criminal may be getting the benefit of this doubt. There does not seem, however, to be a very good case for this, at any rate in the instances where the eventual fate of the criminal turns on the skill and effort of doctors in saving the life of the victim. To what extent con-

[1] *Leviathan*, ch. 30.

siderations such as these make it reasonable to discriminate between intention and the actual commission of a crime need not be considered closely here. For it is plain that, apart from very exceptional cases, it is intention that matters for the legislator as for the moralist; for it is by punishing (or rewarding) intentions that we can modify the conduct of our fellows in the future. If we knew the intentions directly we could disregard the effects, *but this rarely*, if ever, happens, and therefore we have in actual practice to take account of what people can, or can not, actually accomplish, as helping to determine what is the nature of their intentions.

But the fact that the postulate of freedom, as it arises on the present view of responsibility, is of this somewhat incidental nature, while it does not strictly overthrow the view that responsibility can be conceived in the way we are discussing now, shows how far removed it is from what we normally think. For there can be cases in which punishment would be quite appropriate in the absence of the freedom that matters on this view—the freedom to effect an intention. This would happen in cases where some evil intention had been frustrated by factors not anticipated by the agent—if, for example, his gun had misfired or he had been struck by paralysis. But we normally take the relation between the postulate of freedom and responsibility to be much more direct and invariable than that. And this brings me to the matter which needs most to be stressed in regard to the view that responsibility, in the properly moral sense, can be fully described in legal or quasi-legal terms as liability to be punished or rewarded, namely the extent to which it is a departure from what we normally feel bound to believe.

A recent contributor to *Mind*,[1] Mr. P. Nowell Smith, puts the essence of the view we are now discussing very clearly. He writes: "If a man steals because he has decided to do so, we can prevent his doing so again by causing him to decide otherwise. If he expects to be punished, then in addition to the motive that tends to make him steal there will be a powerful motive tending to make him refrain. Now the fear of punishment has no such influence on the kleptomaniac; on the other hand, psycho-analysis, by removing the subconscious cause of his

[1] January, 1948.

tendency to steal, may achieve the desired result. Nor is this merely an interesting but unimportant distinction between kleptomaniacs and thieves; it is the very basis for the distinction."[1] But can we accept this? Does it not overlook something quite fundamental? Do we not believe that, whether or not the theft is one where punishment is appropriate (whether as a deterrent or, if we accept the retributive view, for its own sake), the conduct of the thief acquires immediately an evil quality, not possible in the case of the kleptomaniac, in virtue of wilful violation of an obvious duty? Is not this the fundamental consideration where moral distinctions are concerned, and is not the denial of this a repudiation of all that we normally understand by moral good and evil, however the writer may conceive the ends in terms of which the suitability of modifying conduct by punishment and reward is determined? There are, moreover, cases in which punishment would be the best way of restraining children, lunatics, or animals. But clearly we do not consider the latter to be responsible in the properly moral sense. But if we do not, and if we are to hold that there is more to the distinction between the thief and the kleptomaniac than Nowell Smith suggests, then it is not so apparent that we have an easy solution of the problem of moral freedom in terms of the freedom to do something other than we do if we so desire.

VII

The course described, however, has attractions, not only for supporters of naturalistic ethics, but also for others who are much less entitled to pursue it. Sir David Ross, for example, is firmly opposed to any attempt to define ethical ideas wholly in terms of our own reactions or those of other people. And in conformity with this he admits that the 'freedom to do', in the sense of a power to carry our purposes into effect, has little significance for ethical theory. For we blame those who have failed to carry out a wicked intention quite as much as those who succeed. Yet Ross seems to think that a freedom to intend to do something if that is what we most desire will suffice in ethics. But if we are right in our previous argument, it is very hard to give any meaning to this freedom to intend if, like

[1] op. cit. p. 60.

Ross, we hold a determinist view of the way our intentions are formed.

Account has already been taken earlier of Ross's distinction between three senses of right and wrong action. He argues that obligation in the strict sense must refer to intention rather than outward performance, and so to rightness in the strictly subjective sense, because the most that we can really control is our own intention. We cannot guarantee the result. This is sound enough so far as it goes. But it is an odd view to adopt if we also believe that we are bound to intend in accordance with what we most desire at the time. Ross himself has insisted that we do not control our emotions and desires; we cannot 'summon up' motives at will, although we may cultivate them. But that makes it strange to argue that we control our intentions in any sense which would not also apply to the motives which are believed to determine them.

The main reason for Ross's failure to appreciate this is the divorce of moral worth, as he understands it, from any sense of doing one's duty, and the assumption that blame applies to the latter in a way which does not concern the former. But we have maintained that this is very mistaken. The wrongful action by which blame is incurred is also the guilty and morally evil action, and if Ross does not think that emotions and desires are free in the sense which entitles us to say that we have obligations in respect of them, he is also precluded from making moral worth turn, in any measure, upon these features of character, or upon character as a whole. But he is also debarred from ascribing it solely to intentions. For the most plausible view for anyone to hold, if he believes that intentions are invariably determined by character, is that account must be taken of motives as well as intentions in making distinctions of moral value. From this dilemma there seems no escape short of the bolder course of affirming that moral worth belongs to actions which are free in a way in which neither motives nor actions 'from' certain motives are free; in other words, we have to presuppose a power to act independently of our desires and character—a freedom of genuinely open choice. To relegate the problem of freedom to the sphere of a particular meaning of wrongful action, even a legitimate one, in which it does not directly affect moral worth, affords no alleviation of the difficulties of the determinist. It only confuses the issue.

This is in fact one of the main sources of confusion in recent ethics where philosophers have been seriously at cross-purposes with themselves, especially in the controversy about the distinction between "the right act and the morality of the agent", by making extensive appeals to the postulate of freedom without clear recognition of its meaning as a choice between genuinely open alternatives.

This I have discussed more fully in an earlier paper.[1] But there is one matter not mentioned there which I should like to note now. It seems plain that conscience is fallible, and that, therefore, we may do what is wrong with the highest intentions. We normally think that our moral worth does not suffer in such cases, and this is one of the main reasons for the distinction between the "right act" and the "morality of the agent". But it only holds if we think of the conditions of moral value as differing sharply from the conditions of some non-moral good like knowledge. Why, otherwise, should ignorance exonerate? But conduct which is the expression of motives and character has the same inevitability as appears in the course of our thought. And since this is the view of conduct usually adopted by those who have recently stressed the distinction between "the right act and the worth of the agent", their opponents, proceeding on the same assumption, seem on equally strong ground in urging that moral ignorance is itself a moral defect, or, more ambiguously that "we do not believe that everyone ought always to do what seems to him probably best".[2] There seems to be as much to be said on both sides as long as we seek to retain the idea of obligation within a deterministic view.

But to reject determinism is not to imply that any action may be expected from any man at any time; such a position would be as absurd as any position can be. All that is required is that there should be some occasions on which the flow of our conduct in accordance with character is arrested by a contrary claim of duty. This, in turn, also presents many difficulties, of which the

[1] Ch. VI.
[2] John Laird, "On Doing One's Best", *Philosophy*, January, 1931.

greatest, to my mind, is that of reconciling genuine freedom of choice with what we also feel bound to think about causality. But this raises metaphysical questions which cannot be brought within the scope of this paper. I will content myself with the insistence that we can only retain the ideas of obligation and guilt as properly ethical ideas, if we can also believe in actions which could have been other than they were although everything else in the universe had remained the same. I content myself with this because there is another aspect of our problem to which I should like to turn before I close.

VIII

As we have seen, it is when we think of moral evil as guilty or blameworthy conduct that we have also to regard it as wilful violation of law, as disobedience, and, thus, as involving absolute freedom of choice. But, very strangely, it is the persons who seem most assured that guilt is real, and who would most stoutly resist the attempt to reduce it to psychological terms, or to dismiss it as an illusion or some matter calling for mere therapeutic treatment — it is these, religious thinkers mostly and concerning themselves much more than the moralist with the problem of guilt, who also, as a rule, seem most emphatic in repudiating freedom. Even when they pay lip-service to freedom of choice, they belie it in their deepest and most distinctive convictions. This I shall call "the paradox of guilt". It is very deep and persistent, and it presents itself in fiction and general literature as well as in religious thought and reports of religious experience. Where there is the greatest assurance of guilt, there also we often find least concern for the individual and his freedom, and a consciousness of being in the grip of destiny. And, rightly understood, I believe that this has the greatest significance.

Some matters preliminary to the main explanation of this paradox are these.

There is a tendency for religious thinking to be more conservative than any other part of our thought. This is so for several reasons. But the most important reason, perhaps, is the fact that early religious experience carries a certain superficial authenticity which is absent from more mature religious life. This is because man is closer to Nature and more at her mercy. His life is less protected, and the world about him has not been so subdued to his thought as in more enlightened ages. He wages a more constant battle with reality, and there is thus a greater sense of awe and mystery, of the pressure upon him of alien, unrelenting powers and of a world not made amenable to his own will. The problem of subsequent ages, and above all in religion, is to recover this sense of an alien reality, of what is not ourselves or dissolvable into the categories of our own thought, at the level of new attainments and the conquests of the mind, to bend back our powers into contact with things, and thus be more truly and deeply at one with reality than was possible in the cruder immediacy of primitive life. It is this that we seek in the present crisis of western society, but it is not easy of attainment. And the starker, if unedified, realism of remote times confers on their religious life in particular a genuineness which may be equally present in more sophisticated experiences, but is rarely so obvious. And, therefore, the religious ideas which have taken shape in earlier and darker periods of society are apt to carry with them afterwards a peculiar claim to be the most essential and authentic versions of religious truth. But primitive society pays little heed to the individual; it identifies him, in his moral activities, with his community, with his family or his tribe; and the inexorable rule of custom operates with little regard for such niceties as the distinction between the purposes and the effects of actions. Accidental wrong initiates as surely as the most open maliciousness the savage alternation of retribution and retaliation. It is thus not surprising that so much in our religious thought, hailing from this source and also made more inflexible by its origin, should lag behind more enlightened views about freedom and accountability.

In reinforcement of this, it is worthy of note here that the assertion of guilt incurred in other ways than by avoidable human action, is bolder in times of confusion, like the present, when there is a recrudescence of the primitive and pagan attitudes which lurk beneath the surface of our civilisation. This seems to point to a deep kinship, and not to a mere accident of the times, as might be well brought out from a close study of the course of religion in Europe of late.

But, further, there is a very important way in which it is natural for religion to fill us with a sense of unworthiness, to make us "as dust", "as nothing"; the fleeting and unsubstantial aspect of existence is contrasted with the permanent realities of religion. But this, as has often been remarked by writers on "the sublime" and "the holy", is not moral unworthiness, but, rather, a general sense of unworthiness induced by the confrontation of the individual with the absolute perfection which he senses in his religion. God is all, man is nothing, his "days are as grass, as a flower of the field so he withereth". But this general sense of the dependent and limited character of finite being, and sometimes of utter hollowness, is easily confused with a sense of moral unworthiness, especially in those undiscriminating formative periods in which the more permanent idiom of religious utterance is coined. Moreover, the sense of the distance of the finite creature from the absolute perfection of religion does sharpen a man's ethical consciousness also and make him more vividly aware of the evil nature of the sinful acts that he has performed. And this makes it easier for the feeling of nothingness with which we are overwhelmed in religion—but that is only one aspect of the matter—to present itself also as an all-pervasive consciousness of sin.

With the greater progress of religion other factors enter in. This in particular. As religion becomes more completely moralised, and takes its place as the main source of refinement in ethics, the individual often finds himself confronted with exacting ideals which he is not able to embody to the full in the circumstances of his time and his society. The visionary must carry his neighbour with him, and this means some lowering of standards, much as the socialist today has to belie his principles about the ownership of property until he can persuade his society to accept them as a rule of life for the community as a whole. Some compromise is unavoidable, and the structure of society itself, moreover, impedes moral effort in some ways—even if it helps it in others. Hence, to borrow the title of a notable book, we have "moral man and immoral society". But this adjustment to a more common denominator rests very uneasily on a sensitive conscience, and the more sensitive are also often the most prone to measure themselves, not by what is attainable in the special situation in which they are placed, but by the ideals which glow more brightly ahead, by "impossible ideals" and "patterns laid up in heaven". This also leads to a sense of sinfulness and guilt not resting on individual choice, a matter that is no less distressing to the individual because it has such little foundation. It is significant that the idea of a tainted and fallen nature became most distinctive of Christian thought when the church was passing through a similar crisis. The early disciples of Christ obeyed his revolutionary injunctions—much more revolutionary than we usually acknowledge—with a great deal of consistency. But by the third century the church, for good or ill (but more for ill, I think), had immersed itself more completely in the world, and had to regulate its life by a "relative" rather than an "absolute" law. It was then, in the teaching of St. Augustine and his successors, that the notion of a tainted nature, of unavoidable sin, and the hypostatising of the universal nature of man in the doctrines of the Fall and of universal guilt acquired their ascendancy in Christian theology. They have had most prominence subsequently in times of similar crises, in the nationalist upheavals of the 15th century and in great modern wars when Christian ideals are most obviously strained.

This is not without its sinister aspect. For the idea of unavoidable sin is easily exploited. It presents an attractive way of turning the edge of inconvenient standards. The ideals remain in our midst but go unregarded. And Christians have in fact often, singly or collectively, sometimes with more, sometimes with less, deliberation sheltered from the rigorous exactions of their Christian allegiance behind the doctrine of the radical corruption of man and the domination of his life by impersonal evil forces. Something of the glow of the ideals is retained, or, at the level (rare, I believe) of crude expediency, their prestige, without too inconvenient an exaction of obedience. Such accommodation accounts for more in the history and thought of Christianity than is commonly realised. Along with this there go a delight in denunciation, in exploitation, without great emotional and spiritual cost, of the dramatic possibilities of a tragic situation, and, by a subtle inversion of pride, in vilification of self. Of these there is much evidence at present. The result is twofold. On the one hand, we have an alienation of religion, and often of ethics, from the business of living, a serene irresponsibility; ideals become, not rules of practice, but standards by which we are judged and condemned, salvation in turn being mediated in the cosmic drama of religion independently of our will. On the other hand, we have a sullen despair and pessimism, an enervating sense of the futility of all human endeavour. Both attitudes are very marked today, and they call for the bold and sustained intervention of the moral philosopher. But I mention these matters here mainly because of the lease of life which is lent in these ways also to the paradox of guilt.

But we have yet to offer the main explanation of this paradox and the reason for its significance. This presents itself when we consider the function of morality in the economy of life as a whole. Mention has already been made of the need to discover reality anew, and at a new power. And it is here that morality serves us so well, for its discipline is unlike any other, not excluding that of suffering and pain. For, although reality impinges upon us in pain with a peculiar insistency, this is because in a measure it has become ourselves. It is subjectively mediated, as also in perception where the pressure of reality upon us is rudest. Even in art where reality is made anew, where it is most individualised and expressive, and when the day-to-day rigidity of things is broken, when they stir and become articulate, even there our minds are only turned outwards to reality, as plants to the light, because of its fascination. Art could do nothing with us if it had no appeal. Neither would there be forgetfulness of self in personal attachments were not our affections involved. But morality knows nothing of this, there is no subtle transformation here, no fusion of reality with self. Morality provides no lodgment for the real in our own affections. And this is why the sense of reality is sustained by the moral life, and kept from distortion. Duty does not beguile, it commands; it can have no lure. What is not self is starkly before us, insistent, not to be denied; we are left with it as in an utter void. If we prevail there is a tremendous sense of exultation, a heightening of all our powers; the sheer, rugged, external shape of reality recedes; it is serene again. If we fail there is a diminution of our powers, a desolation, a kind of doom or death which is the penalty of sin. From this we may escape in part by sharp awareness of guilt and confession, and by the thrusting of the evil nature of surrender to self deep into our consciousness in condemnation and remorse;[1] and by grace, even more, the inward flow of reality begins again. What we are told of this in religion is often repellent, because the idiom and structure of religious thought hardened so much at the time when it was still mingled with a barbaric ethic. But the alienation of self from reality in moral failure is often so overwhelming, and most of all for religious minds, that we come to regard that failure, not as the cause, but as the effect, of some general impotence, of a doom in which we are caught up, of evil forces warring in all our members. Hence it is that the deepest consciousness of moral evil, and the sharpest recognition of it as guilt, often carries with it the belief so contradictory of all morality, that our guilt is itself the working out of some radical weakness in our own nature.

This, and much else in the relations of morality and religion, and of both to all forms of experience, we shall understand much better when religious thought is able to mount to the level of our other attainments. We shall then have the clue to the crisis of which so much is heard today, but which is not quite so peculiar to our time as is thought.

---

[1] It is by confusion with this that the notion of retributive punishment acquires some plausibility.

Chapter VIII

SOME AMBIGUITIES OF MYSTICAL THOUGHT[1]

I

I SHOULD like to begin this paper by asking the general question 'How do we come to have knowledge of God? One answer that suggests itself, and will perhaps occur before any other to philosophers, is that we know God by reason or taking thought. This is not the answer which the layman might be most inclined to give. He would probably refer us, in the first instance, to the Scriptures and revelation; and we shall have to say a word about that in a moment. But it will be well, in the first place, to say what needs to be said for our purpose about the sort of considerations which have been uppermost in the past in philosophical accounts of religion.

How far, then, will argument take us? A long way, I think. But this does not mean that we have to accept any of the celebrated arguments for the existence of God as usually stated. Not that the arguments are quite unsuccessful; on the contrary I think that they are very important, but they are important, not for something which a particular argument establishes to the exclusion of others, but for something more fundamental which they all express. And I would like to suggest here to those who concern themselves much today with the traditional arguments, and to Catholic writers in particular, that they will employ themselves best, not in considering new variations and combinations of these arguments, but in pressing behind the particular form of this or that argument to the original principle which they embody.[2]

What is this principle? The answer is not easy, not because

[1] Based on an address delivered to the Northern Universities Philosophical Conference and published in part in the *Hibbert Journal*, July, 1950.

[2] It seems to me that this is what Dr. E. L. Mascall does, in effect, in his impressive discussion of the existence of God in the first part of *Existence and Analogy*. Cf. also articles by Dom Illtyd Trethowan in the *Downside Review*, Vols. LXIII—LXIV.

the principle itself is in doubt, but because it is peculiarly difficult to formulate. Usually, I think, it would be stated by saying that reason makes some demand that reality should be a whole. And I do not know that we can better this, but it is none the less (as I think must be the case, for a reason to be specified, with any formulation) not very satisfactory. 'Demand', in the first place, is a somewhat ambiguous term. It has an ethical flavour, but the principle in question, if it can be classified at all, is not ethical but logical. Nor does it in any way turn on individual enactment. For that would expose us at once to the accusation of wishful thinking. It represents something we are bound to think about reality. But much the most peculiar characteristic of it, and that which makes it so hard, if not impossible, to find a quite adequate formulation, is that although we must say that reason makes this demand, and that it is implicit in all thought, it is none the less by its very nature a demand which cannot be rationally met. It would not, I think, be wrong to say that if we could think that it could be met it would be nullified. This may sound very mysterious, but mystery and paradox, much though we should normally shun them, are not, I think, to be avoided here. This is the one point where philosophy must take its life in its hands, and reluctance to do so, and to perceive that this is just where it is necessary, lies behind much in our present attitudes towards speculative thought and the peculiarly sharpened divergence of views in philosophy. But perhaps it will be here also that extremes will begin to meet again. But that is another rather long story, not to be unfolded here. To return, we have, then, the view that reason transcends itself by positing something which would defeat itself if it could be rationalised. This is why the celebrated 'arguments', in their more explicit tangible form, are so easily criticised. For if we say, for example, that everything must have a cause, and that, therefore, there must be some original cause of all things, we invite the comment, that, on our premise, the original cause must itself have a cause, and so *ad infinitum*. 'Ground' is, for this reason, a slightly less misleading term, but if we use 'ground' in any way in which it would normally be used, the same objection arises. And there is no meeting the objection except by insisting that we are referring to something quite without parallel, but which is none the less quite inescapable for us. And if any are repelled by the air of mystery here, or, as many will no doubt do more resolutely than ever at present, deny that there is any compulsion upon us to think in this way about reality, or to posit any unity which is not identical in ultimate principle with the various ways we coordinate experience, we can at any rate give some indication of the ways the compulsion arises; and that, rather than general argument about it and about, is clearly the more satisfactory procedure.

Let me do so, but very summarily, for these are not the matters that should most engage our attention tonight. It will suffice to mention some bewildering features of space and time, and to submit, that, although they are by no means new, but in some ways as old as Zeno, and very familiar since Kant, nothing has been said to abate the bewilderment they cause, when properly perceived, and that there can never be any expectation of abatement. Let us think first of space. On the one hand, it seems impossible to think that there could be any end of space. For to put it quite simply, as it should be put, however far we go in space it will still be possible to go on again. If some astronomer were to tell us on the basis of some highly improbable calculation from the movements of heavenly bodies known to us now just where the furthest orb could be found, there would clearly be no *a priori* reason, or anything arising from the nature of space itself, which would preclude there being constellations as far removed from that again as it is from us, and yet others as far again, and so without end. We simply cannot believe that there can be a point beyond which we cannot go. Nor is there any new theory about the nature of space which could affect this. Such theories are in any case, I think, suspect. For space—but I shall wish to qualify this in one way later—is just something given or ultimate in our experience, a 'form' if you like, of which no analysis into anything other than itself is possible. We all know it (but see below) but can say nothing to explain its ultimate nature. Most so-called theories of space confuse certain ways of taking measurements in space with the nature of space itself, and whether or not this applies to all such theories, doctrines which tell us of the curvature of space, etc., whatever their importance in their proper context, have hardly any bearing on the nature of real space, and need not be considered in any way before we can all see what anyone could see without the slightest scientific knowledge, namely that there is no point beyond which we must think it impossible to travel in space. Theories which deny this are in much the same case as the theories which hypostatise atoms and electrons, etc., as if they were some mysterious entities of which account could not be given, in principle, in terms of observable facts. But what then? What of it if space has no end? Just this, that this is also something which we just cannot believe. The nature of this compulsion I know not how to expound, and I am sure that many who will readily accept my first point, will say they find nothing bewildering in the notion of endless space. To me, I must insist, it seems to be something the mind just cannot accept, and not because imagination wearies, as has been suggested, and sets an end to space, but because it affects us, in my case almost with the force of some physical impact, as sheer distortion of what must be the case to try to think this kind of infinity real. And I would like to submit to you that this is not due to some logical confusion or bedevilment of our minds, much less is it something capable of psychological cure, but just an ultimate impasse from which, if we examine carefully what we feel bound to think, there is just no escape.

The parallel in the case of time is even stronger. It is plain that we cannot think of a first moment of time, for whenever it be posited there must be a time before that, and before that again. Nor, again, will any appeal to 'theories of time' modify this. But, on the other hand, simply to acquiesce in this kind of infinity is also impossible. It would be like saying, 'we have always been travelling, and yet we have reached a particular place'. To say that there has always been time, and that yet we are now at the present, and there clearly is a present however hard to define, is just impossible. With no beginning of time we simply would never reach now. Further argument will not help here. But I put it to you again that we have here a real predicament of the human mind from which it cannot ever extricate itself.

But neither is the mind content to remain in this predicament.

For we just cannot accept sheer contradiction, and we are directed in this way to the notion of an ultimate nature of reality which has a wholeness that takes us altogether beyond what we must now call the 'phenomenal' world of our thought. I will not amplify this; nor do I claim that I can do anything like justice to this view in such a short compass. It will suffice to show what I think can be attained in this way. But a word of warning must be added. For once we accept the notion of ultimate contradiction—ultimate, that is, for us—we open the door for all manner of abuses. These are rank in recent religious thought where the fact that some paradox is inescapable in religion has afforded a cover for facile and very irresponsible indulgence in paradox, and the exploitation of problems to which there is a simple solution. The word 'paradox' is perhaps partly responsible for this. For it is an ambiguous word, not representing plain contradiction, and yet not clearly dissociated from it. Properly a paradox is some sharp and suggestive opposition of apparent differences which will point to a more comprehensive view of the facts, or it is verbal confusion, as in the well-known philosophical paradox that I may have a duty to do what is not my duty, the word 'duty' being used in two very different senses here, and the paradox, as Moore has shown, being perfectly innocuous. This, incidentally, is one of the paradoxes which theologians have been most ready to exploit. But although we need so much to guard against this and similar distortions of the ultimate predicament of the human mind we must not boggle at finding ourselves, inescapably as finite creatures, in this predicament, or refuse to accept it as fair intimation of a transcendent reality.

So far, then, argument takes us—if argument it is—although we should need to say a great deal more to set forth this position properly and to meet various criticisms. The gain is, I think, considerable; and we should not underestimate it or be disconcerted on account of its apparent thinness. For if we sought to go further in this particular way we should defeat ourselves by surrendering what is most essential, namely the idea of transcendence. The gain is none the less a substantial one, and something of the kind I have described seems to me to be an element in all religious experience, even at the primitive level, although encrusted over in that case with much other matter of which the anthropologist could tell us best. It is, of course, rarely formulated in abstract terms, and it would take us too long here to consider carefully how this more formal element in the life of religion is related to its other features. For what we need most to stress for the present purpose is that, however important in itself, the knowledge of God derived from the transcendence of reason by itself, or as an implication of all experience, will not meet the full demands of religion.

This is not because the God of religion is other than the God of the arguments, albeit some writers tend to suggest that they wish to take up that rather odd position. But we need to know God in a further, more specific, way for the purpose of religion. And it is very unfortunate, to my mind, that those who have pointed the way most effectively to our more formal knowledge of the transcendent have been very imperfectly aware of the limitations of this approach. For the God of religion is one who has dealings with individuals and makes his presence peculiarly significant for them. He is the 'Living', Creator God, a God who meets men and stands expressly athwart their particular destiny. There is thus an 'encounter' of man with God which becomes a way of life and the supreme articulation of all that has worth for us. This is one reason why Emil Brunner, with whose view here, but in little else, I am in full sympathy, complains that "the theory of transcendental philosophy is too abstract and rational to do justice to real religion".[1] "No proof of the existence of God", he declares, "leads to the *Lord* God; by this I do not mean that such 'proofs' have no value, but that they do not lead to the Knowledge of the Living God".[2] "The God of philosophy is an abstraction; he is not 'the Living God'. The Living God is not known through thought, nor through conclusions drawn from the structure of the universe, nor through profound meditation on the nature of spirit; He is known through revelation alone".[3] This tends to accentuate too sharply the distinction between the 'God of Philosophy' and the 'Living God'. But with the main substance of the claim that

[1] *Revelation and Reason*, p. 261.
[2] op. cit. p 45.
[3] op. cit. p. 44.

religion requires more than a formal knowledge of some ultimate ground of all being, even when its transcendent nature is fairly grasped, I am in entire agreement.

The oftquoted cry of Pascal—'the God of Abraham, Isaac and Jacob, not the God of the philosophers and wise men'—thus strikes an important keynote for modern religious thought. And it is, in my view, an exceptionally important achievement of recent theology to have grasped so clearly at one and the same time the notion of the transcendence of God and of his character, in religious life, as a 'living' God, and above all to have sensed an essential affinity between these two. The importance of this view of religion may be well discerned by comparing the experience and testimony of peoples like the Hebrews whose genius is primarily religious, with those of peoples like the Greeks whose culture is not so expressly religious, and who were drawn to philosophy and science. For the notion of God, for the latter, culminates in the idea of an ultimate form or principle of being, or of an 'unmoved mover' rapt in contemplation of his own perfection, whereas the God of the Hebrews is the God who shapes the destiny of his chosen people, who makes his 'name' known to them and sends his word forth by his prophets and 'in these last days to us by his Son'. But how is this intrusion of a transcendent God into particular existences possible; how can God, to be God, make himself explicitly known to man?

The problem would clearly be very much simplified if we could moderate our notion of the transcendence of God. This is what humanism, which for this purpose must include most forms of idealism, has done. It represents God as the fulfilment or completion of what we already find in our own experience. The normal processes of understanding, if carried to completion, would give us God; in essence divine and human are the same. We therefore need only to look for the main patterns in our own experience to be assured of our clues to the nature of God and his will for us. Indeed, on some views, and those perhaps the most consistent, there is more than an identity of principle, the finite being a mere limitation of the Absolute—a view which presents idealism with its notorious problem of 'saving the appearances'. Some kind of pantheism is very hard to avoid on this view, as critics such as Brunner, to mention him again, have stressed. And it is, moreover, because they associate the more philosophical approach to religion too completely with the kind of idealism in question here, among other things, that Brunner, and others of his school, are so anxious to belittle the place of reason in religion and so suspicious of it. This is the essence of Brunner's complaint that the God of philosophy is a God who 'can be thought', a God who 'is already present in the depths of reason', and whom we can discover for ourselves by seeking. That he is so seems to me true as already indicated, and there is not the least harm in thinking this provided we understand it fairly as also a transcendence of thought. But we go grievously astray if we also think that the nature of God can be conceived in terms of our thought. To be God he must be strictly transcendent, but in that case how can he be known except generally and negatively as implicit equally in all things, an absolute mystery? This is the problem of revelation, the main as it is the hardest problem of religious thought, and one which religious thinkers are extremely reluctant to tackle fairly. In illustration of this let us now look at one of the main answers.

II

The answer on which I wish to comment here is not easy to designate, mainly because the terms we associate with it cover a deep ambiguity, and because, on account of this ambiguity, it is not very certain when this answer is intended. This is the view that there is in a literal sense an immediate access to God or some direct acquaintance with him. Religious thinkers, and others reporting their religious experience, very often tell us, in describing their sense of the nearness of God and the closeness of their fellowship with Him, of an immediate or intuitive knowledge of God. But it is never very certain when these terms are to be taken strictly. For it would be possible for an awareness of God to be very intense, to banish all else from our thought, to overwhelm us with the sense of His presence and to rid us of all thought of ourselves so that we have little sense of our separate identity, and yet, as seems to me inevitable, not be in the strict sense immediate or direct. It would not be out of place to use these terms, for no terms other than these or their equivalents will suit the peculiar intensity of the experience and the sense of certainty which it involves. But we have none the less to remember their equivocal nature.

The ambiguity is paralleled in the case of our knowledge of other finite minds. None of us will deny that there are occasions on which we feel particularly close to other persons, in experiences of love (or hate), for example, in the sharing of some common enthusiasm or in some moment of crisis. But those who hold, as most philosophers do, that our knowledge of other minds is indirect, find no particular obstacle here. They can well admit these peculiarly intimate relationships, and approve the ways in which they are normally described, without abandoning the view that our knowledge of others is bound to be indirect. The issue is unaffected by the particular quality of some experiences. For if, on reflecting on our ordinary relations with other persons, we find that our philosophical account of them must be in terms of some kind of inference from our own experience, there is nothing to preclude our extending the same explanation to other cases of especially intimate relationships. These will be intensifications of the normal process, and they will turn, not on anything in the general nature of our knowledge of other minds, but on the particular content of that knowledge and our own reaction to it. The ordinary person, and philosophers when not engaged in philosophy, never trouble about the properly philosophical question of our knowledge of other minds. We take the naïve, unsophisticated view, as we do of sensible things. We go about in the full confidence that we have contact with others in our normal dealings with them, and it is only to be expected that some of these contacts should count much more for us than others and keep other persons more vividly in our thought. Nothing more need be involved in intimate relationships with others, and citation of these relationships, therefore, even if not, as I take it to be, wholly irrelevant to the philosophical question, is quite inconclusive.

This will hardly need to be laboured in this gathering. But the point is none the less worth stressing. For the parallel ambiguity, in the case of our knowledge of God, is a genuinely vicious one. It is very hard to know in many cases just what we are to understand by the claim to an immediate or intuitive knowledge of God. Not that this can be avoided in the normal reports of intensely religious people. If questioned, the probability is that they would be suspicious of any hint of mediation in their experience, and reaffirm its stark directness—'God has spoken to me', 'it was the voice of God I heard'. The whole experience will seem to be jeopardised if it is qualified. But this is probably because such persons cannot properly understand the question or reflect philosophically upon their experiences; they would be disconcerted also to be told that our knowledge of other finite persons is indirect. But one is entitled to greater precision in the case of those who write about religious experiences, and here it is for the most part lacking—a lack which is peculiarly felt in studies of mysticism.

There have, of late, been several very enlightening accounts of mysticism, notably those by William James, von Hügel, Inge and Underhill, but these writers have been content for the most part with a psychological account of the states they describe and the general authenticity of the claim to a union with God. The question which is of most interest to philosophers, the epistemological one, is rarely raised, and never to my knowledge quite unambiguously. Evelyn Underhill, for example, repeatedly speaks of a "conscious union with a living Absolute",[1] of "the science of self-evident reality",[2] of "conscious relation with the Absolute",[3] or, quoting Tauler, of man's spirit "being so sunk in God in divine union, that he loses all sense of distinction".[4] In mystical experience, she tells us, a man "passes over into that boundless life where Subject and Object, desirous and desired, are *one* . . . . In the mystic this union is conscious, personal, and complete. 'He enjoys', says St. John of the Cross, 'a certain contact of the soul with Divinity; and it is God himself who is then felt and tasted'. More or less according to his measure he has touched—or better, been touched by—the substantial Being of Deity, not merely its manifestations in life".[5] But these and similar statements, while adequate for certain purposes, and those perhaps the purposes

---
[1] *Mysticism*, p. 73.
[2] op. cit. p. 73.
[3] op. cit. p. 81.
[4] op. cit. p. 84.
[5] op. cit. p. 73.

the writer has mainly in mind, leave many questions unanswered. 'Conscious relation with the absolute' would cover a host of things, ranging from the formal knowledge of God, supplied, in the way discussed earlier, by reason, to a literal union with God. Nor is the further information that, in mysticism, 'Subject and Object are one' as helpful as it seems. For just in what sense is distinctness surrendered? Is it in any sense radically different from that in which the lover completely 'forgets himself' in adoration of his beloved, the artist in his work, etc.? Some mystics distinguish between distinctness and separateness, and this is certainly helpful, but still not unambiguous. For even if, as I take to be the case, it is not seriously intended to question the ultimacy of the distinctness of finite persons, but only to stress how oblivious of this the mystic becomes, this still leaves unsettled our main question at the moment, namely whether the 'contact' with the absolute is strictly immediate. The importance ascribed to symbols in mystical experience suggests very strongly that it is not. Underhill reminds us that "the mystic, as a rule, cannot wholly do without symbol".[1] But, setting aside the qualification 'as a rule', the position is still not clear. For the reason adduced for this necessity for symbols is that "his experience must be expressed if it is to be communicated, and its actuality is inexpressible except in some sidelong way, some hint or parallel which will stimulate the dormant intuitions of the reader, and convey as all poetic language does, something beyond its surface sense. Hence the large part which is played in all mystical writings by symbolism and imagery".[2] It is stated also that "the greatest mystics . . . . distinguish clearly between the ineffable Reality which they perceive and the image under which they describe it . . . . The object of their contemplation 'hath no image' ".[3] One sympathises with Underhill's fear, which inspires so much of her writings, that the authenticity of mystical experience should be queried by reduction of it to the symbols in which it is expressed. But we should expect a writer who is so interested in art,[4] and so fond of stressing the resemblance

[1] op. cit. p. 79.
[2] op. cit. p. 79.
[3] op. cit. p. 79.
[4] She was also herself a poet of no mean order.

between art and religion, to have appreciated also the peculiarly intimate relation between artistic experience and the communication of it, and thus to have seen how indispensable the symbol is for the individual who has the religious experience as for those to whom it is to be communicated. Whether one could at the same time distinguish between the truth which we know symbolically and the symbolic apprehension of it is a hard question. I imagine that Underhill would answer it with confidence in the affirmative, and that this predisposes her to believe that we can perceive the 'Ineffable Reality' 'without image'. But this would still leave the position a little uncertain. For the intention may be merely to suggest that we can dispense with images of certain kinds, those which constitute the more common coin of mystical exchange. And, although it is sometimes hard to avoid the conclusion that the union of the mystic with his God is held to be strictly intuitive or direct, one is reluctant to ascribe to a thinker so acquainted with religious thought and testimony as Underhill an explicit assertion of a view which, as I shall stress shortly, is contrary to the almost universal testimony of religious experience. My impression is that she never really faced the issue.

The position is little improved when we turn to Inge's discussion of these matters. He opens the chapter on 'The Meaning of Mysticism' in his latest book[1] with a number of definitions, of which I should like to quote the following:[2]

"Mysticism is the immediate feeling of the unity of the self with God; it is nothing, therefore, but the fundamental feeling of religion, the religious life at its very heart and centre. But what makes the mystical a special tendency inside religion is the endeavour to fix the immediateness of the life in God as such, as abstracted from all intervening helps and channels whatever, and find a permanent abode in the abstract inwardness of a life of pious feeling." (Pfleiderer).

"True mysticism is the consciousness that everything that we experience is an element and only an element in fact; i.e. that in being what it is, it is symbolic of something more." (R. L. Nettleship).

---

[1] *Mysticism in Religion.*
[2] op. cit. p. 25.

Of these, and other vaguer definitions such as 'some communion between God and the individual', Inge declares, "these definitions make it quite clear what mysticism means. They agree together".[1] But that seems to me to be just what they do not do. For it seems to me to be quite a different thing to hold (especially in the sense which would be intended by an idealist like Nettleship) that everything is 'an element' of something more and symbolises it, and to refer to the 'immediateness of the life in God' as such, as abstracted from all intervening helps, etc. Just what sort of immediacy has Inge in mind?

The position is complicated for Inge by his Platonism. And this brings us to a point of much importance. For the influence of Platonism on mysticism, both in theory and practice, is very great—but not to the advantage of mysticism. This is not to deprecate the influence of Platonism generally but merely to hold that it has relevance more to the rational than to the mystical aspect of religion. Plato (or at least Plato the philosopher) had little appreciation of the nature of art, and therefore his followers are not likely to have the right view of the elements in religion which have most affinity with art. The result has been that, in addition to prescribing for mysticism practices alien to its real spirit, the mystic intuition has been sought in terms of a Platonic 'glimpse' which is the culmination of a rational process, thereby, by attempting to travel further along this route than it is possible to go, seeking a strictly immediate knowledge of God rather than the radically different intuition of a symbolic awareness which cannot be rationalised such as we have in art, and such as seems to me to characterise mysticism when its course is not complicated by alien theories. The symbolic element in genuine mysticism seems to me essential, as I shall stress again. But for the moment it will suffice to suggest that the ambiguity of which I am complaining is due, in no little measure, to a very unfortunate assimilation of Platonism to mysticism.

As a further consequence of this, in the case of Inge, the issue is also obscured by speaking as if the immediacy of mysticism meant no more than the certainty of our hold on the principles of Truth, Beauty and Goodness and the intimation they are

[1] op. cit. p. 26.

assumed (in a very general way) to afford of the presence of God. This sometimes leads to the identification of mysticism with spiritual experience in the very broad sense of any awareness of value, and its immediacy becomes no more than the independence of our appreciation of value of particular rites or dogmas, and their openness to all. Nor is the position much improved by reviving the distinction between God and the Godhead, for, besides the fact that this is a very hard distinction, little indication is given of any modification it involves in the account of the principles already noted. Finally, it is worth noting, as an example of the way Inge fails to deal squarely with his problem, that he reminds us of the condemnation of ontologism (which view of the intuition of supreme reality also, incidentally, lacks clarity) by the Catholic Church without relating this to the fact that this Church has never condemned mysticism as such, albeit not so well disposed to it perhaps as Inge would wish. But we cannot go further with this historical excursus now, close though its bearing is on our main theme. It must suffice to suggest that the time has now come when, with all the vast and suggestive material that has been accumulated about mysticism at our disposal, we should approach this subject with more severely philosophical purposes, in other words ask the more appropriate philosophical questions.

III

An ingenious attempt is however occasionally made to by-pass some of the philosophical questions we wish to raise about mysticism, and especially the more difficult epistemological questions. These are the questions, what precisely do we mean by immediacy in this connection, and how can we claim a direct or intuitive knowledge of God without presupposing that the secret of His transcendent nature is laid open to us. The attempt to evade these questions takes the form of supposing that we can have some union with other beings without any meaningful content of knowledge about them. This seems to be the daring course taken by exponents of the *I-Thou* relationship in recent religious thought. Like most who have read Martin Buber's classic *I and Thou* I have a great admiration for it. That he says in a beautiful way a great deal that is true about the life of religion and most relevant to the present state of our culture seems to me plain. But it is also impossible to avoid the impression that the *I-Thou* relation is held to be a bare relation of terms without content, a 'pure relation' and no more, whatever that means. This relation is not confined to persons, it extends to other creatures and things, and the context of each *Thou* is the *Eternal Thou*, 'the Centre where the extended lines of relations meet'. But this does not mean that the world of things, and the relation *I-it* by which it is experienced, is unreal. "As we reach the meeting with the simple *Thou* on our lips, so with *Thou* on our lips we leave it and return to the world";[1] "spirit can penetrate and transform the world of *It*".[2] "All revelation is summons and sending".[3] "For the spirit is never independently effective in life in itself alone, but in relation to the world; possessing power that permeates the world of *It*, transforming it",[4] the problem being to ensure by 'reversal' to the life-giving *Thou* relationship that we are not enslaved by the "world of *It*" and leave it "no longer penetrated and fructified by the inflowing world of *Thou* as by living streams".[5] We must arise out of the 'world of *It*' to 'genuine meeting', but, with this understood, "He who truly goes out to meet the world goes out also to God".[6] This is finely thought in many ways, and is highly relevant both to the subtle forms which idolatry may take and to questions of practice and social relations where personal contact must redeem and fructify the increasingly impersonal relations of men in present society. But the latter distinction is not quite so novel as some portentously suggest today, and it is a relative one. Our dealings with others are rarely, if ever, quite impersonal, and, on the other hand, personal relationships, far from being without content, are peculiarly rich in it. That seems to be what Buber denies, so afraid is he of persons being treated as things. He declares:

"I do not experience the man to whom I say *Thou*. But I take my stand in relation to him, in the sanctity of the primary

[1] *I and Thou*, p. 111.
[2] op. cit. p. 100.
[3] op. cit. p. 115.
[4] op. cit. p. 50.
[5] op. cit. p. 53.
[6] op. cit. p. 95.

word. Only when I step out of it do I experience him once more. In the act of experience *Thou* is far away."[1]

And again:

"The relation to the *Thou* is direct. No system of ideas, no fore-knowledge, and no fancy intervenes between *I* and *Thou*."[2]

And yet again, even more explicitly:

"Further, no 'going beyond sense experience' is necessary; for every experience, even the most spiritual, could yield us only an *It*. Nor is any recourse necessary to a world of ideas and values; for they cannot become presentness for us. None of these things is necessary. Can it be said what really is necessary? Not in the sense of a precept. For everything that has ever been devised and contrived in the time of the human spirit as precept, alleged preparation, practice, or meditation, has nothing to do with the primal, simple fact of the meeting. Whatever the advantages in knowledge of the wielding of power for which we have to thank this or that practice, none of this affects the meeting of which we are speaking; it all has its place in the world of *It* and does not lead one step, does not take *the* step out of it. Going out to the relation cannot be taught in the sense of precepts being given. It can only be indicated by the drawing of a circle which excludes everything that is not this going out. Then the one thing that matters is visible, full acceptance of the present."[3]

However unwarranted it may, then, be in some respects, to accuse Buber of other-worldliness, the fact remains that the crucial living 'relation' which is so central to his thought is placed altogether outside experience.

This is even more marked in the case of one of Buber's closest followers and one who has paused in more philosophical reflection than Buber on much that the latter says as a poet and seer, namely Karl Heim. Heim is well aware of the extent of the confinement of each to the mode of his own experience. He declares, in words which, if not very novel, are significant in the context of a discussion of the *I-Thou* relation:

"If I am in the one (world), if I am the person I am then the

[1] op. cit. p. 9.
[2] op. cit. p. 11.
[3] op. cit. p. 77.

SOME AMBIGUITIES OF MYSTICAL THOUGHT 195

world of the other is altogether shut out from me, and *vice versa*. Even the body to which I address myself as his body belongs, to the extent of all it contains, to *my* world. It is not a part of the other's world which projects directly into my world, but a part of my world, from which I am able, with the aid of familiar analogies, to draw conclusions about the existence and the inner constitution of the world of the other. It is not as if my world had an opening, a window or a door, through which the other's world might enter, so as to come into direct contact with my world. My world is, on the contrary, an unbroken, self-contained continuum. It embraces the whole earth, the whole Solar System, the Milky Way, and all the bright starry heavens. In this space I may wander at will, crossing the oceans, flying through the stratosphere, overleaping millions of light-years; but I remain evermore within my world, the world as I see it. I cannot take the smallest step outside it. I can never come face to face with the world of another. For me that other's world is at once unapproachably far off and incredibly near at hand. Both worlds are infinite. There is no wall or partition at which my world ceases to be and the world of the other person begins".[1]

But instead of regarding this as special indication of the fact that all communication must be indirect, and can only be significant as deciphered by each from terms that are private to himself, Heim resorts to the desperate expedient of lifting all knowledge of persons to a plane apart from all other knowledge of particulars. We have *a priori* knowledge of others in the same way as we have *a priori* knowledge of space and time, the particular point of contact being found in experience, on analogy with particular spatial relations. But this, it seems very plain, will not do, notwithstanding the ingeniousness with which Heim develops his doctrine of 'dimensions', and the incidental light he throws on many matters in philosophy and religious thought. For to the peculiarly intimate relations of persons abstractions like 'space' and 'time' hardly afford suitable analogies. Persons are known as individuals, and it seems to me altogether impossible to conceive of the relations and 'meetings' of persons in any way that is divorced from the deepening of our particular knowledge about one another; and we must there-

[1] *God Transcendent*, p. 86.

fore conclude that the subject-object relation in finite experience cannot be transcended in 'pure relation'.

One must of course admit that there is one mode of our knowledge of God which is *a priori*, the formal knowledge of God discussed at the start. But Heim and Buber are not thinking of this but, on the contrary, of the immediacy of the God of revelation felt as a presence by the individual. And however insistently and finely it may be added that this must lead to a 'hallowing' of the world, we cannot but suspect that the refinement of our relation with God to the point of a divorce from all finite significance and evaluation[1] can only lead in practice to diminishing regard for the latter.

At the same time we must give to Heim and Buber the credit of a very jealous regard for the transcendent character of God. They also see clearly that to claim an unmediated *knowledge about* God is to question His transcendence. This, most of all, is why they deny a specific content to revelation, and substitute for it bare relation and meeting. "We have 'known' it", writes Buber, "but we acquire no knowledge from it which might lessen or moderate its mysteriousness. We have come near to God, but not nearer to unveiling being or solving its riddle."[2] We must respect this, but we must also protest that revelation without content is neither significant nor true to religious experience. At the same time I think it is much less at variance with religious experience than a doctrine which, by ascribing a content to a strictly intuitive knowledge of God, presupposes such access to Him as would plumb the mystery of His nature.

IV

In support of our last contention let me now add some further observations on the idea of 'immediacy' as it bears on our problem. Indication has already been given of the vagueness of this term. Let me now give one further illustration of this from our use of such terms as 'immediate' and 'direct' in ordinary parlance. Suppose I were to tell a student, "I have heard indirectly that your grant will be renewed", I would probably

[1] "Man receives, and he receives not a specific content, but a Presence, a Presence as power". *I and Thou*, p. 110.
[2] *I and Thou*, p. 111.

mean that I had heard about the renewal of his grant from someone who had access to the official information but was not in a position to announce it officially. But now suppose I were to say, "I have at last heard directly that your grant will be renewed", I would mean that the information had come from an official source. We are all familiar with distinctions of this kind. But what after all is this 'direct' information that I receive? It has probably been dictated in the first instance to a secretary who sent it on to me via the mail van and a number of post-office employees. In some ways it is very indirect. The position of the word 'immediate' is very similar. To 'come immediately' may mean coming this very instant or in a few hours or even in a few days. In other words the difference between 'direct and indirect', immediate and mediate, is usually a relative distinction within processes which are all in some more fundamental sense indirect or mediate. And it is well to bear this in mind when we consider the uses of these terms in philosophy and religious thought. To give sharpness to certain comparisons we may have to be very emphatic in our insistence that some communication is direct in spite of the fact that the difference is one of degree and not absolute. This, I think, accounts for much of the ambiguity which we have already noticed. Those who claim that they have some immediate knowledge of God, or of some finite minds, are probably claiming something very true and important, and they hold very firmly to their view for this reason. But the true significance of what is described as immediate knowledge may be found, on careful analysis, to consist in certain sharp contrasts between various ways of knowing, all of which may have *some* element of mediacy in them.

An excellent example of this is the case of paranormal awareness, such as telepathy. In cases of this kind we seem to dispense with the ordinary media of knowledge. For example, it has sometimes been known, at the time of some fatal calamity, such as a shipwreck or a railway accident, for someone far removed from the scene of the calamity to have an experience which appears to be connected with it, either in the form of some vague feeling of discomfort or presentiment connected with persons involved in the calamity, or, in some cases, by having some impression of the events themselves, or something closely resembling them, such as cries for help. Here then we seem to have some knowledge of events which is independent of the ordinary sensory means of acquiring information. No one has told the percipient of the happenings in question, and this telepathic awareness is therefore different even from the most sudden communication along ordinary channels. To be told almost immediately by telephone would be quite a different matter. And so we incline to say that here we have direct or immediate communication; and for certain purposes there is no objection to this way of speaking. But in other ways it may be very misleading. For it does not seem in fact that we need to postulate more than certain ways in which occurrences of a certain kind influence our minds. What form this influence takes is another matter, and several theories have been propounded to account for telepathy and kindred phenomena. We are not concerned with these now. But, in the last analysis, all we seem entitled to conclude is that certain experiences, which the recipient of a telepathic communication has, have some peculiarity which entitles us to connect them with other occurrences in some way not to be explained by ordinary causal processes. But there is no reason to suppose that we dispense in such cases with mediation of all kinds. If a person has telepathic awareness of a shipwreck, for example, he usually *sees* or *hears* something, and even if the thought of a shipwreck were to enter his mind, connected perhaps with special times and persons, without any sort of image, we should still be only entitled to postulate a peculiar way in which occurrences, whether physical or mental, affect certain minds. Even when the effect is intended there is no reason to suppose that it is direct in any sense other than in dispensing with certain sensory media which are normally required for communication. As Professor Price puts it: "As with Telepathy, so with Clairvoyance, the bare empirical facts are *correlations*: between the percipient's images or hallucinations or utterances on the one hand, and certain facts about material objects on the other—facts not accessible to him by any form of normal sense perception nor by inference".[1] To suppose more than this, where com-

[1] *Philosophy*, October, 1940, p. 379.

munication with other minds is concerned, would be to suppose that we could strictly 'enter into' the mind of another person or introspect or 'own' his experiences as if they were our own. Of this the facts of paranormal psychology afford no evidence; and what is more, from the nature of the case they cannot do so. For I think that reflection will show that communication in the sense last suggested is inherently impossible for us.

A case where we seem to come nearest a communication that dispenses with all mediation is that where we seem to apprehend the occurrence apprehended in telepathy or clairvoyance in all its details. Professor Price gives us a good example:

It is the example "of Madame Morel which occurred in March 1914. An old man had disappeared from the village of Cour-les-Barres (in the Department of Cher, in Central France). He was repeatedly and carefully searched for, but could not be found. Madame Morel, who was in Paris and had never been in the Department of Cher, was given a scarf belonging to the old man, and told to 'look for' its owner. She said she saw him lying dead on the ground, in a place which she described in detail. She also gave a detailed description of the appearance and posture of the body. Asked to say how he had got there, she gave a detailed account of the route he had followed, and of his feelings on the way. People on the spot then followed the route Madame Morel had described, arrived at the place she had described, and found the body lying there. The details she had given about the posture of the body and the clothes were verified exactly. The place also corresponded exactly to her description, with one instructive exception. She said that the body was lying near a rock. Actually it was a piece of a fallen tree which did look like a rock".[1]

This example raises several questions that we need not consider here, and we need not try to determine whether this was a case of clairvoyance or telepathy. For even if we suppose that it was telepathic, and that the medium had access in this way to what the old man thought and felt as he proceeded on his way, there is, none the less, no reason to suppose more than that the medium had thoughts and feelings and images closely similar to those which the old man himself enjoyed. To go

[1] op. cit. p. 377.

beyond this would involve us, in the first place, in very serious difficulties about Time. But this is not my main reason for contending that, in examples of the kind considered, or even in cases where there is sheer transference of thought without the aid of any visual imagery, there can be no literal sharing of the experiences of others, but only correlations and similarities which entitle us to deduce certain relations between occurrences, such as that some communication is being made to us by highly unusual means. My main reason for this view is the completeness of our confinement to the 'ego-centric predicament' so far as the modes of experience are concerned—a matter which philosophers have often stressed but which we seem even now not to have fully appreciated.

To discuss this in detail would take us very far afield. I will content myself, therefore, with a brief indication of what I have in mind by a further reference to the problem of space.

We are all familiar with the distinction between public and private space, and there can be little doubt that some useful meanings can be found for this distinction. But to suppose that public space can be regarded as some literal duplication of space as I find it in my particular experience seems to me quite impossible. We could not think of such a duplication except in some way as part of the space we actually know. But it also follows from this that we can have no clear conception of what space is like for other persons. I can only know it as a form of my own experience. And many of our problems about space would, I think, be very much simplified if we appreciated this better.

Take the old question: 'Where are the objects I see in the mirror?' It seems to me that we have no reason to say that they are on the surface of the mirror, and yet they are extended surfaces related in some way to the 'actual' objects in the room, a relation which could never be eliminated by the 'wildness' of the images. But is there no problem of an overlap of such relations with that of other objects outside the present field of sense awareness—the furniture next door, for example? This seems to me a very real difficulty which we simply cannot dismiss by a facile repudiation of the reality of mirror images, etc., but it is not a problem that arises within my private experience, for when I view the objects in the next room the images I see now in the mirror will be non-existent. It is only when we think of *other* persons perceiving the room next door at the same time as we look in the mirror that there is a real difficulty, and this difficulty, I suggest, is in no way insuperable (as it would otherwise be) if we make it quite clear that the extendedness of objects for other persons must be radically different from what it is to me, and something of which I can form no clear conception.

These are not matters I can amplify now. I merely wish to emphasise the completeness of the confinement of each person to the particular modes of his own experience. There is, of course, nothing very disconcerting about this to any who can accustom themselves to the oddities and departures from naïve views that are inevitable on any philosophical analysis. On the contrary, it is rather exciting, like Spinoza's doctrine of infinite attributes. Nor is communication ruled out. But it does clearly follow that there can be no strictly immediate access to the mind of another. For that, it seems plain, presupposes that we can see things *strictly* as another person sees them and know *precisely* what the world must be like for him, and, furthermore know it for the whole of his experience; for I do not see how we could really 'get inside' the mind of another person without knowing at least the structure of his world as a whole. It seems therefore plain that no communication to us from outside can be meaningful unless it is intertwined with elements of the peculiar private experience of each individual.

But if difficulties of this sort arise when we think of a strictly immediate access to the mind of another finite person, how much more formidable are they bound to prove when we think in similar terms of our union with God. For to suppose that we could ever see anything as it appears to God seems altogether absurd. It would mean that we would be no longer finite beings. Some writers have attempted to meet this by frankly accepting the notion of mystical experience as 'absorption' in God. But that, in addition to many other difficulties, means, not that we have direct union with God, but that we are annihilated. We cease to be as finite beings who can recognise themselves as distinct individuals if the doctrine of absorption is taken strictly, and not as a metaphorical expression compatible with various interpretations of the mode of our union with God.

Furthermore, to have some unmediated access to the mind of another being, whether finite or infinite, would involve knowing what it must be like to be another person. But that knowledge, in point of fact, we never do have, however much we know in another sense about one another. What it is like to be another 'I' must be an absolute mystery to me. This is, I think, the main cause of our troubles about self-consciousness and self-identity. The uniqueness of the experience we have of ourselves in this way is overlooked and we find ourselves seeking for some common factor of self-awareness which we can describe. That is to seek the impossible. But how infinitely more impossible is it for us to fathom in some similar way the mystery of the being of God. That must be for ever hid, not merely in present existence but in all (and to question that would incidentally jeopardise altogether anything we wish to believe about personal immortality).

It was suggested at one time that we could perceive some *part* of the 'Mind' of God directly. But the Church, very rightly in my view, lost little time in condemning this as heresy. For not only does it leave us with all our original difficulties, but it also errs badly by ascribing to God the sort of relation between whole and part which is quite inconsistent with the transcendent unity we find that we have to postulate in the thinking which brings us to the idea of God.

Nor finally is the notion of such access to God as would plumb the mystery of his nature consistent with religious experience. For however much the seer and the prophet may feel expressly commissioned to deliver a message explicitly entrusted to them, or however overwhelmed they may feel by the sense of God's presence, nothing is more marked than the equally emphatic stress on his unfathomable mystery. 'God is a God that hides himself'. 'No man can see God and live'. To deny that is the essense of idolatry, as the genius of religious peoples early perceived. Not even Jesus claimed to know God absolutely. "No man hath seen God at any time; the only begotten son, which is in the bosom of the Father, he hath *declared* him". Jesus did indeed claim to be the supreme revelation, but that is another matter. It was not given to the Son to reveal even 'the times and places'. And how moderate were the claims of Jesus himself in this regard is not perhaps appreciated as well as it should. The wisdom 'God has ordained before the world unto our glory', and which is now revealed 'by his spirit', is also 'hidden' and a mystery which it is the final blasphemy to question.

To lay hold firmly on this is as important for preaching and apologetics as for religious thought. Much unbelief and lack of interest in religion springs from the notion that religion claims some wholly unmediated knowledge of God. But that in fact is what religion hardly ever does claim. And it is much in the interest of religion, therefore, to show that believer and unbeliever alike can heartily join in rejecting any possibility of a strictly immediate knowledge of God.

There remains the question whether the notion of immediacy, in some sense other than the absolute sense with which we have been concerned, has importance for religious thought. I believe that it has, and that when taken in a relative sense the claim of the mystic to have immediate knowledge of God is significant and points to something that is present in some measure in all religious experience. The clue to this further problem must be sought, in my view, in the close affinities of art and religion. But as I have made this the subject of another address, I will not venture now beyond the more negative conclusions of this paper.

Chapter IX

REVELATION AND ART[1]

PHILOSOPHERS have often felt uneasy about the 'ancient quarrel' between poetry and philosophy which obtrudes itself so sharply into the *Republic* of Plato; they have sought in various ways to compose it. But few have felt that there is any need of a similar office in the case of art and religion. Between these two there seems to be an obvious affinity, whether we think of their early beginnings or of their subsequent development. The nature of this affinity is another matter about which more will be said in due course; and there will no doubt be sharp divergencies of opinion here. But that there is some essential affinity between the arts and religion few will, I think, deny. Nor, I imagine, will there be many to question the further contention to be made later, namely that the relation between art and religion is of great importance for the understanding of both.

There have of course been notorious quarrels here also, and they have been very bitter. But they have owed their peculiar bitterness to the fact that they are quarrels within the family. Bursts of puritanical fervour have led to the fierce condemnation of the arts in general as well as to the abjuration of art in religious worship. The artist, offended in turn, has hastened to repudiate religion, and, even when passions have cooled and amity has been restored, he has remained deeply suspicious of the restraining hand which he feels religion is only too ready to place upon him. But it does not need much discernment to see how much the antagonism owes to the perversion of an essential affinity, and that, when viewed in a wide perspective it will be found to be mainly a protest against the corruption of religion or the prostitution of the arts. The initial harmony rarely takes long to restore. The puritan soon acquires religious habits which, in their simple form, are as artistic as any; and the artist,

[1] Presidential Address to the Mind Association delivered to the Joint Session of the Mind Association and the Aristotelian Society, July 8th, 1949. *Proceedings of the Aristotelian Society*, Supplementary Volume XXIII.

wearying very quickly of his sojourn in the far country, begins to feel the stir of mysterious heart-aches which are strangely like the religious longings from which he was so sure that he had emancipated himself; quite often these mount into a passion which brings him hasting back with the extravagant single-mindedness of the penitent prodigal. We are on the way to this in the atheism of an Omar, a Shelley or a Housman where the disguise is so easily penetrated that the devout have seized upon their works as readily as any, finding in them much to sustain the life of religion.

These are matters which I need not elaborate. They are familiar facts to all observers of art and religion. But I must hasten to remove an impression which my remarks may already have left, and which would be quite out of keeping with what I propose to maintain.

This is that I wish to take up the view which would commonly be expressed by saying that religion is after all 'only poetry'. Many, I think, are attracted to this view at present, and I can hardly think of anything more detrimental to the true interests of art and religion. The view in question is usually an excuse for taking neither art nor religion very seriously, and in particular betokens a vague and curiously uncritical desire to retain something of the trappings of religion without its shattering demands. This goes with a very outmoded view of the arts, outmoded at least so far as the opinions and attitudes of the artists themselves are concerned, which makes art merely the expression of a private emotion, some pleasing relief to our feelings, and not a searching exacting experience which has little to do in the first instance with self. To be rid of this enfeebling romanticised view of art is an important step in the true appreciation of religion. The evasions and superficialities which prompt these attitudes, the proneness to withdraw from reality into a comfortable world of our own, is also reminiscent of a view of religion which had much vogue in the nineteenth century and is still far from being abandoned, namely the view that religion is morality 'touched with emotion'. This view is associated usually with Arnold, but it is well to remind ourselves in passing that there is a great deal in Arnold's teaching about religion, and that not merely on its ethical side, to say nothing of his poetry, which takes us a long way at any rate from the cheaper and more vulgar forms of this attenuation of religious claims. But we must not stray down that tempting by-path. Suffice it to note that the attempt to empty religion of all but its ethical substance is only another variation of the misguided attempt to succour religion by abating its claims, which is often the intention when religion is said to be 'merely poetry'. For this I certainly hold no brief. And in turning your attention at the start this evening to the affinity between the arts and religion, the last thing which I wish to do is to commend to you some attenuated form of religion, shorn of its peculiar rigours and exactions as religion, or to moderate the claims which religion makes upon the mind, as indeed on the whole person.

Let me be more explicit. The relation between art and religion in which I have an interest is that which has a bearing on our knowledge of God, and I doubt very much whether any relation between them which is not derived from this has any importance.

Nor is this apparent merely in the nature of religious art. For although the fact that art comes so easily into the service of religion and that some of the finest creations of art are explicitly religious—not only when we think of architecture, music, poetry, painting and the spoken word, but also in the case of the less familiar arts—is deeply suggestive, the relation between art and religion can be considered with least danger of confusion and prejudging of issues, if we think, not of explicitly religious art, but of the relation between art as such and religion. And if this were not the case we should have to say more than I could venture to say directly in this address in answer to the charge that it is an accident of particular times and cultures that so much of the greatest art of the past, and not only in Christian countries but generally, is so deeply imbued with the spirit of religion and directly concerned with it. I shall in fact have nothing to say about religious art as such; nor is the subject one on which I am competent to offer any expert opinion. It is with the relation of art as such and religion that I am concerned, and it is surely this relation, persisting when we are not considering explicitly religious art, which is most likely to be illuminating.

But we must guard against one further misunderstanding

here. For it might be thought that the reason why we should not concern ourselves directly with religious art is that the art which is made subservient to some purpose outside itself fails to be art. That certainly happens, and it is as likely to happen in the case of religion as anywhere, especially in prose and poetry. The attempt to clothe certain preconceived religious ideas in poetic form has often been the bane of artistic genius. But there is none the less religious art that has not been defiled at all in this way, and some of this, as hardly needs to be stressed, in literature as in other forms of art, ranks among the main works of artistic creation. This, as I have hinted, is significant. But it is also a matter whose significance, at least for religion, can only be seen when the general nature of the relation between art as such and religion is understood. And it is this basic essential relationship solely that I wish to stress.

But how does this relationship of art and religion appear, and where precisely does its importance lie? Its importance lies, I submit, in its bearing on a certain mode of religious awareness, and in coming now to closer grips with our subject, some observations must first be made on the general problem of the nature of our knowledge of God. How, then, can God be known? To some extent, I think, by reason or taking thought. But this does not mean that we have to accept the traditional arguments for the existence of God as usually stated. The view that I take is that these arguments fail in much that is often claimed for them, but that they do express a certain 'demand of reason', to use a stock term for a principle which is peculiarly difficult to formulate. This is the demand that reality must be a whole. That there is this demand, but of course a metaphysical and not an ethical one, is a view which would take more space to defend against recent criticism than would be warranted here. But we must at any rate emphasise one peculiarity of the 'demand for wholeness', namely that, although it is posited by reason, it would defeat itself if we could think that it might be met at the rational level. This sounds very paradoxical, but I do not think paradox can be avoided here, much though we should normally shun it. Rational processes have an incompleteness in which reason cannot rest content, and we are brought in this way to the notion of a transcendent nature of reality. But while

I believe this traditional view can still be maintained, and consider it most important to maintain it, it has also to be stressed that there are sharp and severe limitations to this approach to religious problems. For the most that we can attain in this way, without undermining the argument for transcendence itself, is a purely formal knowledge of some ultimate ground or principle of reality of whose nature we can form no conception. This falls very far short of the needs of religion. For the God of religion is the 'living' Creator God who makes His Presence felt by individuals and communicates with them. How, then, is this particular knowledge of God obtained; how can God, to be God, make himself known?

It has been held, in particular by idealist writers, that there are certain patterns in our experience which afford a clue to the transcendent nature of reality, divine and human being in essence the same. But to query the absolute nature of transcendence in this way is to empty it of real significance. At the same time, to hold, as some mystical writers do, that there is some strictly immediate knowledge of God, is equally futile. The idea of immediacy is notoriously ambiguous, but to claim in a literal sense an 'immediate union' with God involves, besides the peculiar difficulties that attend the notion of immediacy where communication is concerned, the absurdity of claiming to see things as God sees them, to have a transcendent experience. The idea of 'absorption' in the divine nature makes this less fantastic, but it also means that the finite as such is eliminated. To avoid these difficulties, Buber and others of late have argued that union with God need have no content of knowledge, that it is a 'bare relation'. But that is a peculiarly difficult view, and even if it were not, revelation without content seems hardly adequate to the claims of religion itself. But if there can be no strictly immediate knowledge of God, how can particular knowledge of Him be claimed without presupposing such power of determining the ultimate nature of God as would deny his transcendence, in other words, without toppling over into what has so aptly been called 'the pit of anthropomorphism'?

It is here that consideration of art is important. For we have in art an awareness of reality in a form that is least reducible to the categories of our own thought, the world being thus presented in a way that has clearer traces of a sphere beyond that of finite experience itself. Acknowledgment of something resembling this in art has recently been made by writers on psycho-analysis who have stressed especially the element of mystery in art, but they have sought to explain this entirely in terms of the haunting of the conscious mind by elements from other mental levels, or from some remote period in our own history or in that of the race. A similar account is given of religion, and it cannot be denied that much can be achieved in this way; even if the main contention is found to be unplausible, a flood of light will have been thrown in other ways on the nature of art and religion. This is most welcome in view of the need for improvement in the psychological study of art and for a subtler psychology of religion—in both these respects psycho-analysis is likely to count a great deal. But the case for the view that what is most distinctive of art and religion can be adequately described on the principles of psycho-analysis has still to be stated properly. There are ways of improving on what Freud himself has taught, and the hints thrown out somewhat cryptically by writers in general sympathy with his view and more abreast of other developments in philosophy, as, for example, in Mr. Wisdom's recent paper on 'Gods',[1] deserve much more exhaustive presentation. If, in the light of ampler and more considered statements, it is felt that the case has been made, we shall have to conclude that the problem of revelation as normally conceived is a bogus one, that the enigma is after all, not God, but the self. But that does not seem to me likely. And the 'analytical' approach appears to err in particular in its treatment of art, to keep to that for the present, in its failure to do justice to the peculiar process of illumination which is as distinctive a feature of art as the element of mystery itself.

For the artist is, in the first instance, a seer, and his essential function, in his relation to others, is to make them see something to which they are normally blind. This may be something in nature or in human life; it does not matter which. But we must in some way be made aware of objects and events in a fashion which is like seeing them for the first time. The artist

[1] *Proceedings of the Aristotelian Society*, 1944-45.

wrests their secrets from objects and makes them glow with a distinctiveness which escapes normal consciousness of them. This illumination of the world, which almost amounts to a transformation, is the essential feature of art, and where some special sense of clarity and penetration is lacking, where there is no heightened consciousness of inhabiting a world which thrusts itself upon the mind with a peculiar sharpness and insistence, there is no art.

It does not follow that art must be simple and easy to appreciate. Indeed, a very plausible case could be made for the view that, in the growing sophistication of modern culture, and the greater domination of the intellect within the whole range of experience, some obscurities of style are inseparable from any artistic effect. That view, and it has notable adherents,[1] cannot, to my mind, be maintained at all points, but it is very instructive. Some resistance to be overcome, to some extent by deliberate application, is, in many cases, the most effective means of inducing the sense of an encounter of self with reality which we must substitute in art for the easy acquiescence of day to day. But however true this may be, and by whatever inversions of his main purpose the artist must take his course at certain levels of culture, however he may need to bewilder and baffle his audience, the ultimate aim and sanction of this incidental confusion of overt intention is the greater clarification of something different from this of which no indication is possible other than that which the artist gives in the adoption of these procedures. That this puts many serious pitfalls in the path of the artist will be very evident, and it is even more evident that the task of distinguishing between what is spurious and false in art is a peculiarly tricky and delicate one in times of cultural growth and transition. Similar dangers beset the theorist of art when he tries to specify particular and detailed features of art and its modes. But these are matters which need not trouble us now. All that we need to do at the moment is to insist that, underlying all the incidental obscurities of art, there must be a rarer illumination than anything we can achieve in ordinary thought, if also of a very different nature.

It is in neglect of this that most philosophies of art have

[1] Cf. Herbert Read, *Collected Essays*, pp. 89-100.

erred. For they have centred attention on matters incidental to the essential artistic illumination which should be their main concern. This holds especially for theories of art which consider it exclusively in terms of the psychological state and reactions of the artist or his audience. The commonest form of this error is the still very prevalent belief that the essence of art is the expression of emotion. This view is attractive because of the prominent part which emotion plays in artistic experience. But it is also very seriously misleading. For however much the emotions bound up with an artistic experience may become fused in our thought about it with the experience itself, and however dependent we may be upon these emotions when we attempt any specification of that experience other than a revival of it, the emotions themselves are secondary and derivative. They depend upon and presuppose the more essential process of illumination which is so much more elusive than its accompaniments where specific description is concerned, and indeed beggars description of what is most distinctive of it as art.

The undue prominence ascribed to emotion in aesthetic theories is also encouraged by the contribution of emotions of the right kind to the inducement of the attentiveness favourable to artistic creation or enjoyment. How far some emotional preparation of this kind is indispensable is a hard question, the more particularly as its importance need not turn on its being prolonged. Since it may be almost instantaneous, and since it will merge immediately in the emotions consequent on having the essential artistic experience, the problem of its invariability sets introspection a peculiarly difficult task. Almost equally hard is the question of the part which the inducement of certain emotions plays in the symbolic representation by which artistic awareness is possible. But whether emotion is indispensable in any or all of the ways we have noted, its prominence when rightly understood should make us all the more resolved, whether as artists, critics, or philosophers, not to be diverted by it from the main matter of the peculiar apprehension of reality which it subserves.

But why peculiar? We must here go back to the point already made. For what is made plain to us in art is not the rational connectedness of things which we apprehend in science and everyday thought. Art concerns not the universal, but the individual, aspect of reality. It is for this reason that it does not follow any predeterminable course or admit, in essentials, of rational analysis. Art uncovers for us the character of particular things in the starkness and strangeness of their being what they are. It is mercilessly intimate. And this is why Plato, from whom most philosophers of art down to the most informative critics of the present take their cue in defiance of Plato's own aberrations here, took such a low view of art. For Plato was led by considerations which we need not specify now to elevate universal rational truth at the expense of complete derogation of any other mode of awareness normally attainable. The particular historical event, the unique specific reality, had little importance for him. But this is just what fascinates the artist, and however much he may draw for his purpose on harmonies detected for him by reason, this is always in the service of some quite independent way in which he puts himself and others in touch with reality in its more distinctive individual aspect.

The artist thus looks at the world more squarely than the scientist, and without the disinterested distant perspectives of science. Its impact upon him is ruder, and he is himself more committed in his work. But for the same reason his work has also severer limits. The limits of science lie only in the absolute mystery of the ultimate transcendent wholeness of things. But the limits of art lie directly in what is perceived. For the more the artist invests the commonplace reality of ordinary experience with the significance of his peculiar individual impression of them, the more starkly do they also present to him an alien irreducible nature. The finer his appreciation of objects the more is their distinctiveness stressed; there are no essential grips, no claims to be staked, but only a relationship which, in becoming more intimate, is in that measure also more precarious and fortuitous; the closer the artist moves to reality the more is it alarmingly aloof, and so, paradoxically but unmistakably, in art there is an unveiling which is at the same time a concealment; in the very process of clarification there is also a deepening of mystery, not in the sense that there is a mystery at the end of every scientific truth, the sense, that is, that the solution of problems sets us *'ad infinitum'* new problems to solve, but in a more absolute immediate sense that that which is made peculiarly plain to us is itself proportionately more enigmatic. Mystery and illumination are one in art.

Some recent poets have themselves come as near an explicit statement of this as poetry dares.

One says:
>   Imagine, then, by miracle, with me,
>   (Ambiguous gifts, as what gods give must be)
>   What could not possibly be there,
>   And learn a style from a despair.[1]

Yet another, a Welsh poet whom it is not inappropriate to quote on this occasion:
>   Light breaks on secret lots,
>   On tips of thought where thoughts smell in the rain;
>   When logics die,
>   The secret of the soil grows through the eye,
>   And blood jumps in the sun;
>   Above the waste allotments the dawn halts.[2]

But even more striking are the following lines in which another poet concludes his own account of the fashioning of 'The Supposed Being':
>   And at last
>   such a being escapes from the sight of my visible [eyes,
>   from the touch of my tangible hands,
>   for she only exists,
>   where all contradictions exist,
>   where darkness is light and the real is unreal and the
>   world is a dream in a dream.[3]

This is not philosophical reflection, but in its own way it comes very near to our theme; it also illustrates it, for what is said as poetry here is sharply defined, but also elusive. We could not lay hold of it in any other way or transcribe what the poet says.

But is not this also how we think of religious experience and revelation; is it not in just the same way that God is said to be at once a 'hidden' God, an absolute mystery, and yet also 'light' and the 'source of light', a God whose ways 'are not our ways' but whose word is yet 'nigh thee, even in thy mouth and in thy

---
[1] William Empson. 'This Last Pain'.
[2] Dylan Thomas. 'Light breaks where no sun shines'.
[3] David Gascoyne. 'The Supposed Being'.

heart'? Perhaps so, you may say, but is this parallel enough to establish a religious view? I do not think so, and I do not know how such a view could be established had we not already implicit in all our thought, in the way indicated earlier, the notion of some ultimate ground of all being. But granted this formal awareness of a transcendent reality we may, I think, fairly fix a particular point of contact with it in the apprehension of reality which leaves its alien distinctive nature, its 'otherness' in the popular term of today, most unimpaired.

This is a position in which we may be fortified by consideration of the way in which we also become aware of one another's minds. For, as Professor Price has shown,[1] we become aware of one another, not by analogies, much less by intuition or direct acquaintance, but through the way something is communicated to us which could not have arisen from our own thought but affords us essentially new information. The details of this view must be sought in Price's own account, and I must also add that I should consider it wrong to look for any close analogy in details when the same idea is examined in connection with our knowledge of God. For God has no specific location, like other persons, much less a visible body. But we may well follow the analogy to the point of seeking our particular knowledge of God in that aspect of reality which, in the words of a modern theologian, is not known as "a truth that already lay in the depths of reason",[2] but which is alien and other, bearing in what is most distinctive of it the stamp of outsideness.

In conjunction with our view of art, this will, I think, eventually bring us to the view that art is itself a divine revelation, although it need not always be acknowledged to be such. But it does not follow that there is no revelation other than in art as usually understood. For there is no reason why we should not have an impression of reality similar in substance to that which we have in art, and having significance in the same way, without there being needed the peculiar aptitudes which art requires. This seems to me to happen in more distinctively religious experience where elements of present experience so

[1] 'Our evidence for the existence of other minds'. *Philosophy*, October, 1938.
[2] Brunner, *Revelation and Reason*, p. 367.

shape themselves as to become articulate for us in a non-rational way very similar to art but also pre-eminently expressive of a transcendent reality. To illustrate this in detail is not possible now; nor can we examine the conditions which make it possible. But some indication may be attempted of the implications of a view of religious experience derived, in the way suggested, from study of its close affinity with art, and of some of the consequences, for religion and religious thought, of adopting such a view.

There is one matter that needs to be especially stressed. It is that, on the present view, there can be no test of the validity of a religious experience, in its essentials, outside the experience itself. This does not mean that the distinction between what is genuine and spurious is easily blurred, any more than in art, which must also authenticate itself, we are slow to perceive the difference between a sentimental film and a splendid drama. Nor does it follow that there is nothing for reason to do nor any function for natural theology. Art criticism and theory of art are not debarred by the self-authenticating character of art. But in art and religion alike the province of rational consideration must be very carefully and nicely judged.

It is here that religious thought and theology have erred most in the past, sometimes, as in the case of some exponents of mysticism, by seeking to take us altogether outside the sphere of finite experience, or by refusing to accord to reason any function in respect of what we apprehend in religion within our own experience, or, in what is now by far the commonest case, by seeking to rationalise, sometimes exhaustively, those essential elements in the life of religion which most resist reduction of that kind, in the latter case neglecting the crucial fact that symbolism in religion is essential and not incidental. For, in our view, symbols in religion are, not merely in practice but in principle, untranslatable in their ultimate meaning, as the symbols of logic and mathematics plainly are not.

It does not follow that the more overt content of religious symbols, or what they seem to convey explicitly, is unimportant or devoid of religious significance. To suggest that would be foolish. But it is only in a very special way that rational content becomes important for religion. It does so so far as it enters,

P

together with the evaluation of its elements, into a whole of a very different nature in which it has no isolable function. This does not mean that as rational truth it is negated; it can only contribute to religion because of what it is in itself, but it becomes important for religion because of something more which it renders possible. This something more is not added to, or superimposed upon, what is explicitly said. A transmutation occurs by which ideas, in a new medium, and in combination with other factors, acquire a further recognisably religious import. Of this it seems to be one peculiarity that it invests with significance, at once and in the same way, a whole corpus of experience, although it often has a focus not very different from that of finite communication. And although the distinctiveness of the religious awareness is to be sought in the quality of the awareness itself, marked peculiarities of it may be found in features such as I have noted. At the moment it is the unique and essentially symbolic nature of religious truth that I stress, together with the equally essential integration of other experiences into it.

There is a close parallel in the case of poetry. No one who knows his business appraises a poem in terms of its literal meaning. But that meaning matters, and the poem would not be possible without it; for poetry is rarely if ever mere incantation. If the overt meaning is inoperative the poem is at least imperfect; and a great deal of understanding is needed to appreciate even very simple poetry. Its form, for example, must be recognised, and there must be that understanding by which the interplay of associations from which poetic images derive their power is rendered possible. Sometimes this rises to hard intellectual effort. This is still incidental to the meaning and the merit of the poem as such. But it is none the less indispensable, and its being incidental to the truth of the poem as poem warrants no relaxation of its discipline; this holds so far as it is concerned.

In the same way the inclusion of various modes of experience within religion, and some sort of transvaluation of them, leaves the inherent nature and forms of those processes themselves unaffected. Failure to appreciate this and to grasp the relation of subsidiary processes to the religious truth they subserve has kept many from acknowledging the peculiarity of the latter, and others from doing it justice.

Thus the claim that religious truth is not just 'a set of propositions' will find an echo in many quarters today. The positivist, for example, in his own way, will welcome it, but only in the sense that religious terms, being, on his view, devoid of content in themselves, have no significance except as expressions or evocations of feeling, or as 'mere exclamations' (whatever that means). This is plausible, and it is foolish to deny that it is, but it is so only because religious ideas are true for religion not because of the truth of what is explicitly said (although if they are true in this sense that truth remains unimpaired and important for religion), but because of something further which happens in religion to these ideas. This it is which gives to positivism a kind of half-truth which makes it, here as elsewhere, so attractive at first; but the matter is none the less falsely conceived in denying that religious symbols have meaning in *any* sense.

It might of course be answered that meaning can be so understood that the positivist is not committed to this denial—in some causal way, for example. But to raise the general question of the nature of meaning, although an inescapable task in a full presentation of the present view, is hardly practicable now. I must presume therefore to be rather dogmatic and say that the positivist case, to my mind, is more effectively stated in denying that religious conceptions have meaning than in holding to the view that they are meaningful but in terms of the effect of holding them or of some similar distortion of the ordinary meaning of "meaning".

It may be countered that my own account of meaning, so far as the main contention is concerned, is equally novel, and ascribes to terms a meaning other than their ordinary meaning. This I fully allow, and my chief concern is to show that there is such meaning, but this usage none the less conforms with the unsophisticated meaning of "meaning" to the extent of finding its truth or falsity in what it claims in itself, and not in its incidentals. And I maintain, but without further argument here, that this is something we know to be ultimate about the nature of meaning, and to be jeopardised at our very greatest peril, as, to my mind, recent philosophy abundantly proves.

There is of course much extenuation of the positivist position in general, so far as the claim of truth for religion is concerned, in the fact that emotions play so prominent a part in religion as in morals and art. They also seem to shape themselves particularly closely here to the essential experience. When confronted with that which beggars normal description, it is thus tempting to seek a reduction to emotive terms. But that is none the less hasty; and Plato did well to point out the perils of impatience in philosophy; the positivist pays by missing what matters most.

The present view invites comparison also with the 'orthodox' insistence that religious truth, not being a set of intelligible statements to be straightway appraised for their truth or falsity in the ordinary way, requires for its acceptance some 'act of faith' in the way of a decision or commitment of the whole person; some kind of choice is involved. Now, as normally presented there is nothing at all to be said for this view; and I can only describe as outrageous the procedure of identifying a choice of the sort in question with moral choice, and importing into this terrain a whole body of quite alien ethical conceptions, to the great confusion of ethics and theory of knowledge. And yet, in some sense, there seems to be something in this notion as in most ideas to which the religious consciousness clings in spite of their seeming so repugnant to us as normally stated. It cannot be true that we can strictly choose to believe or not to believe; and to arraign those who repudiate some religious notion on the ground of their reluctance to make a decision in its favour, or to meet their perplexity in that way, can only be aggravating in the extreme. But may we not conceive this matter differently?

I suggest that we can, and that it is no trivial advantage of the view commended in this address to allow of accommodation of the 'act of faith' without offence to either moral or intellectual integrity. If religious truth involves rising from ordinary awareness to a grasp of a meaning interfused with ordinary meaning in a way closely similar to artistic experience, then we need not be surprised or repelled at the suggestion that this only happens to the extent that we submit ourselves to the process by mastering much initial reluctance. That there are many inhibiting factors is not surprising. Are there not plenty in art? Does not the artist cast his spell upon us, and are we not inclined to resist this, especially so far as it seems to suspend our other more critical faculties? Is it not just on this score that the 'witchcraft' of the artist has so often been violently denounced, from Plato onwards? Is not this the real source of the 'ancient feud', and is it not the case that only when the feud is composed by what we can fittingly describe as an act of faith on the part of the 'rational man' and the 'power of grace' in art, do we rise to the triumph of artistic perception? It is no accident, in my view, that the notions of 'faith' and 'grace' take their place so appropriately both in religion and art, and to suggest that they do so in utterly different ways seems hardly convincing. Religious people may resent what they incline to regard as the assimilation of religion to art, and they may feel that something is seriously lost in the process. But assimilation is not what happens here, not, at any rate, in the sense of surrendering something which is distinctive of religion as it is not of art, and presenting it in a new guise. Nor is it held that exhaustive accounts of the religious meanings of faith and grace are possible by considering only their similarities of functions in art and religion. But these similarities are held to be none the less essential, and it is now being maintained that the 'surrender' and 'commitment of the whole person', so much travestied and cheapened in religious practice as in religious thought, consists in essentials in just this highly delicate matter of yielding our personality as a whole to some kind of experience, a 'possession', which, being in its whole tone strange and different from ordinary processes, and requiring some superseding, but not the suspension, of ordinary critical power, is bound to present itself as some kind of 'venture' and surrender of self. No one likes 'to be carried', and with reason; for we know well what excesses of sentimentality and delusion are possible thereby. But that is a risk we must take. We may really come to disaster and feel that our integrity has been really 'stained'. That will be followed by a deep sense of bitterness, especially at ourselves, a sense of having compromised ourselves, rising on occasion to sharp reproach, and from this we can only be truly 'redeemed' by another 'venture' which, in such circumstance, we shall be all the more reluctant to make but which, possibly by the additional effort needed to make it, will lead to a new and wonderful triumph in which the old 'lapse' is obliterated. These are all recognisable religious moods, to which centrality is commonly, and to my mind rightly, given in religious thought. Nor do I wish to hold that they can be fully understood in disregard of ethical factors. I shall consider more ethical matters in a moment, but except where confused with ethics, as, unfortunately happens very extensively, and not least today, they are not regarded, in the first instance, as ethical, but rather as distinctively religious moods by religious thinkers themselves. And in this, notwithstanding the distortion which arises from not rightly understanding the relation of ethics to religion, the religious thinkers seem to me to be entirely right. But once this is understood, and once we have also the right conception of art, the sting of the usual objections to pointing the parallel, as we are doing here, between art and religion is easily lost, and nothing is imperilled for religion, but everything gained, by regarding the surrender of oneself to a religious truth needed to apprehend that truth as being closely similar to the way we must yield ourselves to a work of art before its magic can work upon us.

It is tempting to follow the comparison out in greater detail, but I must forbear here; and in any case the task is as much a task for the psychology of religion as for epistemology. And this is a point, incidentally, where it is of most importance to set the psychology of religion on the right course, and to see better just how the interesting facts brought to light by the psychology of religion should be understood. That will enable us to ask new and probably highly rewarding questions in the pursuit of further psychological investigations. And this is one of the ways in which I think, as I said earlier, that we stand in need of a better, more soundly conceived, psychology of religion.

Our theory seems fruitful also in another direction. For are we not told also that religious truth, by contrast with a mere set of ideas, is 'given in events'? It is 'truth in history'. Now this also opens out much possibility of nonsense, and of sententious exploitation. The ease of its acceptance recently in orthodox circles suggests that it will follow the time-honoured course in being speedily travestied or taken as simply another 'accepted view'. But here again we have in fact the reverse of what we should expect. A principle may be established by facts but it does not consist of them; and, in maintaining that religious truth is given in history, religious thinkers do not have in mind at all the way observations of particular events support a theory in science or 'everyday' thought; or, if they do, they are much to be reproached for seeming to say something novel and arresting. But it seems certain in fact that what they intend is different, as will be plain to any who consider the changes that have come over the religious scene since the great days of nineteenth-century idealism. It is not the elements of induction that are being taught us; and history is assigned a much less equivocal position than it enjoys even in the more historically orientated rationalistic systems of the last century. Facts are not, in the prevailing religious view of history, just testimony to the truth, most certainly not in the normal inductive sense. Rather is it held in some much more radical way that the truth is 'given' in the facts; and perhaps we should say that it is the facts. But as it stands, unless we are to resort to sheer mystification, this is quite impossible. A fact as such is not truth, but that about which we have truth, and, in any case, truths of the order of the religious doctrines commended in the terms now in question, the doctrine, for example, that men are sinners and need to be saved, are not historical facts in any normal meaning of the words.

Is there then any substance in the view that religious truth is given in history? Not, to my mind, in the sense that a number of quite unacceptable and inconsistent intellectual principles can be redeemed and placed above rational criticism by affirming that they are not, after all, intellectual statements but some kind of event. We shall certainly not play that game. And yet here again there is also something which lends some cover to the dogmatic theologian. It is not without justification that he has recourse to the claim that truth, for him, is a blend of thought and event. 'Truth in history', understood in the present radical sense, and not as idealism thought, rings the bell somewhere. And may not this also take its place well in our theory? How?

By abandoning, in the first place, in a much more uncompromising way than the theologian is prepared to do, the claim to be dealing in intellectual statements, however necessary in a subsidiary way such statements (but not necessarily those we encounter in dogmatic theology) may be for religion. Once we bring ourselves to do this, we shall, I think, then be in a position to see that there can be a perfectly legitimate sense in which truth and event may be fused. For may it not be that the conversion of rational statement into symbolic religious truth should happen sometimes, and perhaps mainly, in the linkage of such a statement with experience of arresting fact? May not the touch of such fact be the magic we need, not, it must be stressed, to make the incredible credible at the ordinary level, but to bring it, whether credible or not in itself, into life in a totally different medium of truth? And is not the parallel with art significant again? For there also the particular seems in some way indispensable. It is concretion that we stress especially in theories of art today.

This last matter helps to give point to a sharp and important distinction between the present view and another which in some ways it closely resembles. This is the view, commended so ably in Edwyn Bevan's notable *Symbolism and Belief*. Bevan distinguishes between two classes of religious symbols. The first is that 'behind which you can see'. An example of it would be the idea of the virgin birth for a Christian who had ceased to believe in the virgin birth in a literal sense, but found it a convenient way of representing to himself certain things which he did believe about Christ or his teaching. I doubt, however, very much whether symbols are used in this way in religion in any important respect, if indeed at all. It seems most unlikely that anyone who did not strictly believe in the virgin birth could be helped by toying with it in this way; he would certainly be better advised to centre his mind directly on what he did strictly believe than to confuse himself by so artificial a make-believe. But there might be a sense in which the stories about the birth of Christ, even if not literal fact, could in another way tell something important. But what way would that be?

The stories, in the first place, could fill out the picture of the setting in which Christ appeared and the impression he made; and few, I imagine, would deny this or question its importance.

But the stories could also, I think, say something more distinctive which we could not reduce to any other terms but which, as in all art, would need to be accepted on its own basis. And this, I think, could be of great religious value. Nor need it be much hindered by lack of literal belief if religious imagination is properly at work. But this is certainly not what Bevan has in mind in proceeding to symbols of the second order, namely 'those behind which we cannot see'. And it is his view of these that I wish mainly to note at the moment.

Of these Bevan says:

"The other class of symbols are those behind which we cannot see, such as many ideas we use to represent the life of God, if, as we are told, they have only analogical, and not literal, truth. When we speak of the love of God or the will of God, we know that we are speaking of something different from any love or any will we can know in men, and the idea of 'love of God', 'will of God', may, in that sense, be regarded as an element in the life of man taken to symbolise something unimaginable in the life of God. We cannot see behind the symbol: we cannot have any discernment of the reality better and truer than the symbolical idea, and we cannot compare the symbol with the reality as it is more truly apprehended and see how they differ. The symbol is the nearest we can get to the Reality".[1]

Here again we have symbols we cannot translate, and these are taken to be the ultimate forms of religious truth. But beyond that point I can hardly follow the author. For he proceeds to provide a test of the adequacy of these symbols that is not very intrinsic to their own nature. The test is a pragmatic one. This is not because Bevan holds a pragmatist view of the nature of truth. He insists in particular that the symbols do represent the real nature of God, but the only way in which we can know that they do so, it seems, is because of their effect on us. If we are helped to live better lives by thinking about God in a certain way we can rest assured that this representation of Him is sound. But I doubt very much whether this is what happens in religion. Is it really some indirect overall warrant of this kind that we claim for religious ideas? Is there not something more immediate, more inherent to the idea or experience itself that commends it

[1] *Symbolism and Belief*, p. 257.

to us? Bevan's procedure savours much more of a philosophical apologetic for religion than of the spontaneous welling-up of the religious experience. The response of the religious mind, however subtle and involved its presuppositions may be found on analysis to be, has also this much of simplicity that it is elicited directly by what it perceives to be inherently appropriate to it. Nothing seems plainer in religious experience than its claim to authenticate itself, and to propose a wholly extrinsic criterion seems to be as little in keeping with it as it would be to propose a pragmatic criterion of art.

Does not Bevan's theory also fall down on the more strictly logical ground that a test such as he has in mind presupposes an independent knowledge of the ultimate nature of God which, on Bevan's own admission, we cannot have? How otherwise could we know that God desires us to live in a certain way, or, in some similar fashion, decide on our criterion? I do not think the notion of transcendence itself, and the demand for wholeness which brings us to it, can be interpreted, without contradiction, in terms of a perfection which stands in so apprehensible a relation to finite evaluation as this, although it has often been thought to do so.

These objections, it seems to me, hold for most that is commonly claimed about 'analogical' knowledge of God. The idea of analogy is no doubt important in many ways. But we have to distinguish between two possible usages of it. The first is when we use conceptions that prove to be significant in certain spheres to illuminate other departments of experience, or to provide some general co-ordinating principle or 'viewpoint' by which we bring the facts of experience as a whole to a focus. A famous example is Aristotle's use of biological ideas to explain the moral life and provide the basis for a teleological view of the world. Butler's 'analogies' are not very different in principle. And, to give a recent example, it is something of this kind that Professor Emmet seems to have mainly in mind in her account of 'metaphysical analogies' in *The Nature of Metaphysical Thinking*, although her view seems to include some further extension of 'analogy'. Professor Price had recourse to the same notion when, on a similar occasion to the present one, he raised the question of alternative ways of mapping experience as a whole. But while analogies may be most helpful in these ways, the question for us is whether they can be extended to determine the nature of a transcendent reality—a second, quite distinct usage. However 'important', to use Professor Emmet's term, analogies may be from our point of view, what grounds can we have for supposing that they remain so beyond the bounds of experience as it must be for finite beings?

Of those who have had recourse to the 'doctrine of analogy' in religion the thinkers whose work deserves most respect have been markedly cautious in their use of it. A typical statement is that it is 'not misleading' to think of God as Goodness or as Love. I find it hard to give this any meaning, but even if we could, the formal attenuated knowledge so obtained is very far from the fullness of religious truth in actual religious experience; and those in the past whose names we associate most with the doctrine of analogy have been foremost themselves in insisting that it needs to be supplemented, the central position being given to revelation—a point on which for once I think traditionalism is right. What I wish to stress, in particular, in respect to the doctrine of analogy, is, not that it fails, as I think in fact it does fail, in its extension to a transcendent reality, but that it is far removed from religious experience. For abstract conceptions of wide generality can only acquire the veridicality of unmistakable religious awareness to the extent that they convert themselves into something very different in a vivid experience of individuals.

This goes also for dogma. But there is much besides that needs to be said about dogma from our point of view. Dogma arises when religion is in decay. When some great religious exhilaration is dying down, when the life is ebbing from it and vigour and vision are lost, the attempt is made to perpetuate it by holding on to some literal meaning of the symbolic expressions in which it maintains itself, these being no longer effective in their own way. There arise in this fashion rational religious systems little related to real religious experience and also but little able to sustain themselves in the face of rational criticism. But it is here that there is invoked the uniqueness of religious truth as 'the word of God', not the word of man.

One must not, so it is implied, expect full conformity with ordinary rational standards; for it is a transcendent reality that is being known. But this is perverse indeed, for the transcendent is being invoked as a *deus ex machina* to reinforce the weaknesses in processes in which it does not otherwise exhibit itself —a very different matter, I must stress, from finding the idea of transcendence involved in the limits of rational processes as such.

It does not follow that the dogmas could not become themselves in turn, in a new setting and environment, a source of genuine religious life. But they can do so, not as dogmas, but as elements in another medium which probably recovers much of the significance of the original symbol, although this, I should imagine, can happen only when the dogmas are either being blindly believed or clearly discarded as dogmas; and that will be very rare in a period like ours.

But this makes it hard to defer any longer the question of the relation of symbolic religious truth to truth in its other forms. This is a hard question; and the most that I will venture to say now is that the sort of awareness which I ascribe to art and religion may use other beliefs without always having reference to their truth in their own sphere, but that, being radically different, it does not thereby suspend or disrupt the standards of truth that obtain at the rational level; it rather confirms them by deepening regard for truth as such. And thus, although religion may use a mistaken belief, about religion or any other matter, provided it is honestly held, as a term in what it says itself, there is implicit in the religious attitude a profound regard for consistent and honest thinking, as for the proper fulfilment of all other propensities—a matter to which I shall return.

To go back to the question of dogma, it is a consequence of the reduction of religious inspiration to the empty husks of dogma, that the latter, not being able in the least to convince on their own behalf, require the support of an appeal to authority; and this, as hardly needs to be emphasised here, is a source of many evils of which there are abundant examples to-day; and it is also in itself an inherently evil suspension of the free play of the human mind. There is of course a place for authority in matters of thought, but only in a secondary way which requires to be based, in the first place, on individual insight. But that is not how dogma perpetuates itself, but by making authority the final court of appeal. And among the ill-consequences of this is that the question of revelation itself is not properly raised. For this reason, among others, there has been little effective discussion of it in the past. An appeal to authority silences questions and comparisons, and those who enjoy a privileged position as custodians of truth, whatever that position may be, are hardly likely to give real encouragement to an investigation which, whatever its findings, is by its very nature not likely to enhance their prestige, but rather to reduce it.

Nor is this a matter of the past, or of some particular religious tradition. It is common to Protestant and Catholic alike, and if anyone cares to consult the volume entitled *Revelation*,[1] in which leading representatives of various Christian bodies throughout the world offered a carefully considered statement of their views, he will find that at some point or other, sometimes in more, sometimes in less, subtle forms, the issue is made to turn finally on some kind of appeal to authority, the most vicious and essentially irreverent example being, not the highly objectionable prevarications about the nature of the Church as, at one and the same time, a determinate body and a vague community of all believers, but the erection of some blind esoteric acceptance of Christ, as in fact the guarantor of accepted dogma, into the basic principle of Christian faith. Even where reliance on dogma is most condemned, it is often dominant in these subtle ways.

But an even more vicious consequence of the conversion of significant symbol into the dead letter of dogma, is that religious truth is so abstracted from all other processes of thought and experience, and is made to involve, not some supersession, but a direct violation of their own principles in their own spheres, that these processes are themselves thereby brought into condemnation. This is carried out with ruthless consistency by Barth in the denunciation of all finite thought and endeavour. But there are few theologians who can dissociate

[1] Edited by John Baillie.

themselves altogether from the notion that human thought and action are, by the very fact of being human, essentially tainted.

This is not the place to expose all the glaring confusions in the doctrine of essential human corruption, or to show how crude, and how vicious in its effect, is the notion of collective guilt which it usually involves. I have tried to do that elsewhere, and will only repeat here that few ideas seem to me to have been as productive of evil consequences, recently as in remote times, as the traditional doctrine of the Fall. But not the least of the counts against it is the obstruction it has caused to genuine thought about revelation, for it has induced men to be content with saying that the reason why we cannot see God and His truth is simply our sinfulness. Almost the whole of what has been traditionally thought about the crucial question of revelation (but I speak mainly of Christian thought) has been distorted and blunted by association with it in this way of mistaken ethical ideas. The problem of revelation becomes thus essentially the problem of the cure of sin. And this obscures the fact that, however closely moral considerations bear on the question of revelation—and that they bear on it very closely, but not in the way traditionally thought, is my own firm conviction too—none the less there is a quite distinct epistemological and metaphysical problem of the mode of revelation itself and its possibility. The problem has been largely by-passed through preoccupation with specious ethical and quasi-ethical notions; and this has been to the detriment, especially in days of enlightenment, not only of specialised religious thought, but also of the general life of religion. For in the absence of unstultified thought about revelation, the claims of religion are apt to present themselves in terms to which men can attach no importance and which they will often, and rightly, deem preposterous and without basis in any experience they recognise.

I must here add a word (but obviously very briefly at this stage), from my own point of view, about the relation of ethics to revelation. It is widely accepted that progress in religion consists of the greater moralisation of religion, and although this should not, in my estimation, be regarded as an exhaustive account, there seems to be little doubt that it is substantially sound. But in that case it seems to be a further merit of the view advanced in this address that it leads to precisely that expectation. Stress has been placed on the close relation between the peculiar awareness of a reality not ourselves in religion and other processes of thought and action. The uniqueness of religious truth has not been understood, as seems commonly to happen, in terms of complete isolation from other experiences, but quite the reverse of this, as embodied in them. The more we attain it therefore, and also in proportion to its fineness, the more should we also expect, in the absence of some incidental complicating factor, an improvement in the tone of experience as a whole. And as it is a peculiarity of religious truth to deepen especially the sense of reality as other than ourselves, it ought to make us especially aware of the moral demands in which that which, in finite experience, is most distinctively not ourselves confronts us most unmistakably and sharply, and so thus also to refine our perception of those demands. A deepening of religious insight is thus also a refinement of moral sensibility; and where there is little evidence of tender conscience, the claim to much spirituality is therefore immediately suspect—which is in fact precisely how we react in practice.

But there is more yet; for the relation is twofold. It is in moral experience most of all that revelation is formed. This has sometimes been understood in terms of arguments from ethics to religion. But I doubt very much whether arguments of this kind succeed or count a great deal in religion. There is something else, however, and that of the very greatest importance for religion, namely the way it is possible for moral experience to pass beyond itself and to be thus transmuted into something —shall we call it holiness?—which is most like art although not the same, and is articulate as art is articulate. This is more pervasive than art, and does not depend in the same way on special aptitudes. But I know not how it can be described except in terms of its resemblance to art, a resemblance which is in some ways paralleled when scientific perceptiveness, as sometimes happens, and especially in mathematics, arranges itself into something quite different and becomes art—a phenomenon which has often led to gross obliteration of the quite fundamental difference between science and art. It is in this transmutation of our deepest and clearest moral experiences (including, of course, contemplation of goodness in others) that we have the most unmistakable sense of communication to us from a sphere which is otherwise shut to our minds, and of a Presence which is as infinitely near as it is disturbingly remote. And this, most of all, is why the corruption of the moral life and its distortion—especially in religion itself—is the gravest threat to religion.

I may be asked 'Why should science be left so completely out of account? Has it not also its splendours and visions, have not men of science been moved by their science to a profound sense of the beauty and majesty of God? Is not God especially present to them in creation?' I answer, yes, but in two ways; firstly because the richer and more comprehensive our thought, the more are we also aware of its limitations, and thus have our minds directed to a transcendent reality. But as already observed, the illumination of the scientific mind may also convert itself into poetry without change of substance (as a drawing may be seen as a staircase or as a cornice), and in the same way the 'religion of science' is science, by a rare alchemy, reducing its abstractions to particularity in a sense of the holy.

But this cannot happen without constant renewal of vision by contact with other modes of religious insight. Otherwise it will become a fashion and pretentiousness. And this brings me to a point I would particularly like to stress, in coming to a close, namely that, if our view of religious experience is sound, religion stands in pre-eminent need of being continually renewed and given fresh forms. This does not mean that the past can be ignored. It could not be ignored in art either, the parallel being again much in point. Tradition and novelty are the twin terms of the perennial problem in both spheres. And, just as it has been wisely said by many of late that ethics loses its power because its conceptions are dulled by reiteration and association with stale situations, so also we must insist that there is need, even more persistently and urgently, to recreate the religious vision and renew the life of religion in its most relevant contemporary applications, conserving the old only in the new life of the present—never in the letter for letter's sake.

This, and the other conclusions to which we have been led, have a close bearing also on further aspects of contemporary thought and culture—on the much discussed question of the nature and scope of philosophy, for example; for may not much that is suspect to-day in traditional philosophy be given its place in the light of a sound view of symbolic truth? We seem also to be brought very much into line with the contemporary protest against the abstractness of modern culture. This protest seems to me well-founded and important, however ill-considered the form in which it is sometimes made, and however irresponsible and pretentious it may be in some forms of existentialism. The pulsating expressive flow of living reality must be redeemed. And if a historical allusion be allowable at this stage, this, it seems to me, is what we sense especially if we ponder, as, I suggest, we ought to ponder very carefully to-day, the corrective to his own abstractions and his misconceptions of art which Plato glimpsed in his all too occasional accounts of δύναμις, a power engendered in the interaction of mind and things. Had this notion been given more prominence by Plato, and thereby in subsequent speculation, the course of thought, throughout the ages, and of history as affected by thought, might have been vastly different. There are signs to-day that, in some curious ways at least, and in the exigencies of the present crisis of culture, this notion is beginning at last to come to its own. And with it, among other boons, will come a better understanding of religion.

Chapter X

ON POETIC TRUTH[1]

> Reason has moons, but moons not hers
> Lie mirror'd on her sea,
> Confounding her astronomers
> But, O! delighting me.
> RALPH HODGSON.

I

POETRY has to do with reality in its most individual aspect. It is thus at the opposite pole to science, and out of its reach. Studies like *The Road to Xanadu*,[2] highly valuable though they may be in one way, do not help us in any measure to understand what poetry in itself is; nor do they heighten substantially our appreciation of poetry. This may seem rather obvious, but it is not in fact idle to say it. For our thought is apt to be unduly coloured to-day by the progress of science, and some of the votaries of science are prone to regard it, in the Biblical phrase, as 'profitable unto all things'. These are less naïve to-day than their prototypes a century ago, and they have a subtler psychology at their disposal when they turn to art. But their view is no less pernicious for that reason. Science has very certain limits, and we only bring it into contempt by forcing upon it a forlorn and unnatural enterprise beyond its own terrain. Some scientists, and they include eminent persons like Julian Huxley, have made that mistake in regard to our ideas of right and wrong, and have endeavoured to develop a science of ethics. It is not to the purpose here to expose the confusions involved in this particular act of aggression on the part of science.[3] Science has nothing to do, in the final analysis, with our ideas of right and wrong. And it is also true, quite apart from ultimate questions about the meaning of value, that

[1] A lecture delivered to the Poetry Society at University College, Bangor, and published in *Philosophy*, July 1946.
[2] A detailed study of Coleridge's *Kubla Khan* in terms of the poet's experience and reading—J. Livingstone Lowes.
[3] The matter is very fully discussed by C. D. Broad in *Mind*, October 1944, pp. 344-367.

we cannot give a scientific analysis of art. Science may indeed help us to understand matters incidental to the pursuit of artistic activities. Harmonics will tell us a great deal that bears upon music, the chemist can instruct us in useful ways about paints, the psychologist can tell us much that is of interest about the mental processes and states of the artist and his audience, but the essential thing which is music or painting can never be taught or described in this way. In its essentials every art is as far removed from discursive thinking, and as far out of the reach of analysis and rules, as it is possible for any experience of self-conscious subjects to be.

This is because art has to do with reality as individual and concrete. That is not all that we can say about it. An isolated fact, a unit or atom, cut loose from the universe, has no significance for the scientist, the philosopher, or the poet. It derives its significance from the reality to which it belongs. But this may present itself to us in more ways than one. One way is that of the scientist. The table before me will have little significance for any of us if we simply stare at it. Indeed, I could not be aware of it as a table if I did not do a great deal besides looking at the colour. To see things in their true perspective, for example, we require to draw very extensively upon experiences that are past. All that we see and hear is given a meaning in this way and becomes a coherent world in which we can act with intelligence and foresight although the actual elements of which it is made, taken in separation from one another, would leave us with a chaos rather than a world of things which we understand and control. It is the function of science to complete this interpretation of facts, both for the sake of completer knowledge in and for itself and to enhance the control we have to exercise over our environment. The scientist can tell me much about the table which I cannot know from ordinary observation. But however exhaustive information of this kind may be there is something which it does not cover, and that is the particularity of this table here and now in this room. The table cannot be reduced, as has sometimes been supposed, into a collection of universal qualities. There is something 'given', a matter of fact, particulars, irreducible data with which explanation ends. This is apt to disconcert us because it sets so definite a limit to the strictly rational operations of the intellect. And some have succumbed to the temptation of representing the reality of various things in terms of their relation to other things and the rules which determine these relations, reducing an object to what we know about it and can describe. One celebrated thinker of the last century, namely T. H. Green, regarded the universe as a 'system of all-inclusive relations'. But this will not really do. The particular, the given, refuses to be conjured away. It remains a stubborn, disconcerting factor of experience.

This is not the only reason for the limitations of science. For the nearer we get to *living* realities the harder it is to attain scientific precision. An organism seems to respond as a whole and thereby reacts on its environment in a way which cannot be described by mechanistic rules. Its own nature enters more completely into the events of its own life, and this self-determination, the taking up of our environment into ourselves, is very extensive in the experience of self-conscious or thinking beings. This is one reason why there cannot strictly speaking be a science of society, and why it is misleading to describe psychology as a mental science. But the point that has most importance for our purpose is that there is in reality, whether we think of it as inanimate or animate, human or sub-human, an aspect of individuality at which every form of rational explanation stops short.

II

What has this to do with poetry? I shall come to that shortly. I want first to take note of one thinker, in some respects the greatest there has been, who took a very bold course with this problem of the individual. He was Plato. For Plato the only reality that mattered is exemplified best for us in the principles of mathematics. The aim of our lives should be to draw ourselves away as much as possible from the unsubstantial fluctuating facts of the world about us, and establish some communion with the abiding or 'eternal' objects which are apprehended by thought and not sense. This was the source of Plato's asceticism. We must so discipline our material appetites that the soul may disentangle itself from the world of the senses and rise, in his own notable comparison,[1] like the God Glaucus out of the sea, into the realm of limpid unresisting abstractions, unresisting in the sense that the mind can master them and master completely, understand without remainder. This is not a venture in which we can ever be wholly successful, not only in the present world where we can never shuffle off our mortal coil, but under any conditions. For the grip by which abstract conceptions cohere and by which our thought is enabled to pass from one truth to the other, as in a system of geometry, presupposes some principle which cannot be itself explained in that way, and whose nature can only be discerned by a noesis, a glimpse or intuition. But this supreme vision is a vision of some condition of abstract principles,[2] and it comes as the culmination of a long and arduous struggle to break our association with the world of the senses and accustom ourselves to abstract thought, the 'silent communion of the soul with itself'. In that rarefied atmosphere, we come to our own, we encounter what is most 'familiar' in the sense that it is akin to our minds, and we are thus no longer at the mercy of the alien unmanageable facts which enslave and bewilder the majority of men. This striking, if, as it may also appear when presented without equivocation, rather extravagant view, has many features which cannot be properly exhibited in a brief reference; its ramifications in the spheres of politics, education and religion, are very extensive. But it must suffice here to note the dismissal of the individual and particular facts of experience as of no importance in themselves. At best they can serve as counters or diagrams by which we direct our thought about the objects of the discursive intelligence, much as the triangle we draw on paper helps us to discover and explain geometrical truths about the triangle 'in itself'. This was carried by Plato to the point of disregarding the observations by which scientific hypotheses are substantiated in various fields; and thus, although he can be quoted for the view that leaders of society require an extensive training in science, this has to be understood in a highly specialised sense which would hardly win the approval of the scientist to-day.

[1] *Republic*, 611.
[2] It makes little difference here that they are also thought of as entities or things.

For, while the latter may, as in the case of Adams and Leverrier, 'calculate a planet into existence', the calculation is the result of careful observation. Whitehead is the thinker of to-day who holds a position most nearly resembling that of Plato, and I do not think that calculation will quite yield the results he expects, however important it may be as a factor in scientific procedure. An astronomer would not get very far with the counsel that Plato gives him in the following passage:

"These ornaments of the heavens, since they adorn a visible sky, should be thought to be the most beautiful and to have the most perfect nature amongst visible things, but to fall far short of those true adornments, those movements wherewith pure velocity and pure retardation, in true number and in all true figures, are moved in relation to each other, and wherewith they also move that which is within them, which matters are to be apprehended by reason and understanding, but not by sight ... Then we must use the adornments of heaven as models in our study ... But in respect to the relations of night and day, of days and months, and months and years, and of the other stars to sun and moon and to each other, do you not think that he (the philosopher) will regard with astonishment the man who considers that these objects, bodily and visible as they are, are ever invariable and never decline from their courses, and will think it absurd to make enormous efforts to apprehend the truth of these matters? ... Astronomy, then, like geometry, we shall pursue by the help of problems, and leave the starry heavens alone; if we hope truly to apprehend it, and turn the natural intelligence of the soul from uselessness to use."[1]

[1] *Republic* 529, Lindsay's translation, Everyman Edition, p. 255. The student who is introduced to the *Republic* mainly through Nettleship's *Lectures on the Republic of Plato*—a work that is little likely to lose its value for the purpose—is apt to be misled at this point. For Nettleship represents Plato as merely insisting on the need for an "interpretation of sense" (p. 276). On this view all that Plato wishes to deny is that "we ever get at the truth of astronomy by simply looking" (page 272). But this is only one of many cases where exponents of Plato have endeavoured to make his view more acceptable by representing him as exaggerating for effect. If we blur the dualism of Plato we miss his intention entirely and fail to appreciate the precise nature, and the importance for Plato, of logical considerations upon which his view was based quite as much as upon the analysis of perception. The more we study the movement of Plato's thought

This shows very clearly the extent to which Plato was prepared to go in dispensing with any observation of facts. While the scientist to-day is concerned with particular facts or 'specimens' only in so far as they exhibit or confirm his general rule, the rule can only be established by its conformity with facts. This is largely what the scientist has in mind when he prides himself on thinking realistically. But Plato would describe himself as a realist in a very different sense, namely in the sense that it is by breaking away from the world of facts that we make genuine contact with reality.

The bearing of this on our problem will begin to unfold itself if we note next the sweeping condemnation of the arts, and of poetry in particular, which we find in the dialogues of Plato. For this is not some wholly mysterious aberration of a man of genius, a cultural blind spot not capable of explanation in a normal way. It is sustained and deliberate, an integral part of the thinking of one whose ideas were never allowed to settle in stagnant pools. There are no compartments in Plato's philosophy; on the contrary his thought was unified to a fault. Neither could we ascribe his view of the arts to aesthetic insensibility. That is the least plausible of all suggestions. For the literary excellence of Plato himself is as notable as his power of thought. He was born into a civilisation that accorded to the poet a pride of place in education and culture. Homer and Hesiod were especially revered, they were the scriptures, the holy writ, by which the character and outlook of the young Athenian were shaped. They were taught with a remarkable thoroughness which does not seem to have detracted at all from the enjoyment they continued to afford, an achievement which would repay closer attention, I am sure, by the educationist to-day, for its secret, if it can be discovered,[1] will take him a long way towards the solution of what may well be regarded as the greatest intrinsic problem in education. And Plato, being favoured by fortune in his circumstances as in his

---

as a whole the more evident also will be the completer rationalism of his final views. Nettleship, as is usual with idealist expounders of great philosophers, is somewhat prone to interpret Plato in the light of his own idealism.

[1] We have to remember, of course, that there was little else for the Greek to be educated upon.

natural endowment, had the full benefit of this training. He knew the poets of Greece, and their spell is unmistakably upon him in all his writings. Ridicule does not prevail against it; it is more subtle than the 'slyness' of Socrates, and makes itself evident in the very tone and temper of the passages most critical of art, to say nothing of the apt and discriminating quotations in which the dialogues abound. The artistry of Plato himself will be equally evident to the most cursory reader. In range of literary power alone his peers are not many. The skilful opening, capturing attention while it lightly touches on the matters that set the main course of the dialogue, the play of light and shade, the delineation of a character by a few deft strokes, the apt word and the trenchant sentence, the memorable simile and the sheer triumph of imaginative writing in myth and allegory, this, and much else, and, above all perhaps, the impression that is always conveyed of a master who is never overborne himself by his art, this reveals that fullness of literary genius by which the very structure of literature itself is fashioned. No praise seems too extravagant for Plato the literary artist, and yet it is he who would expurgate Homer out of recognition, who would forbid all music except the very simplest notes on the lyre and pipe, who instructs aspiring young men to cast aside poetry and painting, with other childish things, on reaching maturity, who rates the poet well below the statesman and the soldier[1] and not very far from the usurper and tyrant enslaved by his own thoughts and passions as well as by his bodyguard. It is he, at the close of his *Republic,* who adds the final touch to the ideal city which he has built with such cunning and care by firmly, all the more firmly because also a little wistfully, turning the poets away as ones with no part whatever in drawing the 'pattern that is laid up in heaven'.

"Let it, then, be our defence now that we have recurred to the subject of poetry, that it was only to be expected that we should expel poetry from the city, such being her nature. The argument compelled us. And let us tell her also, in case she should accuse us of brutality and boorishness, that there is an ancient quarrel between philosophy and poetry. Phrases like 'the bitch that at her master yelps', 'the yelping hound that in

[1] *Phaedrus* 248.

assemblies of the fools exalts its head', 'the conquering rabble of the over-wise', the statement that 'the men of subtle thought are beggars all', and many others are signs of this ancient antagonism . . . We are conscious of the charm she exercises upon us. Only to betray the truth as it appears to us is impious . . . As men who have loved but have come to the conclusion that their love is unprofitable, though it may cost a struggle yet turn away; so likewise, though by reason of the love for such poetry that our nurture in beautiful constitutions has bred in us we shall be glad of any manifestation of her goodness and truth, yet until she is able to defend herself, we will not listen to her without repeating to ourselves as a charm this argument of ours and this incantation, for fear of falling again into that childish love which is still shared by the many".[1]

So the poets leave. Was there ever a problem that could perplex more the student of literature, has the paradox a rival in the history of great thinking? I doubt it, and I doubt even more whether there is any more instructive.

III

Instructive? Now why? Let us first dispose of some fairly incidental matters to which undue weight has often been attached. Firstly, as I have said, the Greeks took their poets very seriously, and not altogether with the right kind of seriousness. The poet was, for them, inspired, not in the sense we would nowadays give to the term, but more in the sense in which devout persons used to believe in the literal inspiration of the Bible. God spoke in the words of the poets as He spoke to the Hebrew by the mouth of His prophets. And this has obvious dangers, for it carries with it a conviction of very immediate, if not of literal, infallibility, an attitude that could not fail to be confusing, and sometimes also ludicrous and mischievous in practice. And this was undoubtedly happening in a real and serious measure in Greece. Plato was aware of the danger. He also understood well the moral and political dangers that lurked in the excessive excitability of the Greek temperament. There are many passages in the dialogues which represent the poet as the purveyor of excitement, as one who was made to pander to

[1] *Republic*, 607-608, Everyman Edition, p. 353.

a licentious and enervating emotionalism. And when we remember this we may be tempted to conclude, as many have in fact done,[1] that Plato was opposing, in somewhat extravagant and misleading fashion, not poetry in itself but a particularly misguided view of the function of poetry. That will not, I think, really hold. When we have made the fullest allowances for the circumstances in which he wrote, including the deliberate use of poetry for mystification by the sophists, the condemnation of poetry in the *Republic* and other dialogues remains far too consistent and direct to be a kind of inverted defence of poetry, or a case of exaggerating for effect. This matter would take long to debate thoroughly, and many pens have, in fact, been kept busy upon it, but I have little doubt that Plato really and consistently considered poetry and all other forms of fine art to be debasing and mischievous, an excuse for shallow sensibility, the

[1] Among the most interesting and scholarly attempts to substantiate this view is that of R. G. Collingwood ("Plato's Philosophy of Art," *Mind*, April 1925). He does not ascribe to Plato "the puritanical moralist's objection to art as such" (p. 169). The purpose of Plato, according to Collingwood, is to show, on the one hand, "that art is not knowledge" and "cannot be praised for its truth", but that, on the other, it is "symbolic of philosophical truth" (p. 163). Plato, it is urged, is in this way bringing out the true function of art. And that is where I cannot accept Collingwood's view. For while it is contended in the present paper (see below, Section IV), that art does express truth symbolically, what it does symbolise, on our view, is an aspect of reality other than that which can be comprehended intellectually. (Is not this the most distinctive form of symbolism?) On the view that is, rightly I believe, ascribed to Plato by Collingwood, art would have only very low value. It would do imperfectly what is done better by the strictly intellectual operations of mind. And this, as I take it, is just what Plato does say. Art is a propaedeutic to knowledge; and it is to be encouraged only within the strictest limits and dispensed with on reaching intellectual maturity. One finds it hard to see how this could yield the conclusion that Collingwood expects of it, namely that the quarrel between philosophy and poetry is that of "rivals for the supreme allegiance of mankind" (p. 170). It may be true that Plato "felt within himself a real conflict between the claims of his literary genius and those of his philosophical" (p. 170), but that is not how he himself understood the incompatibility of art and philosophy. The quarrel originates precisely where art makes a claim, quite preposterous on Plato's view of it, to be a serious rival to philosophy for our allegiance, and hinders the work of philosophy. The very tone of the relevant passages in the *Republic* fully bears this out, and I am sure we cannot get a true view of Plato's thought as a whole unless we take his condemnation of poetry and the arts quite seriously.

The student who wishes to pursue this matter closely will find a valuable guide to the relevant passages of Plato's dialogues in "Plato and the Poets", G. A. Hight, *Mind*, 1922.

nostalgic indulgence of an effete and unhealthy mind. And this attitude is, I think, integral to the philosophy of Plato, his genius compelled him to carry his point unswervingly to a conclusion so little respectable (much less so, for example, to the Greek than the communism of wives and property) that a lesser mind would certainly have cast about for a means to avoid it. It was the penalty of genius to pay the price of a principle without remission. I suspect it cost Plato more than we think. In that case the deeper are we in his debt; we learn so much more from him because he could not prevaricate.

What do we learn? Just this; that poetry has to do with reality in that concrete and individual aspect of it which the mind can never tackle altogether on its own terms, with matter that is foreign and alien in a way in which abstract systems, ideas in which we detect an inherent pattern, a structure that belongs to the ideas themselves, can never be. It is never familiar to us in the way in which Plato wished the conquests of the mind to be familiar. On the contrary its function, the salve which it brings to mankind, the need which it meets and which has to be met in some way in every age that is not to become decadent or barbarous is precisely this contact with reality as it impinges upon us from outside, the sense that we can touch and feel a solid reality which does not wholly dissolve itself into the conceptions of our own minds. It is the individual and particular that does this. And the wonder and mystery of art, as indeed of religion in the last resort, is the revelation of something 'wholly other' by which the inexpressible loneliness of thinking is broken and enriched. To know facts as facts in the ordinary way has, indeed, no particular power or worth. But a quickening of our awareness of the irrevocability by which a thing is what it is, has such power, and it is, I believe, the very soul of art. Whatever the device adopted its purpose is to make us see things as we have never seen them before, see the familiar for the first time; and thus there are no exclusively poetical or artistic subjects, anything may be a proper subject for a poem or a painting or a song. This has often been urged, but rarely, I fear, for the real reason; at best it is usually a vague empirical generalisation. But the real reason is just this, that any device which makes us see any kind of object, in the material or mental sphere, with a sense of wonder that it should be this and not that, is an artistic achievement.[1] This is why we use the word creation. All things are made new in art, they are made for the first time, they count for their own sake instead of being pointers by which we move about in our own orbit. This may refer to a specific object that we know or to an imaginary one. The choice is at bottom immaterial. What matters is that the sense of some otherness in reality should be stirred. But this is obviously easier when our attention is turned to the unfamiliar, to events in a remote past, to fairyland and eldorado. It is the same awareness that we have when there is a sudden fall of soft snow. There is a feeling of wonder, an inexpressible delight in being alive when we first turn out into the new snow. The sense of the unfamiliar is not, I believe, all that we can say about beauty in nature or in art. To that I shall turn again in a moment. But it is essential. The light in a picture must be the 'light that never was on land or sea', for it must make us see what we could not normally see, not necessarily, or indeed usually, by superimposing something on the ordinary sense, but by making us aware of the familiar as we are not normally aware. There must be a miracle. Whereas we were blind we now see, and the miracle is greatest although not always in its ultimate consequence the most sublime, when it evokes this new awareness in an ordinary context—so much so as almost to frighten us.

But no fact is a bare fact, no individual is a universe in itself, and just as it is the function of the scientist to exhibit to us the abstract rational connection of things, the necessities which our mind can follow and understand, so the artist exhibits affinities in the *actual* structure of objects by which their significance is deepened and enhanced. All facts have 'ragged edges', as one great man put it. They are torn out of some context, and these contexts are not wholly those which science or philosophy supplies. There is a possibility of seeing things, even the humdrum and trivial, in a way that goes surety for the supreme worth of the whole from which they derive, and there

[1] I believe that this is what Gerard Manley Hopkins really means by "inscape" notwithstanding the Platonism that colours his account of it. For an excellent discussion of the topic see *Gerard Manley Hopkins*—John Pick.

are relations of things, harmonies, in which this worth of the whole articulates itself with greater completeness. But we have to be careful here, for we must not lose sight of the fact that every individual reality is potentially poetry. How this is related to the harmonies to which a completer significance belongs is not easy to determine, although I am certain that there is such a relation. Neither is it possible to add much about the fuller significance which belongs to some artistic contexts,[1] and which makes it proper to speak of suitable poetic themes provided we are careful to identify such themes with a special kind of context and not with any kind of fact as we ordinarily know it. Even if it promised to be fruitful, and I doubt it, we could not embark on this further inquiry in the space at our disposal. What I desire to stress is that there is a unity rooted in the individuality of objects and discovered in a different way from the apprehension of rational connections.[2] The 'idealist' philosophers in the last century provided a good way of denoting this when they spoke of a 'concrete universal', but they failed to do the fullest justice to this important conception, for they continued to think of the unity concerned as a rational one, and capable, in principle, of being understood through and through. They did not relate it sufficiently to the awareness we have of a reality impinging upon us, although some who were of that 'idealist' persuasion had the awareness of this character of reality in no small measure.

IV

To reveal this otherness of reality and the context in which it matters most is the function of the artist. The result is not achieved in any way resembling the deliberate procedures of science. For the artist is dealing with matter that he never subdues. There are no directions to be given, no rules or formulae by which his real work can be done. Some study of technique is, indeed, possible. We can distinguish the different forms of art, and within an art such as poetry distinguish one

---

[1] The general question of the objectivity of value does not come within the scope of this paper.

[2] If I understand aright this is what Berdyaev means when he urges that "Unity in reality does not resemble unity in thought" (*Slavery and Freedom*, p. 75).

mode from the other. This is also normally helpful to the poet, especially by making him familiar with certain forms or media upon which his genius may exercise itself. But knowledge of this kind will never take him very far, or ensure for the reader much appreciation of poetry. We may know all *about* poetry and miss its essence. It is much more important that the poet should familiarise himself with what has been finely achieved in art, concerning himself with such factual matters as are required to know the media for what they are. But the trick must work or, if you like, the miracle must be accomplished, in a way that cannot be described or anticipated, and it sometimes happens where there is very little technical equipment or analytical knowledge of technique. The artist hits on the right symbol, some way of arranging colours or sounds or words in a way that makes the real nature of the world break upon our mind. And this is what we mean when we say that art is essentially symbolic. It does not describe or analyse, and it has no method in the strict sense. Method only concerns the incidentals of it, some exhibition of conditions in which the miracle usually happens. But the conditions are never exhaustive, they will never give us the result themselves. We must walk in ways that are haunted by beauty, and we may be lucky, but it is luck, or, if a more dignified term be preferred, grace. Vision is vouchsafed to us, and while we can say, within some limits, when it may happen, we cannot say why. A certain kind of diligence will help, in particular, as was remarked, the continuous attention to what has been finely achieved in art. We must continue to look at pictures or to read poems, until we see with ever finer perception how excellent they are. But why they should be so we can never say, the most that we can describe, as distinct from just having the awareness of beauty, is certain regularities that are really incidental to artistic awareness itself. What can be described or explained is not art.

This is why an artist who sets out to compose with a very clear notion of what his achievement is to be and how it can be accomplished, whose heart is not constantly a-flutter with the fear of failure, stands little chance of success. A true poet or a novelist may indeed know much about the incidentals of the course he proposes to follow, but unless there is ample room for him to take himself by surprise the prospects are bleak. What his art will be really and truly as art he cannot know until it is accomplished. In some rare matters it may even be accomplished before he turns to the technicalities, but that will only be in a very specialised sense. The technicalities in that case will be the equivalent of the treatment a craftsman may give to a work of art, making the materials serve more completely the purpose which the artist has already indicated with precision. In any sense in which it is a part of the artistic achievement the material has to be chosen and formed with renewed artistic insight at every stage. That is why the experience of artists is often unutterably tragic. For 'tasks in hours of insight willed' cannot here be 'in hours of gloom fulfilled'. And this is but to say again that the artist is not to be saved by 'works', even by that very special kind of artistic perseverance, namely living in the atmosphere of great art, which is usually helpful. In all essentials it is *sola gratia*—as in religion if the matter be properly understood, which is very rare among theologians. And the mistake which many men of genius have made is to seek to direct and canalise their art in a way that is wholly incompatible with its continued spontaneity. The artist can only succeed so long as he continues to be hitting on novelties which quicken an awareness of some otherness in reality that we cannot express in the ordinary conventions of language, that cannot, indeed, be expressed at all in the usual sense, but only suggested.

An obvious form which suggestion of this kind takes is direct comparison, in the simile, or image. What we see is seen more vividly in relation to something else, something like it but also different. Consider a line from one of the much maligned Georgian poets:

"And when the downy twilight droops her wing".[1]

The comparison deepens the impression of a slowly enfolding darkness which the poet is anxious to convey. Personification has a similar effect. These are fairly obvious examples of a procedure which in all its forms consists in drawing some kind of comparison, exhibiting affinities by which objects become

[1] *Brumana*, James Elroy Flecker.

vivid for us and acquire a significance which cannot be reduced to rational terms.

The moral of this view for the artist himself has already been drawn. He goes sadly astray if his artistic activities are made to conform to some purpose or rule independently conceived. The temptation to rationalise art in this way is greatest in literature, where, as in the case of didactic poems, principles that are deemed to have much importance in themselves, especially in the sphere of morals or politics or religion, are thought to acquire a further lustre by having an artistic form imposed upon them. But that, in fact, is precisely what we cannot accomplish. An idea has no importance for the artist as such outside his work of art. It does not bring any capital of its own to invest in an artistic undertaking. The soundness or impressiveness of the ideas expressed in a poem is irrelevant to its merit. But that is not, perhaps the best way of putting the matter. The truth is that the rough distinction we make for some purposes beween form and content in art is apt to be more misleading than helpful.[1] The unity of artistic creation precludes any separation of its elements. What the poet has to say, in other words, is not what he seems to say on the surface, not the meaning we might give to his work if we considered it as philosophy or science. It is the expression of this meaning in a special way, a fusion of form and matter suggesting something which could not be put in any other way. This constitutes the truth of a poem, poetry is in this sense invariably veridical; 'Truth is beauty and beauty is truth'; where we have a work of art it is a revelation of reality. But this gives no grounds for

[1] It is also very misleading to identify the form with the sounds of the words alone. Artistic relations of sounds that do not depend in any measure on overt meaning are music and not poetry. There is some early poetry which has no syntactical form that we can recognise to-day. If it has no such form it must come very near being music rather than poetry. In some poetry, on the other hand, overt meaning plays much the most important part. Browning provides an obvious example, but it has to be stressed again that Browning succeeds as a poet, not because of the truth or impressiveness of his thoughts in themselves, but because—to draw a distinction that must not be pressed too closely—he is doing with thoughts what Tennyson does with words. Whether there can be poetry of thought alone, a bringing together of thoughts that stirs the peculiar awareness which is art independently of the sounds of words, is an interesting but extremely difficult question.

concluding that a poem expresses ideas which are independently true. That is not its purpose. And when poets have been so false to their genius as to endeavour to be philosophers and poets at the same time they have invariably failed, as they were bound to do.[1] The poet works by a discernment of his own, not by deliberate analysis and synthesis. When he borrows philosophical ideas, and there have been some instances of a successful appropriation of this kind, these ideas are important for the poem only in so far as they have been transmuted by the poet's art and become elements in a whole that expresses symbolically something quite other than the ideas themselves. This happens very rarely, for close adherence to the unity of the philosophical principle or system predetermines the course of the poem too rigidly to allow sufficient spontaneity for the evolving of an independent artistic pattern. Dante seems to have succeeded, even to the extent of presenting an argument in poetry. But it is not the argument in itself that matters in such poems; neither its lucidity in itself nor the importance of the conclusion established by it, are of the slightest account. It has value in the poem only as indissolubly a part of a whole whose value is quite independent of formal or theoretical truth. As Eliot very properly observes, the fact that Dante has behind him the 'exact intellectual system' of Aquinas for which, we may record, Eliot has a special regard, does not make Dante a greater poet than Shakespeare or "mean that we can learn more from Dante than Shakespeare".[2] The most that we can say, and I believe Eliot ought to emphasise this more, is that the artistic sensibility of Dante is all the more remarkable in view of his dealing successfully with material so full of inducement to him to turn from his proper business.

V

The long course of literary activity is strewn with the wreckages of artists lured to their doom by the siren songs of intellectual truth. But this is not the only moral of our view.

Let it be clear, firstly, that it is not the poets themselves that

---

[1] The supreme example in recent times is Bridges in the *Testament of Beauty*.

[2] "Shakespeare and the Stoicism of Seneca", *Elizabethan Essays*, p. 47.

stand in most need of our warning. We must ourselves be sure that we allow the poet to be about his own business. Consider the lines:

> From too much love of living,
> From hope and fear set free,
> We thank with brief thanksgiving
> Whatever gods may be
> That no life lives for ever;
> That dead men rise up never;
> That even the weariest river
> Winds somewhere safe to sea.

This is from Swinburne's *The Garden of Proserpine*, a poem in which Swinburne appears to good advantage. Swinburne is a little out of fashion at the moment, but I have no doubt that he will recover his position, if not in the first rank of English poets, then only a little below it. But most of us would be little inclined to endorse the view that these lines appear to express. Similarly the poem *Hymn to Proserpine* with the sub-title *Vicisti Galilæe*, a remarkable poem little known nowadays, I fear, for anything other than its titles and a famous line, might seem to have little to commend it to a Christian. Is it not a complete distortion of religious truth? But questions of this kind only arise on a very superficial view. The poet is not advancing a theory or rational belief. He is enabling us to see something which we could not otherwise see. And the meaning of the poem as a poem is very different from what it may seem, on the face of it, to tell us. As such it cannot lead us astray. It can only seem to do so if we seek to distil the meaning out of the poem to be judged by ordinary canons of truth. What was said could only be said as the poet has said it.

Incidentally if we consider the matter closely, if we let ourselves come sufficiently under the spell of their poems to read them aright, we are certain to be struck by the affinity between the apparent paganism of a Swinburne or a Housman or an Omar and the infinite yearning that is found in notable hymns and other great religious poems. This will in turn incline us to take a more cautious view of the contempt of earthly things which we may also encounter in religious poetry and prose.

Hymns have often been subjected to foolish and undiscerning comment by those who do not understand what a hymn tries to be.

Unless these matters be borne in mind we shall be in danger of falling into much sophistication that will seriously affect our taste, and which, if we were to carry it out with consistency, as Plato did, would lead to such drastic pruning of our literature that little would survive.

The extraction of a meaning from a poem and appraisement of it by rational standards of truth has mainly been due to enthusiasm for moral or religious truth. But that is not usual to-day. Politics is our culprit, not merely in totalitarian countries where all activities are made to sub-serve a political end but also in democratic countries. Literature of the 'left' in particular is prone to regard conformity with certain social principles as a condition of artistic excellence. The viciousness of this procedure has, however, been obscured for a reason on which our theory has a close bearing. The 'left-winger' is apt to pride himself on being a realist, and realism in the sense that is proper to political thinking has some features in common with the realism which we have found to be the secret of genuine art. This applies especially to the interest in facts as they really are and not as they present themselves under the rosy hues of wishful thinking or distorted by prejudice. Art of the 'left' has thereby been saved from much that is dilettante and artificial. But the gain is won at far too great a cost if it perpetuates the substitution of a spurious realism, spurious, that is, so far as art is concerned, for the integrity that is proper to the artist and the peculiar contact with reality that he can establish. The eventual result will be all the more ruinous to the proper work of the poet.

We have not here, however, the temptation that besets the poet with most subtlety to-day. He is more likely to succumb to the prevalent preoccupation with 'form'. And here it must be said with emphasis that our view in no way minimises the importance of content. It would be fantastic to suggest that the overt meaning, that which we have described as what the poem seems to say, contributes little to the artistic significance and merit of a poem. We merely protest against the abstraction of this content from the whole and appraisement of it by other than aesthetic standards. The 'something said' is important, but it is important for the poem only in so far as the saying of that particular something in a special way is a revelation of reality in the peculiar way we have noted. But it also follows that the form derives its significance from the whole. This is much overlooked to-day among poets and critics alike. And the reason is not hard to discover. So much has been accomplished in the past, so many possibilities have been exhausted, that the need for novelty is both greater and harder to meet. This stimulates experimentation with new forms, and the impression is thereby left that there are poetic forms distinct and complete in themselves and waiting to be discovered, waiting in some dim hinterland until the kindly artist appropriates them. But this is a complete misconception. There are indeed new forms and the future may present us with an astonishing richness of them. But they do not hang on a peg to be reached down like a suit of ready made clothes. Form has no significance except in relation to the reality that is being revealed. Admittedly sounds and colours may be pleasing in themselves, and the association of words may attract in themselves. But this is not beauty and it is not art, even where the sensuous attractiveness is very high as in the case of bright colours.[1] The poet must see what has not been seen before and what cannot be expressed in any other way than by means of the symbols which also make it possible for him to see. There are, therefore, no artistic forms unrelated to new perceptions of reality, and it is idle to strive after new developments in art by pouring old wine into new bottles. The wine must also be new.

Warning may be entered here also against the foolish but prevalent belief that, if art is realistic, it must cling very closely to objects as we normally see them. That is precisely what art cannot do. The genuine artist is never 'true to life', for he is not living normally in moments of artistic creation. He sees what is real, but not as we are normally aware of it. Neither will his feelings be normal, nor those of the characters

[1] It may be objected here that there are good pictures which seem to be nothing but a riot of colours (e.g. some of S. J. Peploe's work). But then the presentation of these colours is deeply significant although they have no obviously recognisable pattern.

whom he may describe. The rages or the sorrows in which he traffics, and the moods by which the *dramatis personæ* of his world are shaken, are not those we normally experience in situations which outwardly resemble those which the artist may portray. Normally, if we are to avoid sentimentality, our feelings, even feelings of deep joy or sorrow, will be subdued. We do not go storming through life like actors in a play. Neither Lear nor Hamlet nor any other great Shakespearean character has a place in real life. But art is never real life. It is life and it is real, supremely real, but it is both these at a new power. The poet sees with a poignancy and penetration that are altogether unique, and that is precisely what Plato failed to grasp when he accused Homer and other poets of ascribing to great men feelings and reactions which we would not, in fact, consider proper in 'real life'.[1] It does not follow that emotion, in so far as its enters into art, must always be exaggerated or distorted. It is irrelevant whether it is so or not. What matters is that the poet must be true to his art and not 'true to life', whether his art be simple or complex, violent or subdued.

This brings us to two further matters. Little has been said in this paper about emotion. But emotion is usually thought to lie at the centre of aesthetic experience. That, however, is not how the matter appears to me. If I am right, the essence of art is insight of a special kind into reality. But such insight is bound to be accompanied by remarkable emotions. Emotions also heighten aesthetic perceptiveness. But emotion itself is not art. Neither is it the business of the artist (as is so often urged)[2] to express emotion. The emotion is derivative and secondary. Its significance depends on the object by which it is aroused. It is the revelation that matters, although the revelation will possess us body and soul, personality being essentially a whole. Subjectivist theories of art mistake the concomitants for the essentials.[3] The positivist does not quite accept this subjectivism,

[1] See *Republic*, 386-391.
[2] e.g. by E. F. Carritt in *The Theory of Beauty*. See especially Chapter X, p. 272; also *What is Beauty?*, Chapter VI.
[3] This goes also for Housman's celebrated dictum: "To transfuse emotion —not to transmit thought, but to set up in the reader's sense a vibration corresponding to what was felt by the writer is the peculiar function of poetry." *The Name and Nature of Poetry*, page 12. In view of the very close affinity of this theory with Expressionism generally it is rather odd that

and his theory has also a further feature in common with the view commended here. This is my second point. For the Logical Positivists whose views have such a wide influence at the present time art is not the communication of a special meaning. It is rather some kind of exclamation[1] evocative of feeling. That suggestion is, I think, quite preposterous. But it can be seen what makes it initially attractive if it be allowed that 'overt meaning', in the sense indicated above, is not the meaning of art as art. It is easy to conclude that if a poem does not depend on its content as such or its apparent meaning, then it has no meaning. As in many other cases positivism owes its plausibility to a half-truth. But a poem or a picture would be nothing without some meaning. There could not even be an exclamation without some specific occasion. The truth then is that meaning, meaning of a rich and new kind, is the very soul of art, it is an awareness and a communication. But it is no ordinary awareness, no ordinary communication.

VI

Hence the predicament of modern poetry. The need for novelty is greater because so much has been notably achieved in the past. The shock that takes us out of ourselves is harder to induce in an age when clever schoolboys can imitate their anthologies with remarkable facility. Poetry is too hard for us because it is also, in one sense, too easy. Originally it may well have sufficed to say 'the grass is green'. The charm of the early poets depends in part on our transporting ourselves into the conditions of their time when many simple utterances had the magic that belongs to the first expression of them. That anyone should think of saying 'the grass is green' without any ulterior purpose might put us into touch with nature in a new way—if it had not already been done. And the trouble by now is that so much has been done. To imitate the past is useless however close we come to our originals. To seek the style of Shakespeare or Milton or Wordsworth is immediately to be sententious and insincere. That was the mistake of the Georgian

---

Listowel, after trouncing the latter very thoroughly (in "The Present State of Aesthetics", *Proceedings of the Aristotelian Society*, 1934-35, p. 119) should approve so heartily of Housman's theory (op. cit. p. 203).

[1] See Ayer, *Language, Truth and Logic*, Chapter VI.

poets. They brought the achievements of the past to a fine flower of perfection, much more so than is generally allowed, but poetry in the Georgian decades was living on its capital. And that is always fatal. For in art the capital runs out immediately if it is not sunk in new ventures. We understand this by now. But we must not for that reason be unmindful of our heritage. For it is only when the past is most alive in the present that we can break most completely with the past. But there must always be adventure, and it is very hard to-day to find new seas to sail. Some poets seek newness by a very great simplicity, dispensing with artifice where we are most given to expect it. They have had much success, but the course they have taken is also full of risks and dangers, for the simplicity that arrests is never far removed from the trite and the banal. The pitfalls are many, but they are not so many, nor do they gape so darkly, as those that lie in wait for the artist who cultivates an artificial novelty. His is the sin against the Holy Ghost that deadens all inspiration. It is the false pride which the shrewd medieval thinker put as the first of the seven deadly sins. To leap into an abyss, to cast ourselves down from high pinnacles, avails nothing. Art has no guardian angels to save us from suicide, or to prevent us from making fools of ourselves before the world. The novelty must be inspired. But there must be a novelty. For this reason poetry always invites us to new adaptations, and the break that is required to-day may be so considerable, the growth that is needed if we are not to sicken and fail may be so rigid, that we may find ourselves groping very unsteadily as though we were cast into outer darkness rather than offered a way of salvation. We may, in fact, have reached a point, in many matters besides art, where men can only continue to live by passing over into something very like a new dimension.

This crisis is most evident in religion. The apocalyptic strain in religious thought at the present time may take some rather extravagant forms, but it has significant implications. Supported as it often is by confusions[1] which a little reflection and analysis

[1] For a brief but most penetrating discussion of these confusions see "The Features and Factors of the World Crisis", by A. E. Garvie, *Hibbert Journal*, Vol. XXXIX.

would dispel, it nevertheless bears important testimony to a sense of urgency, of doom and 'an end of the world', of forces that lead to a cataclysmic change, and this in a way that cannot be treated wholly as an epiphenomenon of political and economic conflicts and privations, or a hysterical fantasy arising out of the stresses of war such as your thorough rationalist would have us regard it. It began before the war, and before the impact of the disorders that led to the war had been properly felt. Those are themselves the symptoms of conditions that lie deeper than moral perplexities and economic confusion. They have a significance to-day that they could not have had before. For, occurring within a civilisation such as ours, they point to aspirations that cannot be met at any level that is naturally reached by the forces released in the fifteenth century. These were necessary, and there is certainly no remedy for the ills of to-day in the attainments of yet earlier ages. Our troubles arise, not from something we have lost, but from something we have failed to find. Digging in the past will not therefore provide easement, however much a superficial pessimism may underrate the blessings of enlightenment. Creeds outworn are outworn for good. The past succours us when the new emerges. And this is the need that the theology of 'crisis' expresses to-day. The theologians do not understand the matter well. They are wedded to a past that is dead and, seeking to contain within it what is quickening now into life, they can only cover their defeatism and reaction by irresponsible play with extravagant paradoxes, the glorification of nonsense. In particular, they know not the difference, fairly grasped in the main (notwithstanding its inadequacy for us) in the notable theological thinking of the past, between making religion articulate and giving an account of religion in terms of the whole of life. That is indeed the crux of the matter. For however ill they may do their own business, an extraordinarily hard one in all conscience, the theologians whose thought is most astir today, Otto, Barth, Niebuhr, Brunner, Berdyaev, do make articulate a supreme need, and one that has now become also imperative, as their urgency shows, the need to infuse into the ages of enlightenment an awareness of reality adequate to their achievements and such as will not be attenuated by them. Amid the strained theorising and the docile acquiescence in the eruption of primitive and pagan forces there is one most welcome and authentic note in the vigorous religious thinking set in play by continental theologians; it is the insistence on 'the wholly other', on a reality that forces itself upon our consciousness and refuses to be managed and mastered. This, at bottom, is why we hear so much of crisis, and of 'existential thinking', thinking that is rooted in the character and experience of the individual. And it may not be possible to apprehend the matter in a way more conformable to our intellectual advances until the religious experience is itself more substantial and extensive—in other and, I believe, apter words, until the 'revelation' and 'revival' has us more in its grip. Bewilderment may then give way to the self-possession, the mastery, of true prophetic awareness. It is here that the affinity of art and religion is most evident to-day. Both have to mediate for us a reality not ourselves, avoiding the romanticism that confuses us with exudations of ourselves and the obscurantism in which the self is lost. It is easy to fail, and failure is rank in the posturings of poets and religious teachers alike. Of success in either regard one thing alone is plain. We must turn our minds out into the world, break out of the routine of our own orbit to voyage among things, we must touch and see; as the scriptures teach, we have to lose our own lives and then we may find that we have saved them. This is what the poet does; conceited he may be and solicitous for praise—what poet is not?—selfish and given to display, but he is this, if at all, as the doctor in Plato's *Republic* is a money maker *as well*— as a doctor his care is for the cure of bodies. The poet as poet is in love with the world, not himself. His pride begins as the pride of achievement and awareness. This is what Dostoievski meant in a celebrated passage where he declares that the world shall be saved by beauty, *beauty that is in the world,* not in the eye of the beholder. The supreme virtue here is humility, for the humble are they that move about the world with the lure of the real in their hearts.

INDEX

Acton, H. B., 90.
Aristotle, 25, 49, 67, 82, 149-53, 224.
Arnold, M., 205.
Ayer, A. J., 252.

Baillie, J., 227.
Bain, A., 155.
Barth, K., Barthianism, 4-6, 9, 11 ff, 18-20, 24, 25, 41, 43, 227, 254.
Berdyaev, N., 243, 254.
Bevan, E., 222-4.
Bosanquet, B., 65.
Bradley, F. H., 3, 112, 155, 159.
Bridges, R., 247.
Broad, C. D., 80, 121, 154, 232.
Browning, R., 246.
Brunner, E., 18, 19, 28-46, 147, 184, 186, 214.
Buber, M., 192-4, 196, 208.
Butler, J., 224.

Camfield, F. W., 12, 15.
Campbell, C. A., 15, 53-5, 90, 121, 141-2.
Carritt, E. F., 13, 22, 141, 251.
Collingwood, R. C., 240.
Croce, B., 87.

de Beauvoir, S., 91.
de Burgh, W. G., 51-3.
Descartes, R., 91.
Dostoievski, F., 255.

Eliot, T. S., 247.
Emmet, D. M., 224-5.
Empson, W., 213.

Falk, W. D., 112, 133.
Field, G. C., 69, 131-2.
Fisher, G. F. (Archbishop of Canterbury), 99-100.
Flecker, J. E., 245.
Flügel, J. C., 162, 164.
Freed, L., 95-7.
Freud, S., Freudians, 1, 32, 146, 160, 162, 163, 209.

Garvie, A. E., 253.
Gascoyne, D., 213.
Gomperz, H., 112, 114, 136.
Greek ethics, 146, 149-53, 154, 156.
Green, T. H., 63-5, 234.

Hartmann, N., 80, 121, 145.
Heim, K., 194-6.
Hight, G. A., 240.
Hobart, R. E., 121.
Hobbes, T., 66, 150, 164, 168.
Hodgson, R., 232.
Hopkins, G. M., 242.
Housman, A. E., 205, 248, 251-2.
Hughes, G. E., 129-30, 134.
Hume, D., 150.
Huxley, J. S., 232.

Inge, W. R., 188, 190-2.

James, W., 2, 188.
Joseph, H. W. B., 126-31.

Kant, 1, 18, 49, 52, 58, 63, 65, 81, 121, 154, 181.

Laird, J., 50-1, 55, 172.
Lindsay, A. D., 73.
Listowel, Earl of, 251-2.
Livingstone Lowes, J., 232.
Locke, J., 79, 110.
Lutheran Church, 24, 25.

Marxism, 87.
Mascall, E. L., 179.
MacIver, A. M., 81, 85, 89.
Matthews, B., 8.
Mill, J. S., 155.
Moore, G. E., 80, 121, 122, 125, 146, 183.

National Socialism, 24.
Nettleship, R. L., 190-1, 236-7.
Niebuhr, R., 103, 254.

Osborne, H., 52-3.
Otto, R., 254.

Parmenides, 3.
Pascal, B., 185.
Paton, H. J., 15.
Peploe, S. J., 250.
Pfleiderer, O., 190.
Pick, J., 242.
Plato, 3-4, 30, 62, 76, 79, 82-3, 150-1, 153, 191, 204, 212, 218, 219, 231, 234-41.
Price, H. H., 79, 198-9, 214, 224.
Prichard, H. A., 78, 80, 128.

Rashdall, H., 112.
Read, H., 210.
Reid, L. A., 134.
Ross, Sir W. D., 36, 49, 80, 89, 120-4, 126-38, 142, 147, 157, 170-1.
Rousseau, J. J., 66.
Ryle, G., 91-2.

St. Augustine, 71, 176.
St. John of the Cross, 188.
Sidgwick, H., 51.
Smith, P. Nowell, 140, 169-70.
Socrates, Socratic ethics, 3, 31, 36, 79, 146-7, 238.
Sophists, 151.
Spinoza, B. de, 79, 201.
Stevenson, C. L., 166.
Stoics, 18.
Stout, A. K., 121.
Swinburne, A. C., 248.

Tauler, J., 188.
Taylor, A. E., 136, 152.
Tennyson, A., 246.
Thomas, D., 213.
Trethowan, Dom I., 179.

Underhill, E., 188-90.
Urquhart, W. S., 18, 24.

Vaughan, C. E., 66.
Vedas, 18.
von Hügel, Baron F., 188.

Whitehead, A. N., 236.
Wisdom, J., 123, 209.

Zeno of Elea, 181.

For Product Safety Concerns and Information please contact our EU
representative GPSR@taylorandfrancis.com
Taylor & Francis Verlag GmbH, Kaufingerstraße 24, 80331 München, Germany

www.ingramcontent.com/pod-product-compliance
Lightning Source LLC
Chambersburg PA
CBHW071815300426
44116CB00009B/1332